WITHDRAWN

Family:
The Good F-Word

Troy Dunn

First edition 2014

19 18 17 16 15 14   10 9 8 7 6 5 4 3 2 1

EAN/ISBN-13: Print: 978-1-939457-02-8
                     ePub: 978-1-939457-18-9
                     Mobi: 978-1-939457-19-6
                     PDF: 978-1-939457-17-2

Book Design: Hagop Kalaidjian, Jacquelynne Hudson
Layout: Dovetail Publishing Services
Front Cover Photo: David Y. Chung
Back Cover Photo: J&B PhotoReflect

Family:
The Good F-Word

Troy Dunn

First edition 2014

19 18 17 16 15 14   10 9 8 7 6 5 4 3 2 1

EAN/ISBN-13: Print: 978-1-939457-02-8
                    ePub: 978-1-939457-18-9
                    Mobi: 978-1-939457-19-6
                    PDF: 978-1-939457-17-2

Book Design: Hagop Kalaidjian, Jacquelynne Hudson
Layout: Dovetail Publishing Services
Front Cover Photo: David Y. Chung
Back Cover Photo: J&B PhotoReflect

Dedication

This book is dedicated to my eight beautiful children: Trey, Trevor, Treston, Josalin, Trendon, Trace, Jennica and Trevin.

I began writing this book in the hopes that I could help others build a life as joyous and love-filled as the one Jennifer and I have been blessed with. But as I wrote, I realized that, to my children, this book is a look behind the scenes of their own mom and dad's marriage, and it exposes a glimpse of the raw truth. Jennifer and I are thrilled about that distinct possibility. We want each of our children to discover that the family they grew up in took an immense amount of work, humility, sacrifice, forgiveness and unconditional love to make it what it is. It is worth every ounce of energy it required.

My dear, amazing children, great families take great work. Mom and I pray you will someday find an eternal companion with whom you can co-found your own beautiful family.

Families are forever.

Note to Reader

Acknowledgments

It is with deep gratitude that I acknowledge the following individuals for their contribution, in one way or another, to this book:

Jennifer: My eternal companion, my high school sweetheart, my life partner. You know better than anyone that this book is a journal of stuff you have taught me through your amazing example! Thank you for trusting and believing. I love you more! To eternity!

Mom (Katie, to the rest of the world): You were my best friend since day one, the first to believe in my dreams, and the one who remains by my side unconditionally. ILYFILYFA (Night, Mr. Moon!)

Jan B.: You are the writing partner authors only DREAM of finding. Thank you for the hundreds of hours you sacrificed to walk this journey with me. I would send you a personal thank you note, but you would likely rewrite it and send it back for review! On to book four!

Dr. Phil: I am honored to know you as a true friend. Your sincerity, your integrity, and your consistent belief in me is so humbling. Thank you for truly walking the walk. It's amazing what can happen when a couple of old Okie football players run into each other at the office.

Robin: Throughout the writing of this book, Jen and I would discuss various values and principles we believe in, and so often, she would make her point to me by using you and Phil as evidence. Your quiet but consistent example has inspired many, I'm sure, but it has definitely impacted our home and marriage. Thank you for your presence in our life.

TJ: Our friendship is unlike any other I have. When we first met, I thought I was meeting a "fan," but I quickly realized you were going to be my newest mentor! Then we became business partners, and now I am grateful to call you my brother from another mother. May the readers of this book seek you out and learn from you as I have.

Lisa C.: I'm not even sure what title to give you because you far surpassed the definition of editor! Writing this book while getting your feedback, insight, and even your challenges to my thinking, was exhilarating and exhausting! I'm so grateful for every single note, each personal insight you shared and every challenge you issued. I grew on this journey. This book is so much more because of YOU!

Hagop: When I turned this manuscript in, it was hundreds of pages of typed text. When it passed through your gifted hands, it emerged into the beautiful layout that is this book. When I described to you how I envisioned it looking, I struggled to put it into words, but I could see it so clearly in my mind's eye. You captured that vision exactly, and then improved on it significantly! Thank you!

Josh: You pushed this across the finish line under extreme deadlines; so glad you came along!

Jay: The day you agreed to publish my book was a very emotional day for me. I was so excited, yet so humbled. You have been so successful at delivering powerful messages to millions of people through publishing. The realization that you had chosen my message as one you wanted to take to the world has been one of the great moments in my life. Thank you for believing in me.

Christ: I would not be my authentic self if I did not include you here. Above all others, you are the greatest influence in my life. You are my Lord and Savior. You are my friend, my brother. I give you the glory for all I have, all I am. I seek you always, in all places, in all faces.

Contents

Foreword

I first met Troy Dunn several years ago when he was a guest on my show, making a personal appearance on behalf of the TV series he starred in at the time, called *The Locator*. Every week on that show, Troy worked to reunite families, often after decades of separation. Now, I have to say that after 35+ years in the arena of human functioning, I'm a pretty tough sell. I have pretty much seen it all and am hard to impress. But Troy Dunn had a uniqueness that caught my attention in a big way. His abundant skills were evident in the joyous reunions that took place. He did an extraordinary job, first in actually finding family members, but secondly and most importantly, in persuading families to meet. He earned their trust by listening carefully to their stories and guiding them slowly and with great sensitivity toward rebuilding their relationships.

The show Troy was doing was a distant second to his top priority of actually helping families to reunite and heal the right way. His compassion was obvious and his agenda clear and concise—he truly believed he could help every family he met. I was very impressed and greatly admired his commitment to trying to heal the world one family at a time. He began what became his life's work by helping his mother, who had been adopted, find her birth mother, and he hasn't stopped since, always looking for new, creative, and better ways to reunite families. That he has succeeded beyond measure is evidenced by the volume of families (40,000 and counting!) who can thank him for their reunions.

His principles and tools for empowering individuals to better themselves and the people around them are sound, proven, and based on years of real-world application. Simply put, his methods work. I truly believe Troy is doing God's work. And I want to put him in the direct path of as many troubled relationships as humanly possible.

And now, finally, he has gathered his ideas and successful strategies for repairing and rebuilding families into a book. With a wonderful combination of compassion, humor, practicality, optimism, and passion, Troy offers the reader an accessible primer to addressing family problems and taking the slow, but sure, steps to fix them. Whether you think your marriage is in its death throes or you just want your family life to be stronger and better, there are answers here that will help every family be the best it can be.

It is a great pleasure to introduce Troy to you in this book. We share many things, the most important of which is how very much we value our own families. Troy is a family man through and through. He is devoted to his lovely wife, Jennifer, and their eight children. (Yes, I said eight children! So we know he must write really late at night!) He tends to his family's needs in the same compassionate way he counsels the people he works with. He walks the walk.

My wife, Robin, shares my pleasure in our friendship with Troy. On one of his first appearances on my show, as she and I walked off the stage together, she said, "I just love him. He is clear and powerful with people when they need it most." With every appearance he and I have made together ever since, Robin's admiration has grown.

Why do I take so much time here to share my personal thoughts and feelings about Troy Dunn? Because I am a firm believer that before you accept any message, you must know who the messenger is. I'm here to say, this messenger, Troy Dunn, is the real deal. You would do well to take the necessary time to not just read this book that is now in your hands, but study it. Ponder it and reread it until the message, the tools, and the strategies within it become a part of you. You are clearly seeking help for yourself and your family. You have taken action by getting your hands on this book. Now have the fortitude to do the work. I believe my friend Troy is capable of facilitating a journey for you that will take you closer to the life you want to live.

—Dr. Phil McGraw

Introduction

At my desk in my Florida office, I keep a small, yellow sticky note taped to the base of a globe that sits on the far corner. It's a note from my mother, and all that's written on it is, "40,000, son. So proud of you."

My mother, Arliene (we all call her Katie), has worked with me for 23 years in our business of reuniting and helping rebuild fractured families, many of whom were featured on countless talk shows and on our television show, *The Locator*. I consider her one of my secret weapons; she is brilliant. One morning she noticed that the little counter on our database, which automatically counts the cases as we resolve them, had quietly clicked to the number 40,000.

To us, that was an extraordinary number, taking us back over two decades to the many brave people whom we have guided on the path to find long-lost family members. These weren't people eager to revisit old wounds, squeeze money out of their parents, or inflict revenge on mothers, sisters, or uncles who had done them wrong. They were, instead, people who were seeking forgiveness, love, and a restored connection to those individuals who were, at one time, the most important people in their lives. And while everyone was unique in his or her quest, they all showed enormous courage in facing the past with the hope of creating a better future. They did so not only for themselves, but for their parents, children, siblings, aunts, uncles, and grandparents, thus expanding the breadth and depth of these 40,000 cases to more than 100,000 family members. We are talking about a lot of change.

And being a part of all that change has certainly changed me as well. I have listened to people's sad, often tragic, stories of how their families broke apart. I have worked with them closely to help mend their relationships through long discussions about the meaning of true forgiveness, courage in the face of adversity, humility and love with no strings attached. We've talked about how to let go of resentment in order to clear the way for new beginnings.

If these reunions were going to be successful, it was imperative that they entered into the search without old behaviors sabotaging their efforts. They needed new, healthy ways to communicate as the groundwork for these second chances at their relationships. I helped them do this through specific exercises. I have learned what works because I deeply embedded myself within these 40,000 heartbroken, angry, lonely, lost, hopeless families, so I could see, firsthand, the peace and happiness they experienced when they reached out and found that person who once meant the world to them. These experiences have made me fluent in a language I never knew existed. I now find myself, day in and day out, speaking the language of *family*.

I speak this language in my home, my office, when I'm out to dinner with friends, and even to unsuspecting strangers sitting next to me on planes. I honestly don't know how to shut it off. I *believe* in the power of family. It is fuel. It is air to me. It sustains me. It gives meaning and life to all that I do and all I care about. And now that I know it, I want everyone to know the happiness it can bring you. By reading this book, I hope you will.

My Own Family

I bring my work home, so to speak. I have a family myself—in fact, I have a rather large family consisting of my wife, Jennifer, and our eight children. And like everyone, we have our ups and downs. There are moments in which we share tremendous joy. And there are moments when the lines of communication break down, when tempers flare and feelings are hurt.

As you probably know, with family comes responsibility, and with a big family such as mine comes big responsibility. We try to ensure that each child receives enough attention, their different personalities are accommodated, everyone gets fed and finishes their homework, they get along without killing each other, that there are enough socks to go around, and my wife and I have time enough to ourselves. Just writing this makes my head spin!

But I wouldn't have it any other way. My family is the most important thing in my life; I cherish my wife and children, and I work hard on our familial relationships. But I am most assuredly a better husband and parent because of my "day job." Having witnessed the devastation that ensues when families split apart, I'm inspired to pay even closer attention to my own family every day.

There are, of course, many serious problems that can challenge a family, such as drugs, alcohol, physical abuse, infidelity, and abandonment. But what I've discovered, and I think this will surprise you, is that the *vast majority* of the damage that causes unhappy families comes from neglect. I'm talking about the simple yet insidious neglect of small but important acts of understanding, love, and forgiveness. Those are the ingredients needed to make and keep families strong and connected, and without them, a family could quickly find itself on a path to ruin.

Constantly ignoring small signs of unrest in your family can slowly create big problems, much in the same way ignoring a leaky faucet can lead to a costly plumbing disaster. Making a sarcastic, hurtful remark, opting for silence rather than discussing issues that arise, playing the blame game with each other, keeping score of snubs or insults—all of these behaviors can extinguish the love between family members. And ultimately, these behaviors can lead even the most caring families down a dark and unhappy road.

By helping other families heal themselves, I've learned that if people would just look out for and respond to early warning signs of trouble, they could avoid years of heartbreak. But I've been deeply encouraged, because I've witnessed families on the brink of dissolution pull themselves back together, back toward being whole and restored. I'm not saying it was easy; they had to work hard to make it happen, but they did it. Even the angriest and most deeply hurt families have done it. I have seen them embrace the tools I give them so they can trade their pain for the joy of feeling loved. Once they get a taste of the enormous sense of security, strength, and happiness that comes with reuniting with a family, its members will do anything to ensure they can sustain that joy and peace.

One of the most important keys to success in a family is to attend to small problems before they become big ones. Even if your grandmother told you that "a stitch in time saves nine," you probably never connected that advice to your marriage. But the fact is that there's no early warning system for couples who are drifting apart. No oven timer dings to alert them that it's time to sit down and talk. Even if an airplane flew over their heads pulling a huge sign that said, "Time for a marital checkup," many people would still have a hard time knowing what to do. My experience has taught me that many people have no idea how to go about attending to their loved ones.

It comes down to having the right tools. It seems like we have tools to fix everything from our clothes to our cars, but hardly anyone has the right tools to repair their relationships. Most of the time, folks don't even know they need them.

But I know you need them—we all do—and I'm here to give them to you. Having spent most of my professional life extending a helping hand to families in need, I've managed to hone in on successful strategies for bringing about positive change. (If I hadn't, I imagine I would have been out of business pretty fast!) I've found what works and what doesn't, and based on my experience, I've designed practical and effective steps you can use to turn your dysfunctional (or barely functioning) family relationships into much happier, more connected family relationships.

This will extend to every area of your life. Living in a healthy home sets you up for happiness and success as a *person,* not just as a wife, a husband, a mother, a father, or any other familial role you play. With the stability of a well-functioning family to encourage you and lift you up, you will become more productive at work, your children will be more relaxed and secure, and all of you will be more likely to thrive at every level. Your days will be markedly different—you might be more joyful, have a brighter outlook on life, and be filled with more hope than you might imagine possible.

Sounds pretty good, right? Wouldn't you like your family to be that way? If you will trust me, I can help you.

My Plan for You

I make no apologies for being one of the world's biggest fans of "family." I've seen so much evidence of its benefits, and it is my daily intention to broadcast the power of a family unit far and wide. A functioning, happy family is the greatest gift you can give yourself, your husband, wife, partner, and children, and really, the world. That's right: I believe with all my heart in the ability of families to do good, not only for themselves, but for everyone they touch. When family members are devoted to each other, they are also good neighbors and good citizens. Their joy and generosity radiate from them like the sun.

As you can probably tell, I'm pretty passionate about this subject. Given even the slightest chance, I will tout the power of the family unit to anyone who will listen. Some folks get really excited about the latest movie that's out, or their new favorite restaurant, maybe their political position or religious beliefs. Me? It's all family, all the time. I can feel the energy and emotion welling up inside me as I write these words; I'm invigorated because I know I can help you. No matter how bad it is, even if you feel like your whole world is upside down and lit on fire and it's only a matter of time before your family is nothing but a pile of ashes, you *can* come out unscathed. It is not too late, and I want to help pull you and your whole family out of the flames.

That's why I wrote this book.

I have crawled into thousands of "burning" families, pulled relationships to safety, and seen them go on to live another day . . . together. But I have also seen others perish, ones who wouldn't listen, weren't willing to try, and refused to reach out and accept my help. Their lives, their most cherished relationships, went up in flames. Sadly, I tend to remember those the most, and those memories are what push me forward to continue my work to prevent other families from giving up on each other.

That's why I've created the Life-Changing Action Plan (LCA Plan), which is the exact program I've used to help so many people restart their families. Using the LCA Plan's tools and strategies, I will be your temporary guide on a journey of personal growth and change, one that will help you restore your family to its full strength. I call myself a "temporary" guide because once you understand and embrace the LCA Plan for yourself, you will become your own guide. That's how long-term change will occur.

The plan has four steps. Step one helps you determine what's wrong with your relationship. You might be thinking, "Oh, that's easy—my partner is what's wrong!" But in fact, the first step of the LCA Plan starts with you! The most successful reunions I've seen were ones in which *all* parties were willing to take a personal inventory and experience some personal growth beforehand. That way, the reunion doesn't simply become a rehashing of old behaviors, which can lead to the very same stalemate that caused the division in the first place. This will be true for you, too, even if the person I am going to "reunite" you with lives right under your own roof or sleeps in the same bed. (That is, if you are even still sleeping in the same bed!) My tools for self-assessment within the context of your marriage will help you clearly see what you've been doing well *and* the areas that you need to work on.

But now I can hear you shouting, "Hey, what about my spouse?"

Well, we'll bring your partner in as we go, but since you are the one who has taken the initiative to read this book, you get to be first.

The second step of the LCA Plan is CHANGE, which I put in capital letters because without it, you will be helpless to fix your marriage. Embracing the idea of change and then stepping into those changes in a consistent and long-lasting way is how you will succeed in re-creating a loving relationship. I know how hard it is, and I imagine you do, too, so I am going to give you some clear strategies to get you started.

The third step in the LCA Plan is aimed at repairing damage and rebuilding your marriage or relationship, no matter what its challenges. There can be a lot of roadblocks here, especially in a relationship with some long-established negative patterns, but I will show you how to look at your differences in new ways that will cause you to *want* to change. I'm betting you're probably not even aware of most of the toxic behaviors that have been keeping you and your partner apart. But in this step, you will learn how to recognize them and then banish them from your marriage. We will also talk about some pervasive marital myths that could be crippling your relationship without you even realizing it.

Step four is about empowerment and how to permanently stabilize your relationship. This is my favorite part, because it will give you hope and the practical skills to make your marriage more fulfilling than you ever thought possible. I begin this section by talking about two of my favorite things: taking responsibility for your actions and embracing forgiveness. There can never be enough of either in a relationship, and I will sell you on the surprising and empowering benefits of both.

Let me be clear: the LCA Plan is not easy. Nothing worth having ever is! But before you start to worry, I want you to know that it is not impossible either. In fact, it's perfectly within your grasp, if you're willing to put in the hard work necessary. Just think of how hard you work at so many things in your life—a project at your job, keeping your house in repair, helping your kids with schoolwork, driving them to their activities. You might not have ever thought about how hard you work, day in and day out, at things that are pressed upon you. In fact, tending to all your other responsibilities could be one reason that your marriage has suffered. There are countless reasons why a marriage drifts into troubled waters, and the

longer you've ignored it or let resentments build up, the harder it will be to change course.

I've encountered some of the worst family scenarios you can imagine, and it takes a lot of soul-searching, forgiveness, and a very deep desire for change to repair and rejuvenate a damaged family. But know this: it is very doable. Let me repeat that. It is *very* doable! Together, we can not only repair your family, but we can get it into better shape than it has ever been. I have seen it happen time and time again. Some of you may have seen these transformations yourself if you've seen my work on *Dr. Phil* or watched my TV show, *The Locator*. People who seemed permanently stuck in old behaviors get a taste of the possibilities that change can bring and suddenly they thirst for more. It can happen just as quickly for you and your family, too.

And I can promise you, in fact, that if you're willing to let go of whatever you are clinging on to, I *will* help you navigate safely out of this and into a stronger, healthier family.

Right now, all you have to do is . . . turn the page.

Why Are You Reading This Book? Set Your Goal for Your Family and Go for It

1

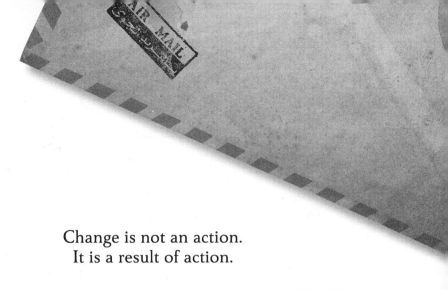

Change is not an action.
It is a result of action.

—Troy Dunn

You picked up this book for a reason, and I'm guessing that reason has to do with your desire, maybe even your desperate need, to make changes in your family. You're obviously looking for answers. Maybe you're at the end of your rope, worn out, fed up, and sick to death of what's going on at home. Your husband or partner just admitted he cheated on you, your daughter is threatening to move to her best friend's house, you're worried sick about money, you're disgusted by how much you're drinking, and you feel like crying all the time.

Or perhaps it's not that dramatic. Maybe you and your partner just don't really talk anymore, let alone have fun together, you hate your job, your kids are busy with their own lives, and you've basically forgotten why you got married in the first place. You feel stuck, stagnant, and worried, but you're afraid to take a step in any direction that will make things worse. Divorce and separation are words that have started circling in your thoughts. You don't want to split up, but maybe you're headed in that direction. You don't know what to do.

Well, I *do* know what to do. I've reunited over 40,000 people with their families over the last 25 years, giving them the tools to cut through the despair, resentments, blame, and anger that have driven them apart, and I've helped them find each other again and enjoy the love, security, and amazing joy that a rebuilt, healthy family creates. The information and tools I use have been road-tested thousands of times on the most troubled of families, people terribly stuck in very dark places. They are angry, hurt, full of pain, and unforgiving, unable to move forward, backward, or sideways. But they have the desire to change. And when I see that desire, even if it's just a flicker, I grab it with both hands and help them. I show them, step by step, the possibilities for change and give them practical ways to initiate those changes. I help them repair themselves and their families. It is my life's work to do everything I can to save families and make them whole again.

And I can do the same for you.

I can't know what's sabotaging your relationship, whether you're completely, desperately unhappy with your situation and on the verge of separation, or whether you're just yearning to get back the magic you once felt toward your partner. Regardless of where you stand, here are two facts you should know:

Fact #1.
There are couples with issues just like yours and your partner's whose marriages fail.

Fact #2.
There are couples with issues just like yours and your partner's who resolve those issues, rebuild their relationship, and live a long, happy life together.

I've seen both of these outcomes over the last two decades. I've seen families with almost exactly the same problems either redeemed by their willingness to forgive each other and move forward together, or destroyed when they couldn't commit to change, so that husbands, wives, and children are cut adrift from each other forever.

There is nothing better than witnessing the incredible joy of family members who have worked so hard and reached out to each other to build loving bonds and connections that sustain them and give them strength to become the best people they can be. It fills my heart with joy every time a successful reunion occurs.

But it is heartbreaking when a family crumbles and falls apart. Those failures haunt me because I know so well what they are missing. When I watch family members sadly go their separate ways, all I can see, in a mirror image, are the smiles, hugs, and bright, happy eyes in the faces of the families who made the courageous leap into joy and forgiveness. As a result, I stand firmly and loudly on the side of reuniting even the most broken of families.

So if you're looking for answers to your troubled relationship, here are the choices I'm offering you:

1. You can stay where you are, frozen in limbo, continuing to move through your life on automatic pilot, holding your partner at a distance, with no hope of change.

2. You can swing the final wrecking ball at your relationship and smash it to smithereens, taking down your partner and children with you.

3. You can take a deep breath and change your life, and the lives of your family members, by rebuilding what you once had or hoped to have.

If you chose the last option, I can help. My four-step Life-Changing Action Plan (LCA Plan) takes you step by step toward living the life you want for yourself and your family.

The LCA Plan

It starts with you! Step one of the LCA Plan, beginning in the next chapter, opens with an in-depth series of questions for you to ask yourself. They are designed to tease out what's going on under the surface of your relationship, some of the hidden influences that drive you and your partner's behavior. You probably already know, or think you know, how your partner's attitudes are undermining your relationship, but do you understand how the influences on *both* of you, from your pasts and your lives now, can also contribute to your unhappiness? Most people are so caught up in their day-to-day frustrations and resentments that they never step back and take a deep look at things. Your answers here will help you do just that, which will be a big help as I guide you through repairing your relationship.

Step two of the LCA Plan is about *change*, how difficult it is and how you need to embrace the whole concept of change if you want to repair your relationship. I will guide you through setting up your own program of change and, most importantly, give you the motivational tools you will need to stick to your program, which is by far the hardest part of change. This section will allow you to make the changes you seek and set you and your partner up for a newer, more fulfilling relationship, one you can build on for years to come. And of course, we will talk about your partner's need to change as well!

Next will come step three of the LCA Plan, the section dealing with what has most likely kept you locked into your negative, unhappy patterns. These are the toxic behaviors that most commonly derail relationships—roadblocks that keep you from communicating with your partner, that build up walls between you, and that undermine your hopes for fixing your marriage. You will be amazed at what you've been unwittingly doing to damage your marriage! Within each chapter here, I will give you tools, strategies, and exercises to get rid of those bad habits and begin communicating in healthier ways with your spouse.

We will also discuss the biggest areas of tension in relationships: parenting, money, and sex. You may recognize yourself in these chapters, and I can help you take the heat out of money arguments and disagreements about handling your children.

Finally, step four of the LCA Plan. This is the good news, the healthy behaviors you can embrace that will set you and your partner on a path toward healing and renewed intimacy. Included here is a second chapter on sex—and the good news is that I will show you how sex can be a huge opportunity for healing. This empowerment section will give you the tools to go forward in your relationship with confidence.

By following this program through to the end, you will be giving yourself and your family a wonderful gift of hope and happiness—a new beginning.

The LCA Plan requires a solid commitment. Depending on the state of your relationship, you may have to work hard to undo the years of damage you and your partner may have done to each other. It also takes a lot of courage to forgive the hurts and insults that may have caused you great unhappiness. And it requires discipline to make your new behavior stick. Sometimes you will have to close your eyes and just *believe* that things will get better.

But I really, *really* hope that you will, because if you do, there will be great rewards in store for you. If you take this journey with me, you will read about other people who've transformed their lives. Their stories will inspire you to shed unproductive and negative behaviors, learn how to accept responsibility for your actions, and embrace forgiveness and change. You will experience more happiness and joy than you ever thought was possible. Your life will get a whole lot better!

What *Is* "Family"?

The concept of family has definitely changed in recent decades. According to the 2012 US census, the number of children living with two married parents was 64 percent, down from 77 percent in 1980, and 28 percent of children live with a single parent, primarily a mother. Within these demographics are further subdivisions of unmarried couples cohabiting, stepparents, children living with grandparents, and so on.

So while in many ways the idea of family no longer assumes the "traditional" structure of a married, two-parent, nuclear family, I find there is still an overpowering yearning to create or re-create a loving connection between family members among the people who come to me for help, regardless of the makeup of each individual family.

I've seen over and over again how a strong family empowers each of its members, building security, self-esteem, safety, love, and joy, and I do everything I can to help people build or rebuild their families. Because of its power to do so much good, in fact, I find it very discouraging and sad how our society seems to devalue the astounding capacity of a family to promote happiness and well-being. The family unit is the very best structure for personal growth, for raising children, for creating successful communities.

I was recently riding in my friend's car as he and I drove through his community. As we passed a particular house, he pointed at it and said, "That's where the Brooks live. They are a really good family." Everyone can name the "good families" in their neighborhood or community. They have an undeniable impact.

What's interesting is that people are always touting the importance of families in the media. Every politician worth his salt says he or she honors the sanctity of families. Celebrities show off their round tummies and reverently extol the importance of families. The baby industry thrives on promoting a sort of saccharine respect for families every time they sell you heated baby wipes.

But the *idea* of family is tossed around like a beach ball at the seaside, colorful and bright but light as air. Families are *fun*. Families are screwball sitcoms, where parents act like kids and kids get all the good lines. Or, in the opposite view, families are dysfunctional nightmares, incubators of hostility and bad behavior, irredeemably damaged. I get all that and, like everyone else, I enjoy some of these images and ignore others. But is that all there is to a family? Either some collection of hopeless misfits out to get each other, or a bunch of hapless parents and their children muddling along doing their best to stay out trouble?

Not to me. Not by a long shot. Being in the trenches with broken families who work *so* hard and truly fight to be together always reminds me that creating a good, healthy family is serious business, and that you have to pay attention to make a family succeed and keep it healthy.

I also have a deeply personal reason for my reverence for families—my own father. As a young man, I witnessed his transformation from being a severe alcoholic to a loving husband and father, an enormous and difficult change that he accomplished through discipline, a strong will, and because of his love for our family. His courage and his determination to keep our family together demonstrated to me back then an essential attribute I have seen, and hope to see, in the fractured families I help today—a strong belief that a family is a *treasure*, worth whatever it takes. My father's belief in our family dramatically changed my life for the better. I grew up knowing I could depend on my parents' love, which gave me security, confidence, and much joy.

I learned as a young man that the words "time," "effort," "loyalty," "forgiveness," "discipline," "restraint," and, most of all, "forgiveness" were the most important in sustaining a thriving family. Many families operate this way instinctively because their members come from families where these values were taught and embraced. But there are many others who don't have a clue, and their ignorance gets them in trouble. Their families fall apart. If they had good information so they could make good choices, though, then their families would prosper.

You might be starting from scratch because no one ever showed you what a healthy family looked like. Well, that's okay. It's not your fault. But you *can* learn what it takes and then apply it to your life. And if your first step is to recognize the value in cherishing your family and keeping it safe and strong, then you're on the right path.

So, based on the many thousands of families I have worked with and my own experience, the answer to the question, "What is family?" is:

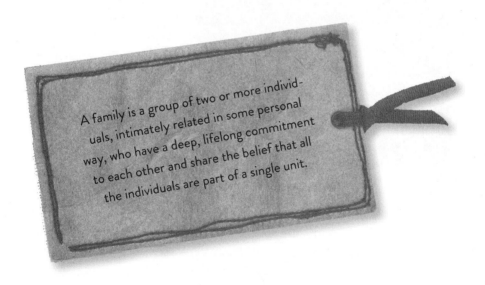

A family is a group of two or more individuals, intimately related in some personal way, who have a deep, lifelong commitment to each other and share the belief that all the individuals are part of a single unit.

This one sentence might sound simple, but it's taken me nearly 25 years to create it. Both in my business and on my television series, *The Locator*, I've worked with so many families in need of repair that I've identified the most important things that make up a successful family. So I'm going to explain this sentence to you in the hope that you will understand and appreciate how much I respect good families. And this is no secret.

My goal is to persuade you of the fantastic joy that can come to you if you work to improve your own family.

Recognizing the Imposters

There are so many kinds of families. Over the years I have worked with heterosexual and gay couples, single mothers, grandparents raising their grandchildren, older siblings taking care of younger siblings, and vice versa. You name it, and I have met them. But no matter how dissimilar these families are, each is composed of people who have pledged themselves to each other for life, for better or worse. They have made a lifelong commitment to each other.

What they are not, however, is *"like a family."*

Married or Single: Who's Happier?

A survey conducted by the Pew Research Center in 2010 asked single people and married people if they considered themselves unhappy, happy, or very happy. Of the married respondents, 43 percent described themselves as "very happy," while only 24 percent of single respondents chose that option.

I hear this phrase a lot. It is part of the fuzzy thinking about the definition of a family. Someone says "the people at work are like my second family," or "our team works like a family." Sure, when you're in the middle of basketball season and you and your teammates are joined at the hip at practice and twice weekly games, or when you're on deadline at work with your team, they all can *feel* like a family. For a particular period of time, there are strong bonds between you and an intimacy that comes with shared experiences.

But families have entered into a lifelong commitment with each other and are bound together in ways that no friends can be. Friends move on with their own lives and their own families. An office mate gets a job at another company and you never see him again, the college football team graduates, your neighbor moves to Phoenix. Even the best, lifelong friendships you enjoy are different from your family ties. They can be strong and supportive but they are still friendships, which is in a very different category from your family.

There is no expiration date on families. You can say, "We're not friends anymore," and it will be the truth. But you can't say, "I'm not a mother anymore," because that's impossible. (Well, you *can* say it, but it won't be true!) You are a parent for life. You are siblings forever. You will always be a grandparent, cousin, or uncle. No matter where you live, how infrequently you speak, how well you get along, or how much you occasionally want to kill each other, you are a part of your family.

"We" Is One

In the definition above, I've referred to the family as a "single unit." This is one of the most important strengths of a functioning family and one that is often the hardest to embrace.

When I played football, I learned what it meant to be a part of the team. We had our main team and within it were smaller units. I was on offense, for instance, and we were separate from the defense. And I played running back, so we running backs felt like a separate unit within the offense. But when we took the field for a game, we pulled all the separate units together and functioned like one team. And that's how we became champions!

So it goes with a family. As a whole, everyone in a functioning family considers the family to be a single unit, the result of smaller groupings within the family. In my household, though my wife Jennifer and I are individuals, we consider ourselves a single unit when it comes to parenting. My six sons definitely consider themselves a unit—they refer to themselves as the "Dunn Brothers." But when necessary, we all know when it is time to come together and act as a single unit in pursuit of the family's main priority, which is to love and protect each other.

But many families that I've worked with have for years carried resentments and the terrible wounds that only family members can inflict on each other. They have abandoned the effort to work as a unit. Because someone has been bruised, he or she has separated themselves from other family members and often has no idea of what a functioning family unit should feel like. So I help them understand how they will thrive when they work together with their family. When people get this, it's like a magic bullet, one that often makes the difference between a successful family and one that falls through the cracks.

The same will happen to you when you embark on the LCA Plan. The tallest buildings are built one floor at a time, and so it will be here. You and I will attempt to build—or rebuild—your family, one person, one heart, one mind at a time, starting with *you*.

Your *Two* Families

For the purposes of this book, you and I will be working with the family you've *created* as the "founders" of your own family. This is different from the family you were born into—your "given" family—which consists of your parents, grandparents, and siblings. You had no choice in the matter of being born—or adopted—into your given family and very little, if any, control over how it functioned. Now that you are an adult, you may have plenty of ideas how to improve the dynamics of your given family, but please believe me when I tell you that these are not your problems to fix! You may choose to work on various relationships within your given family, like being a better son or daughter, or getting closer to your siblings, but the responsibility for the success or failure of your given family rests on the heads of its founders, most likely your parents. I'm not going to address the problems of your given family here, but if you would like to see that unit change and grow, give a copy of this book to your parents!

What I want to talk about is the family you have made. *You* chose your partner. *You* and your partner made a commitment to each other, chose to have children together, chose to make your own family. *You* and your partner are the CEOs of your family, and even if right now you want nothing more than to resign your position, claim your golden parachute, and head to Tahiti, *you* are still in charge. The two of you have a lot of power, more than you probably know, to strengthen the family you have built. And just as the two of you may look around your home, see the stained carpet, the scarred and dinged dining room table, and the paint peeling off the bathroom ceiling and decide it's time to remodel, repaint, or reorganize, you can do the same with your family! Why not make it as warm and loving as possible, a wonderful place for a marriage to thrive and children to grow in? I will help you. So for the purposes of this book, when I refer to "your family," I mean the family you and your partner founded.

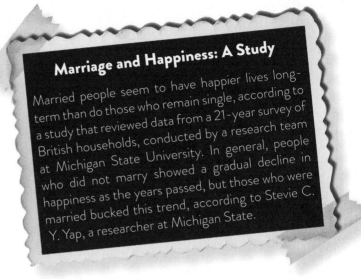

Marriage and Happiness: A Study

Married people seem to have happier lives long-term than do those who remain single, according to a study that reviewed data from a 21-year survey of British households, conducted by a research team at Michigan State University. In general, people who did not marry showed a gradual decline in happiness as the years passed, but those who were married bucked this trend, according to Stevie C. Y. Yap, a researcher at Michigan State.

Give Your Family a Chance

If what I've written makes sense to you, if you're feeling a tiny shift inside your heart that makes you think that maybe there *is* hope for you and your family, then *pay attention!* You are someone who has not given up on yourself or your family! You can entertain the possibility of change, and I can guide you, step by step through that transformation. It will require an honest look in the mirror, the will to change bad habits, and the resolve to let go of a *lot* of hurt, blame, and pain in exchange for apology and forgiveness.

This is not easy, but it has worked for many, many people, and it can work for you. Take a deep breath and know—really *know*—that this is going to lead to a better life. Press on with a positive mindset and confidence! You can do it. I know you can.

Action Starts Now!

You can begin to repair your relationship by filling out the questionnaire in the next chapter, which is the first step in the LCA Plan. One note: I'm assuming that you are reading this book on your own. Some of you will introduce your partner to what you are learning here and some won't, depending on the state of your relationship. If your partner joins you, your work may go more quickly. But either way, the information here will move *you* forward to new understanding and confidence in your relationship. So let us begin.

Life-Changing Action Plan: Step 1
Look in the Mirror

Chapters two and three are all about you—how you think about yourself, and how you think about your life, your family, your friendships, your partner. Like we talked about earlier, you might be thinking, "Hey, wait a minute. It's my partner who needs attention, not me." And you're probably right, because you and your spouse have created your problems together. And you might also be correct in thinking that a lot of the trouble is his or her fault. But if you're going to change things, you need to be honest with yourself and open your mind to the possibility that you've contributed to the mess you're in. Not everything can be the other person's fault. And to help you do that, the next two chapters will guide you through a series of questions and answers about your feelings and attitudes not just toward your relationship but toward yourself.

Many people enjoy these questions. They are carefully designed to help you think about yourself and your marriage in new ways. The insights you gain will surprise you and give you the motivation to move forward in your plan to improve your relationship. So get your pencil out and let's begin the journey.

Know Thyself: Find Out What Makes You Tick

2

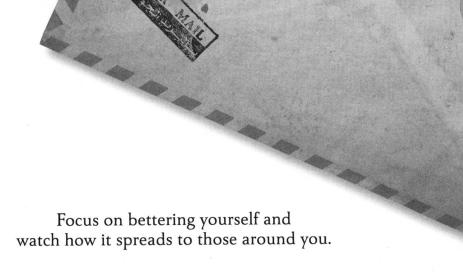

Focus on bettering yourself and
watch how it spreads to those around you.

—Troy Dunn

When your family isn't working, it's hard to remember what a good day feels like. And if you're single, coming off a divorce, or ready to look for a new relationship, you could be suffering from big-time battle fatigue and might be convinced that you're never going to find happiness again.

Discouragement, unhappiness, anger, and hopelessness are your go-to emotions. Even the bluest sky looks gray; that is, if you even bother to look up! But looking up and forward is exactly what I want you to do. I'm going to help you step outside of the drama and disappointment of your family life, or the mistakes you made in a previous relationship, so that you can once again believe in yourself and your family again. I'm promising hard work and much reward.

So let's begin the LCA Plan.

Self-Assessment: How Bad Is Bad?

If someone were to be a fly on the wall in your home, watching you and your spouse eating, sleeping, watching television, checking your computer, putting away the groceries, deciding who's going to pick up your son from basketball practice, and so on, how would they describe your relationship? Loving? Hostile? Noncommunicative? Remind me never to invite them over for dinner?

It helps to get a sense of where you are in your relationship as you figure out a recovery plan.

On the Brink of Disaster?

You might be skeptical that you can ever change your family. You may even believe your family is officially past the point of saving. And I have to be honest and say that there are some families who, for the sake of its members, should be separated, at least temporarily. If, for instance, yours is a family that is dealing with alcoholism, a drug problem, or physical abuse, you need immediate help of a kind I'm not qualified to give. For your sake, and for the sake of any children in your home, I beg you to muster the strength to seek assistance right away. If you're someone who is separated or divorced because of this kind of toxic destruction, you know what I'm talking about, and I applaud you for your courage and would like to help you repair yourself so you can move forward.

If your family is free of drugs and/or other kinds of abuse, you are blessed. You probably don't think so when staring across the table at your partner and all you see is an enemy who shows no signs of understanding or even liking you. And you feel exactly the same way about him or her! Even though you live under the same roof, maybe you spend most of your time apart, and when you're together, the simplest exchange can quickly explode into conflict or even all-out war. Further, the arguments, depending on your family's particular flavor of miscommunication, could be noisy, even verbally abusive, shooting insults at each other like missiles, or they might be deadly silent, with unspoken allegations crowding the air you breathe. Mistrust colors every interaction. You haven't made love in months. You can't remember the last time you shared a smile. Your friends, even your mother, with whom you talk all the time since things are so awful at home, have begun to hint that you should leave. And if you have children living in the type of home environment I'm describing, I can promise you that they're miserable, too, probably acting out in their own ways as they assimilate the behavior they see. You are all exhausted from the battling and you, for one, are ready to throw in the towel.

I don't blame you. Being stuck in a bad situation grinds you down so that changing a family's dynamics can seem as impossible as turning an ocean liner around on a stormy sea. To you I say, read on before you make a decision to give up. Think of the people you know who have divorced and who are struggling with single parenting or a difficult new relationship, and look again at what you have, or could have if you dig in and give your marriage another try.

The "Okay" Families

As sad as it makes me to see horribly dysfunctional couples, almost *more* heartbreaking to me are the many families who are functioning in a sort of suspended limbo. There's little of the hostility and anger you see in truly unhappy couples, but no one's doing high-fives either. These couples, and there are a lot of them, get along well enough, but they are not really engaged in their relationship. And they don't take any steps toward more intimacy because, sadly, they have no idea how much they are missing and how much better their family lives could be!

They suffer from the "okay" problem.

Your family life isn't exactly great, but it's "okay." There are no knock-down, drag-out fights over who's taking out the trash, but on the other hand, no one seems to really talk at all. About anything. Everyone's so engrossed in their own worlds—jobs, schoolwork, sports, hobbies—that there seems to be little overlap, connection, or communication between partners or their children. There are no real special family times, where everyone is together and enjoying each other's company. Instead, the days just go by, one after the other after the other.

So when someone asks how things are, you shrug and say, "Okay."

Really? That's it? Is "okay" really what you were striving for? Does that accurately describe your hopes and dreams in having a family? Is that really why you fell in love, got married, and built a family, so you all could be the "okay" people?

Think about it: Is there any *other* part of your life where you settle for "okay"? Imagine if your friend ate at a new restaurant in town, and when you asked how the food was, he said, "Okay." Would you drop everything to make a reservation to eat there? Of course not! If your latest job performance review simply read, "She's okay as an employee," do you think you'd get a promotion? Nope. There are few areas in life where "okay" is good enough. Why should your own family be just "okay"?

Maybe, over time, you've begun to accept the idea that eventually all relationships hit the snooze button. You're not quite sure how this happened to you and your partner, so you just accept it as the new normal. Besides, when you look around at your friends and extended family, a lot of them seem to be in the same boat. Their relationships aren't really going anywhere, but they're not sinking either. And since you most likely know families who *are* in far worse shape than you, you shrug and tell yourself to count your blessings.

But the truth is that if you are in an "okay" relationship, you are only inches away from a "fantastic" relationship and may not even know it! Imagine if you were running a marathon blindfolded. You have no idea how much farther you have to go before you cross that finish line, but you know that you're exhausted. Your body aches and you desperately want to be done running, so you stop. Then you take off that blindfold and realize that you gave up and stopped running literally two inches away from the finish line. Out of the thousands of steps you've just taken to get that far, it would have taken exactly one more to cross that finish line and step into your victory. That's what's going on if you're suffering from the "okay" problem. You have stopped just short of your potential.

Maybe it's because you're exhausted, frustrated, or just don't know how to take that next step into victory. But given the choice, wouldn't you like to take that final step, to try to make things better? Wouldn't it be nice to rediscover why you and your husband married in the first place? Or why you committed yourself to your partner? And wouldn't it be wonderful to see how great it can be to do things as a real family again?

I'm going to help you take that step up into a whole new level of intimacy, joy and, yes, even romance! You will be able to take off the blinders that have kept you from seeing the incredible potential hiding within the collective heart of your family. This program is tailor-made for you and your family because you have the groundwork already in place by being together, committed to each other, and looking to make things better.

Single Parents

There are currently 12 million families in the United States headed by a single parent, and 80 percent of those parents are mothers. If you are among this number, you are solely responsible for your children, probably holding down a job (or two), and very likely worried about money. You barely have time to sleep, let alone deal with another relationship and/or partner.

And if you are in a relationship, you have a whole other layer of considerations because of your kids. Children in these situations view men through two prisms: their "previous" dad and their potential or "next" dad. That's it. The moment you walk a new man into the house, your child is thinking, "This guy is bald. My real dad isn't bald." Or he's thinking, "This guy looks mean. I want a nice daddy." They are sizing him up as a father before you have even considered him boyfriend material, much less a potential husband. So you can't play with their heads while you're in the process of deciding how you feel about a new man in your life. It's really important to keep your boyfriends away from your children until you're sure the man will be a permanent part of your family.

You can benefit greatly from the work in this book, both by realizing where you may have made mistakes in your marriage or last relationship, and in getting to know a new man in your life. You just have to do it away from the curious eyes and tender hearts of your children.

It Makes This Clanking Sound

When you take your car to the mechanic or call up tech support for your computer, you're asked a lot of questions about what's not working correctly. The professional asks you some questions to get to the root of the problem, and your answers help him or her fix the problem. It's pretty straightforward.

But asking you to identify your family's problems is a bit trickier. Most of the people I help don't know what's wrong, but they can describe what hurts or angers them. Since they're right in the middle of everything and very upset, it's very hard for them to even know where to begin to repair things. Their answers are pretty general and often full of anger and blame toward their partner or themselves. They need help in connecting their feelings to the underlying problem so it can be solved. You might tell me, "I can't stand our fights," which is your *feeling*, but what I hear is the **problem**, which is that you and your spouse need to improve your poor communication skills.

A single person, especially one coming off a divorce, is equally vulnerable to giving up. She's just been through one of the most grueling emotional experiences a person can have. Her whole life may have been turned upside down. She may be in a new house, a new city, or have a new job, and if there are children, you can bet they're acting out due to their own pain. You can't blame her for wanting to curl up in a fetal position and hide from the world.

Well, nothing's hopeless if you're willing to try. And if you've had the courage to get out of a terrible relationship, with all the pain and suffering that entailed, you are obviously a strong person. Why not tap that courage to begin a new way of thinking about yourself and future relationships?

Below are a series of questions designed to cut through all the emotions you're feeling, and the strong (maybe misguided) opinions you hold about your marriage and your spouse, and help you get a more objective view of what's going on in your relationship. Read them slowly and answer them with honesty and care. The process is as important as the answers, because you will start to see things differently.

That's Me?!?

The questions you're about to answer are geared toward helping you think in new ways about yourself, your spouse, and your family. There are no right or wrong answers—only truthful ones.

I love these questions because in answering them, people see themselves more clearly. They start to make connections between their attitudes and their behavior. When they are newly aware, they are then able to open up with their spouses and families. Right off the bat, they become more generous in their assessments of themselves and others. This is a great place to start our work together; it's foundational.

Please give yourself enough time to answer the questions thoughtfully. And please don't answer them just after you've had a big fight with your spouse, because you won't get a true picture of your relationship and feelings.

Instead, center yourself, take a deep breath, exhale, and then once you're calm, read each question, ponder it, and then answer it honestly. Again, there are no wrong answers, and there is no time limit. This is just for you to get a true snapshot of things as they are, or at least how they seem to be to you today.

Note: If you happen to be lucky enough to have a spouse doing this with you, great! You should each answer these questions separately, then share your answers with each other and discuss them briefly, but only briefly. You can print off copies of these questions at www.TroyDunnBooks.com.

You

1. Are you happy with your current employment situation?
Yes   No   Somewhat

2. Are you happy with your physical appearance?
Yes   No   Somewhat

3. Are you happy with your house?
Yes   No   Somewhat

4. Are you happy with the city in which you live?
Yes   No   Somewhat

5. Do you have a close friend?
Yes   No

6. Do you have a hobby?
Yes   No

7. Do you feel you have grown and matured since high school?
Yes   No   Somewhat

8. Do you consider yourself an optimist?
Yes   No   Somewhat

   Realist?
Yes   No   Somewhat

   Pessimist?
Yes   No   Somewhat

9. Have you set goals for yourself?
Yes   No   Somewhat

10. Have you experienced tragedy or loss in your life?
Yes   No   Somewhat

11. If you answered "yes" to the previous question, do you believe you came through the tragedy stronger?
Yes   No   Somewhat

Weaker?
Yes   No   Somewhat

Unchanged?
Yes   No   Somewhat

12. As an individual, do you feel that you are, for the most part, where you wanted to be in your life at this age?
Yes   No   Somewhat

13. Do you believe you have one or more character flaws? (A character flaw can be anything that you believe hinders you emotionally, physically, morally, or financially—such as lying, anger, overspending, jealousy, impatience, martyrdom, greed, drinking, drugs, distrust, exaggerating, stubbornness, arrogance, etc.)
Yes   No   Somewhat

14. If you answered "yes" to the previous question, have you ever made a sincere effort to overcome or eradicate this character flaw from your life?
Yes   No   Somewhat

15. If you answered "yes" to question 13, do you believe your life and relationships would be better if this flaw was no longer an issue in your life?
Yes   No   Somewhat

16. Do you believe you are capable of change?
Yes   No   Somewhat

17. Do you believe some of your best traits/habits/issues are a result of the family in which you were raised?
Yes   No   Somewhat

18. Do you believe some of your worst traits/habits/issues are a result of the family in which you were raised?
    Yes   No   Somewhat

19. Do you respect yourself?
    Yes   No   Somewhat

20. Do you have hope for yourself?
    Yes   No   Somewhat

Your Spouse

1. Are you happy with your spouse's current employment situation?
   Yes   No   Somewhat

2. Do you think your spouse is happy with his or her current employment?
   Yes   No   Somewhat

3. Are you happy with your spouse's physical appearance?
   Yes   No   Somewhat

4. Is your spouse happy with the house in which you live?
   Yes   No   Somewhat

5. Is your spouse happy with the city in which you live?
   Yes   No   Somewhat

6. Does your spouse have a close friend?
   Yes   No

7. Does your spouse have a hobby?
   Yes   No

8. Do you feel your spouse has grown and matured since high school?
   Yes   No   Somewhat

9. Do you consider your spouse an optimist?
   Yes   No   Somewhat

   Realist?
   Yes   No   Somewhat

   Pessimist?
   Yes   No   Somewhat

10. Has your spouse set goals for him/herself?
    Yes   No   Somewhat

11. Has your spouse experienced tragedy or loss in his or her life?
    Yes   No   Somewhat

12. If you answered "yes" to the previous question, do you believe your spouse came through the tragedy stronger?
    Yes   No   Somewhat

    Weaker?
    Yes   No   Somewhat

    Unchanged?
    Yes   No   Somewhat

13. As an individual, do you feel your spouse, for the most part, is where he/she wants to be at his/her age?
    Yes   No   Somewhat

14. Do you believe your spouse has one or more character flaws? (A character flaw can be anything that you believe hinders you emotionally, physically, morally, or financially—lying, anger, overspending, jealousy, impatience, martyrdom, greed, drinking, drugs, distrust, exaggerating, stubbornness, arrogance, etc.)
    Yes   No   Somewhat

15. If you answered "yes" to the previous question, has your spouse ever made a sincere effort to overcome or eradicate this character flaw from his/her life?
    Yes   No   Somewhat

16. If you answered "yes" to question 14, do you believe your spouse's life and relationships would be better if this flaw was no longer an issue in his/her life?
    Yes   No   Somewhat

17. Do you believe your spouse is capable of changing?
    Yes   No   Somewhat

18. Do you believe some of your spouse's worst traits/habits/issues are a result of the family in which he/she was raised?
    Yes   No   Somewhat

19. Do you believe some of your spouse's best traits/habits/issues are a result of the family in which he/she was raised?
    Yes   No   Somewhat

20. Do you think your spouse respects him/herself?
    Yes   No   Somewhat

21. Do you think your spouse has hope for him/herself?
    Yes   No   Somewhat

Your Relationship

This set of questions concerns your relationship—how you rate it, how you and your partner interact, and how serious your problems are. Answering them honestly, as you did with the previous set of questions, will give you some clarity about the state of your relationship.

If your spouse is filling out this questionnaire as well, and you both think that revealing your answers to each other will trigger an unhealthy argument or hurt feelings, then you can agree to share your answers with each other at a future time. After you have received and implemented some of the tools contained in this book, you will be in a better and stronger place to exchange answers and calmly discuss your feelings about each other's responses to these questions.

Whether or not your spouse joins you now, honesty is the goal. This is an excellent opportunity for insight.

1. On a scale of 1 to 10, with 1 representing divorce and 10 representing the perfect relationship, how would you rate your marriage? (Not 10 minutes after an argument or 10 minutes after making love, just overall.)
   1 2 3 4 5 6 7 8 9 10

2. On a scale of 1 to 10, with 1 representing abusive and 10 representing a healthy disagreement, how do you rate the majority of your arguments with your spouse?
   1 2 3 4 5 6 7 8 9 10

3. On a scale of 1 to 10, with 1 representing terrible and 10 representing excellent, how do you rate you and your spouse's overall communication skills?
   1 2 3 4 5 6 7 8 9 10

4. On a scale of 1 to 10, with 1 representing terrible and 10 representing excellent, how do you rate you and your spouse's overall sex life?
   1 2 3 4 5 6 7 8 9 10

5. When you argue with your spouse, does the disagreement stay centered on the issue, or does it turn into name-calling and veer off topic?

Stays on the issue   Veers off topic

6. Do you consider yourself a victim in your marriage? (Signs of this include a feeling of not being listened to, of having your own wishes ignored, of not feeling the relationship is balanced equally between your needs and your partner's, etc.)

Yes   No

7. When there are troubles, do you:
   A. Keep it to yourself
   B. Talk about it with a friend/relative
   C. Talk about it with your spouse

8. Do you believe your worst arguments are about the same issues over and over?

Yes   No

9. If you answered "yes" to the question above, have you or your spouse made any specific attempts to change the circumstances of those issues?

Yes   No

10. Do you believe the challenges facing your marriage are having:
    A. No impact on your children
    B. Some impact on your children
    C. Significant impact on your children

11. Is sex used as a weapon and reward in your marriage?

Yes   No

12. Does your spouse know how you truly feel?

Yes   No

13. Would your marriage be able to move forward if one of you asked for forgiveness and the other offered forgiveness?
Yes   No

14. How often does the thought of divorce enter your mind?
A. Never
B. Only after a bad argument
C. It is always on your mind

15. If you suddenly discovered you or your spouse were terminally ill, would you handle things differently within the walls of your marriage?
Yes   No

16. If you answered "yes" to the previous question, ask yourself what you would do differently.
Write it here: _____

17. Now ask yourself why it would take the discovery of imminent death to trigger that sort of change in behavior.
Write it here: _____

You might want to score your responses, but you can't! This isn't a contest. The purpose of each question is to give you an opportunity to ponder things as they are. You might already feel some shifts in your thinking after identifying how your life has unfolded and changed you.

Embrace those new feelings as you continue on this journey. Your answers will provide you with all sorts of things: areas to focus on, patterns to break, topics to discuss with your spouse, goals to set, motivations for change, and ways to measure progress as you move forward through the LCA Plan. Save these and refer back to them. There is a lot of insight into your life contained in your answers, and you can use them to seek solutions to some of the troubled areas in your marriage, yourself, or both! The great news is that no matter how many negative answers you gave, you don't have to be discouraged. The fact that you are here reading and answering these questions means you recognize that there's untapped opportunity to improve yourself, which means your life will get better.

The goal here isn't perfection. This is the first of many times I will remind you that you, your spouse, and your children are not, and never will be, perfect. But you can strive and work toward improvement. That is what the LCA Plan will guide you to: making a better life for you and your family. And that is what you are doing right now, so let's keep going.

The next chapter will help you understand how the answers you gave here can be used to improve your relationship.

What's It *All* About? Get the Answers You Need

3

> I consider honesty to be magical,
> as it causes truth to suddenly appear.
>
> —Troy Dunn

You might be wondering what all these questions have to do with what you consider the train wreck that is your relationship. Who cares if you like your house or job or whether you're overweight or thin? You're so angry at your partner that you could be living in a zoo and it wouldn't make any difference to you. In fact, you feel like you *are* living in a zoo. And as for your weight, if your partner wasn't so stubborn/selfish/mean/demanding/inattentive, you wouldn't be scarfing down ice cream in the kitchen at two in the morning by yourself.

But guess what? Answering these questions is exactly what you need to do if you're going to commit yourself to the kind of change that will repair your relationship.

I've developed this questionnaire over many years of working with troubled families, because the information the answers reveal allows people to see very clearly how the many details of their lives influence their own personal happiness and growth. Such knowledge is enormously empowering, not just for the relationship, but for each partner in the relationship. Self-awareness lets you step back from the emotional chaos you may be living in and gain some perspective on your situation.

This questionnaire is all about you. Whether you are single or in a relationship, you will learn more about yourself and your motivations. If you have a partner, you will think about what he or she brings (or doesn't bring!) to the relationship. What you learn here will give you a new perspective on your relationship and lead you to rethink some of your actions and personal choices. You will be motivated to continue working on your relationship instead of giving up.

This chapter walks you through the questionnaire and helps you interpret your answers productively. You can find out what you're really thinking! The people I've worked with usually get a lot out of this process, and you will, too. You'll discover things about yourself that you didn't know before, information you can lift from these next couple of pages and place directly into your life.

Warning: If you did not answer the questions in the previous chapter, please do not read any further in this chapter. It is really important you answer the questions in chapter two without having any insight into the purpose of each question. So if you skipped over them, go back now and answer them. Then return here.

Now, here's the cheat sheet to the questions in chapter two.

You

1. Are you happy with your current employment situation?

A lot of people place a significant amount of value on their work and their career. They judge their personal success by their professional success. Many don't like to admit this—they will insist that their job doesn't dictate their personal happiness or their own perceived worth—but evidence points to the contrary. People will skip a high school reunion because they feel they haven't been as successful in their careers as they should have been.

But the fact is that people who are generally happy with their work spread their contentment around. They are more patient with and tolerant of the people and events around them, tend to roll better with the punches, and respond more positively to things. If you are unhappy with your "day job," chances are that you will arrive home after work unhappier than if you felt satisfied with your workday, and your mindset will be a little darker than it would be if you enjoyed or took pride in what you accomplished at work. This "splashdown mood" can and does significantly impact the way you interact with others in your life. You may think your problems are due to other things (usually your partner) when in fact, at least a part of your discontent could be due to your work. An unfulfilling job can leave a hole in your life that is too easily filled by anger toward and impatience with your loved ones.

2. **Are you happy with your physical appearance?**

Everyone feels better when they look good, but almost nobody thinks he looks as good as he should, especially when bombarded with photographs (always airbrushed into perfection) of all the perfectly toned bodies in the world. Your attitude toward your physical looks can affect your relationship profoundly, especially in the bedroom. People who are basically comfortable with their appearance, even if they know they could lose a few pounds, tend to be less self-conscious and more relaxed. But if you've got weight issues, and/or if the fatter you get, the thinner and more toned your partner seems, you can carry your own bad feelings into your relationship. Problems you may be having with physical intimacy can be related to your own frustration with your body rather than your partner's attitudes. Understanding this is very helpful, because if you can see that the reason you're leery of the bedroom is because of your own self-doubt, you might be able to override those negative thoughts and empower yourself to make love to your partner anyway. This could be a very important shift for you and your partner.

3. **Are you happy with your house?**

4. **Are you happy with the city in which you live?**

Questions 3 and 4 seek to discover if your surroundings are causing you disappointment and whether that disappointment is enough to create a disruption in your happiness. If you don't like your house or community, if you're always carrying a chip on your shoulder wishing you lived somewhere else, you tend to be more detached and more critical of things around you, and your dissatisfaction could leak into your family relations. It's likely you may not be in a position to change the house or city you live in, so the best thing to do is to recognize those feelings exist and do your best to separate them out, compartmentalize them, so they don't continue to have an impact on your relationship.

It's tempting to lump them all together by telling your-self things like, "I can't believe he moved me away from my mother and into this godforsaken city to live in this dump!" Even if the facts are true, thinking this way is unfair to your partner. It's highly improbable that he wanted to move to your present location just to make you miserable. His intentions were good, perhaps connected to a jump in salary that would make your lives better, or maybe the move allowed him to pursue a professional dream he had always had but would never have been able to achieve if he hadn't been willing to relocate. Further, his desire to enjoy a house and city are just as great as yours are, so attaching how and where you live to the way you view your partner is unfair and unhealthy.

5. **Do you have a close friend?**

Friendship is an important part of being a happy human. Being able to confide in someone brings enormous comfort when you're feeling low and is even better when you want to share good news. Many people, myself included, consider their spouses to be their best friends. Jennifer and I know each other better than anyone else, we share a lot of history, and we trust each other. If you're having a difficult time with your partner or are now single, you may not be in this situ-ation, but you may have other close friendships you value. And beyond those deep friendships are the many pleasures of more casual, but valuable, friendships that keep you laughing and keep you from crying.

If you don't have many friends or have a hard time mak-ing friends, you could be shutting yourself off from the world around you. When you do this, you can easily put too much pressure on your partner, expecting him or her to answer all your emotional needs.

Conversely, you may have friends but use them as sound-ing boards for all that's wrong with your partner instead of talking things out at home. This is extremely toxic for a relationship. These factors can be adding pressures to a relationship, and it's helpful to be aware of them.

6. Do you have a hobby?

This question might seem irrelevant to your relationship, but those who have hobbies and outside interests tend to have a healthier perspective on their relationships. Doing something you enjoy—playing sports, sketching, painting, reading, collecting, hiking, gardening, tending to animals; anything that helps define you as an individual and brings you personal fulfillment—boosts happiness. A hobby allows for "me" time and keeps people from overthinking everything else in their lives. We sometimes hear about "helicopter parents" or "smothering spouses." These people are usually the ones who need an outside interest the most! They need something else to direct their thoughts and attention to besides the minute-by-minute life of their spouse or child. This question allows you to think about how you balance outside interests and time for yourself in your relationship, and how much emphasis you put on self-improvement.

7. Do you feel you have grown and matured since high school?

Most people, when given enough time to ponder this question, generally arrive at a "yes." It's fair to say that the experiences of life, both good and bad, have changed us in some way. We have learned from our mistakes, kicked old habits, outgrown some behaviors, and perhaps even accumulated a little wisdom.

The reasoning behind this question is twofold. First, I'd like you to acknowledge how you have in fact changed, and really understand that change is possible. This is a very important insight and a valuable exercise, because too often people don't give themselves enough credit for the changes and adaptations they've made in their lives. You have perhaps married or divorced, had children, moved to a new town, changed careers, stopped smoking, learned to swim, drive, cook—the list is endless. You should definitely honor, perhaps even write down, the ways you have changed as you've gotten older. Give yourself a well-earned pat on the back.

And, if you've been able to change and adapt creatively to what life has handed you, you can use this skill to find ways to improve your thoughts about your relationship. You may realize you can repair your family in the same conscientious and forward-looking way you've made other changes in your life.

Please note that I ask this same question in the section about your partner. I've found that while people can recognize and acknowledge how they have changed, they often have a blind spot when it comes to change in others, refusing to honor others who've shifted behavior in their own lives. For the sake of this exercise, I'd ask you to review how you answered this question about your partner and make sure you give him due credit for any changes he has made in his life. It might seem to you that he is locked into his behavior and refuses to change, but it's far more probable that he, like you, has made some significant adjustments in his own life since you have been together. Further, he could do so again! Everyone is capable of some level of transformation—you, your partner, your children—and it's helpful to remember that all of you have a choice in the matter.

8. **Do you consider yourself an optimist, pessimist, or realist?**
    Many people haven't thought about their overall outlook on life, but it's really important to have a sense of how you see the world. It gives you a great tool to check your reactions to things. When you have a down day, do you sink into despair? How easily do you shrug off bad news? When your spouse comes home in a funk, do you join him or do you do your best to help him see the bright side? If you're not sure, and you feel comfortable doing so, ask the people you know best and who you can trust to be honest to tell you. I've found that about half the time, people find they are perceived differently by others than from how they view themselves.

Another reason it's important to know whether you see the glass half-empty or half-full is because your attitude affects how others treat you. If people sense you are open to good news, you'll hear more of it. If, on the other hand, your son comes home with a huge smile on his face because he got a part in the school play and your first reaction is, "Does this mean I have to dig up a costume?" he'll learn to downplay or not share his future accomplishments.

If you think about it, you will realize that this is exactly what you do to others. You probably tend to edit what you tell a friend who always thinks the worst is going to happen, and you share your news in a different way with the friend who will be more upbeat. Why shouldn't everyone, including your partner, do the same with you?

9. Have you set goals for yourself?

I am asking you this to get you to think: Are you working to make things better or just hanging on, hoping they don't get worse? If you realize you're in the latter camp, don't despair. I just want to guide you to step back so you can look at your behavior from the outside. Then you can see whether you're walking in circles or moving forward. You can make the decision to improve your life and set some goals for yourself and your relationship. Goals help you navigate your daily decisions. With each choice you make you can ask yourself, "Which choice moves me closer to my goals?" If you're single or if your relationship is in trouble, you can do this for yourself. If you and your partner are in a better place together, you can set goals for your relationship and your children. Goals really help you move forward in life. Driving without a destination is a risky journey, and you may end up right where you set out to go—nowhere.

10. and 11. Have you experienced tragedy or loss in your life? How did you come through it?

These questions encourage you to think about your coping skills. Generally, when trouble strikes, people respond either with "tools" or "weapons." Religious faith, psychological help, communication, and compassion for others are "tools." They comfort you, lead you to answers, and help you adjust to whatever has happened so that you can absorb your sadness and pain and slowly move forward. "Weapons" are responses like anger, blame, withdrawal into yourself, substance abuse, or simply becoming paralyzed and doing nothing. They can provide temporary solace but don't solve problems. Think about the tragedies you've experienced in your life and whether you dealt with them with tools or weapons. Depending on which you chose, what were the outcomes? If you relied on weapons, could you replace them with tools?

12. **As an individual, do you feel you are, for the most part, where you wanted to be in your life at this age?**

This is a difficult question. It's relatively easy (too easy!) to judge another person and do a quick evaluation about whether she is where she should be at this stage of her life. When we look in the mirror, it's much harder. We lack objectivity about ourselves. But as with all the other questions here, this one can help you stand back and gain a clearer perspective on yourself apart from your relationship. Consider different categories, not just life as a whole. Are you the caliber of partner you wanted to be this far into your marriage? How are you doing as a parent? Where are you in your career? Does your body look and function the way you hoped it would at this age? You can go through a list of areas of your life in this self-assessment. Try to measure yourself honestly. Don't let yourself off the hook if you know in your heart you haven't lived up to what you planned for yourself. But don't be too hard on yourself either. Life has many twists and turns, and most people try to do their best with the hand they're dealt.

This self-assessment can lead you to setting the goals we discussed above. You can begin to let go of behaviors that aren't getting you anywhere and could be damaging your relationship and instead focus on positive change. Even the process of doing this, the shift you feel in taking charge of yourself, is empowering, and the results can be life changing, a gift to yourself and your family.

13. **Do you believe you have one or more character flaws? (A character flaw can be anything that you believe hinders you emotionally, physically, morally, financially—lying, anger, over-spending, jealousy, impatience, martyrdom, greed, drinking, drugs, distrust, exaggerating, stubbornness, arrogance, etc.)**

14. **If you answered "yes" to the previous question, have you ever made a sincere effort to overcome or eradicate this character flaw from your life?**

15. **If you answered "yes" to question 13, do you believe your life and relationships would be better if this flaw was no longer an issue in your life?**

16. **Do you believe you are capable of change?**

    Everyone has flaws. Insecurity, jealousy, vanity, inflexibility . . . and those are just for starters. So don't beat yourself up when you realize you're not perfect, but do try to take responsibility for your weaknesses and acknowledge how they can create havoc in a relationship. If you tend to be stingy and are constantly harping about the cost of everything, for instance, and tend to jump on your partner every time he buys a venti latte at Starbucks, how does that affect your discussions about money? Could you learn to curb your tongue, if not your attitude?

    Questions 13 through 16 continue the process of helping you analyze your own behavior to get a clearer idea of your strengths and weaknesses. If you're recovering from divorce, this might give you some insight into what went wrong in your marriage so you can make some changes in your next relationship. For those in troubled relationships, recognizing your own weaknesses leads you to a fairer assessment of the causes for your problems. Put together, these questions are a very helpful way to begin to think about your own behavior separately from that of your partner. They speak to the areas

47

of change and goals you can set for yourself, and serve as impetus to judge your partner and family with more compassion. People in glass houses . . . . You get the idea.

17. **Do you believe some of your best traits/habits/issues are a result of the family in which you were raised?**

18. **Do you believe some of your worst traits/habits/issues are a result of the family in which you were raised?**

These questions also spark new thinking about all the behaviors—the good, bad, and ugly—that you've picked up along life's way. Acknowledging them enables you not to cast blame but to simply be aware of where you have been and accept some of the less stellar behaviors you might have brought to your relationship. Then you can make some adjustments to lessen their damage. Keep in mind that someday your own children will be asking themselves these same questions and imprinting what they learned at their parents' knees. If you still have children living at home, you now have time to become a better role model, so that they can enter adulthood empowered with positive and productive outlooks. Remember, your role is not to change your given family (parents, siblings, etc.), so don't use these insights to rewrite your given family's history. Instead, use what you learn to shape your created family—you, your spouse, and your children. *This* family is your responsibility.

19. **Do you respect yourself?**

Don't let this question mislead you. I am not asking if you are pleased with every choice you have made in your life. I am asking if you respect the type of person you are, the way you treat your spouse, your children, other people in your life? Ask yourself: Are you a good person? Your answer says a lot about your outlook on the rest of the people in your life. Someone who respects himself is generally kinder to those around him than a person who is truly unhappy with whom he is or who he has become. Someone who doesn't

respect himself can spread his self-loathing to everyone around him. Misdirected anger is a common side effect of self-disrespect.

20. Do you have hope for yourself?

This is a pretty basic question. If you are really stuck and have no idea how to change the bad situation in which you find yourself, if every day seems the same as the day before and nothing improves, you are living in a very dark place.

I ask this question to motivate you, to make you realize that there is always hope. There is always the possibility of changing things for the better. No one—not you, not your partner, not your children—chooses to be unhappy with themselves or each other forever. If you've made the choice to live without hope, recognize that it *is* a choice. Think how your attitude affects the rest of your family. If you can shift your mindset, even a little, you will find you can dig down and find the will and energy to do the hard work to grow and improve as an individual. Doing that, whether you are single or in a relationship, is a big step forward. As a single person, you can begin preparing yourself for a new relationship, if that's what you want, and if you're in a marriage, you will be doing a great service to your partner and your family. Where there is no hope, tragedy looms nearby. Find the hope, hoist it high, and keep your mind and heart on it until better days arrive. And they will.

Your Partner

Questions 21 through 40 are all about your spouse or, more accurately, your perception of your spouse. If the two of you are able to do so without significant anger and drama, it would be good for you to share with each other your answers about how you perceive your partner (and how your partner perceives you). Listen carefully to one another's answers and do not react. I repeat, do not react. One more time—do not react! Just listen. Absorb it. Don't let it evolve into an argument. Let it be an enlightening glimpse into the mind of your partner and his or her perception of you.

It will give you both a fascinating perspective on each other and provide things to think about and possibly work on. Work is good. It's what builds better families.

If you don't feel the time is right for such intimacy, especially if you and your partner are antagonistic toward each other, just hold on to your answers. If you decide to work toward improving your relationship with the insights and tools provided here, there will be some big changes in your relationship, and it will be empowering to look at what you have written now and compare your perceptions of your partner as your relationship improves.

Your Relationship

The remaining questions, for those who are in relationships, are to begin to tease out the problems you face. The first questions help you decide how bad you think things are, so you can begin to realize how much work you have ahead of you in order to repair your relationship, if you choose to do so. Most of the rest of the questions address the common conflicts that create unrest and hostility in marriages. Many of these issues are ones that are discussed later in this book, so if you find that your answers are mostly in the negative columns, there's hope! I've laid out many, many strategies for you to shift the dynamics of your relationship and bring light where there is darkness. Don't forget that I have worked with many people in circumstances very similar to the ones in which you find yourself and have brought them across the stormy seas to calm waters and happier times. Stay in this with me.

Life-Changing Action Plan: Step 2
Change, the Game Changer

I hope you now have a fuller picture about yourself and your partner and can see how your relationship can be strongly affected by how you each see the world.

Opening your mind to the other influences on you both doesn't justify the silences, hostility, and chaos that may be a part of your day-to-day life at home. And they're certainly not excuses for your partner's bad behavior! But the more clues you have to explain what's going on between you, the better your chances of fixing things, which is why we're here.

The bottom line is that if you're serious about fixing your relationship, you need all the help you can get! So embrace all the new information you can, including—*gulp*—if and when your own behavior is driving some of the conflict between you and your partner.

This can be hard. It's much easier to blame everything on your partner and stay where you are—stuck and dissatisfied, but self-righteous in your victimhood.

If you're reading this book, however, I'm guessing that blaming each other for everything that goes wrong somehow doesn't feel very good anymore. You may be deeply discouraged and disheartened, convinced that you and your partner have little in common, that your lives are heading down completely different paths, but there's still a little nagging something inside of you that is asking, "Does this *have* to be this way?"

The answer is no, no, *no!* You *don't* have to spend the rest of your relationship as if you're living in an armed camp, with enemy fire coming from your very own side, or, just as badly, spending your days and nights in a colorless, empty no-man's-land where you and your partner have about as much intimacy as two people sitting next to each other on a bus. You *can* clean up your relationship, communicate in new ways with your partner, and find excitement and joy that you didn't know existed. This book is chock-full of strategies, advice, and insight to help you along the way to a new, satisfying relationship, one that will amaze you in its richness and variety.

And it starts right here, with step two of the Life-Changing Action Plan.

Commit to Change: Overcome Your Fear, Reap the Rewards

4

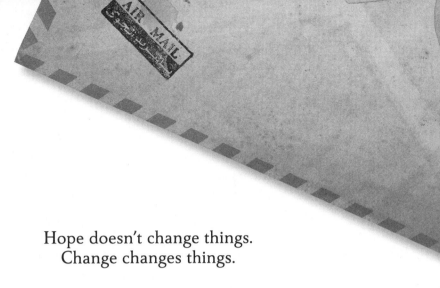

Hope doesn't change things.
Change changes things.

—Troy Dunn

Change is the most important theme of this book. Opening your mind and heart, finding the courage and will to work for changes in your relationship—even when they are uncomfortable, and even when they run smack up against your deepest instincts to protect yourself—will be what carries you to success in fixing your family.

We will be talking about change all the time, with every new strategy I introduce, and with every tool I offer you to replace toxic behavior with healthy ways of communicating. In time, as you begin to see the good effects of the small, incremental changes I suggest, you will find them easier to embrace. You will get excited by them and be energized to move on to bigger, life-changing shifts in your relationship. It will be a gradual, sometimes painful process, and you will at times wonder if it's worth sticking with the plan. You and your partner will need time to adjust to your new dynamic, accept the fact that there will be setbacks, that you will have to readjust and then go forward again as you begin to build a new, kinder relationship. It took a long time for the two of you to get to the standoff you find yourself in, and it will take a steady, consistent commitment on your part to turn the tide.

But many couples have taken the steps that I show you here and have transformed their lives. You can, too.

Are You Ready to Change?

If changing were easy, everyone would be perfect. Depending on your own personal wish list, you'd be 10 pounds thinner, have a great job, a clean and organized household, excellent relations with all the people in your life, and maybe even enjoy inner peace!

And I'm sure you've tried to change some of your bad habits. Maybe you are determined to stick to a new exercise plan, or you promised yourself to keep better track of your finances, watch less television or spend less time on the Internet, or spend more quality time with each of your children.

For the first few weeks or even a month, you're disciplined about your new behavior and you might even have begun to see some good results. But then something happens . . . You've got an early morning meeting at work, so you skip out on exercising that day. You get hooked on a movie on cable and then are too lazy and tired to get up off the sofa, so you stay plugged in front of the television for another hour. Your son begs to spend the night at a friend's house, so you cancel your plans with him. You tell yourself that each lapse is just a one-time thing, but then it happens again, and then another time, and pretty soon your good intentions have gone up in smoke and you're back to your old routines.

Deciding to change and then failing is bad on so many levels. The more you attempt changes and don't succeed, the more you begin to believe that you can *never* succeed, and then, finally, you stop trying.

Why is it so hard to change?

Change, especially *permanent* change, can be one of the most difficult things you choose to do in life. It requires several steps: First, you have to understand why you want to change; then you must have a deep, driving desire to make things better; and then you have to create a road map for accomplishing that change; and then, finally and hardest of all, you must lock doors behind you, not just close them. Have the discipline and commitment to follow through until you've achieved the change. I know it sounds like a lot, and the process might sound daunting, but you can do it. I've seen so many people transform their relationships by recognizing that they had to change, then stepping into that change and rescuing love and trust that had been buried for years under resentments and recriminations. Witnessing their courage as they overcame years of unhappiness to rekindle their feelings for one another is what inspires me to share their success with you. You *can* change. I'm going to show you how.

You've Already Begun the Journey

Since you're reading this book, you've taken the first step toward change, which is the desire to improve your situation. You've shown yourself to be open to the idea of change and are curious about advice on how to repair your relationship. Congratulations! Right off the bat, you're setting yourself apart from other unhappy couples who continue in their damaging patterns like hamsters running endlessly on the wheels in their cages. You are already taking significant steps toward change.

Your next challenge is to decide if and how much you want to truly change your relationship.

This is where you have to dig deep and ask yourself some serious questions. How hard are you willing to work to reach out to your partner so that you can retrieve the affection you once had for each other? And what about your partner? How willing will he be to join you? If he, like you, is tired of your fights and hostility, he might be an ally, and you can support each other. If not, if he is so angry and insists that everything is your fault, can you start following this program alone with the hope that he will come on board?

I'm going to help you set up a template for change so that you can go forward with a solid plan for success. First, let's talk about the motivation you need to keep you on course.

Making Your Motivation Map

Change can't take place without a strong desire to get to a better place. The deeper your family has fallen into trouble, the more challenging your job will be to mend it. What has taken years to creep up and strangle your relationship won't be fixed in a single day. There is a lot of hurt, sadness, and regret packed into your heart right now. But it can be fixed. It can.

So while you're motivated enough to get and read this book, how are we going to keep you on board to stay the course? I've learned there are three things that are the most successful in helping people set up the motivation to make solid and permanent changes in their relationship: fear, helping yourself, and helping others.

Fear? Are you kidding me? I know. It doesn't sound very inspirational to tell you that being scared can move you forward, but think about how it has gotten you to do things you really didn't want to do.

A few years ago, I backed myself into going skydiving, something *I really did not want to do*. Since I knew my wife was totally against me taking such a risk because of our family, I had regularly announced over the years how much I would really like to go skydiving but that I couldn't because she wouldn't let me. I got all the glory of being a daredevil without actually having to do anything—it was perfect. Then, one day she surprised me at my birthday party in front of our family and friends with a gift certificate to go skydiving . . . that afternoon, so everyone could watch me realize my "dream." My heart sank.

Off we went in the car, my wife and kids all excited for me, me looking in the rearview mirror at all our friends following us to the airfield, thinking, "How in h*** can I get out of this?"

In no time I was up in the airplane, strapped to a big bruiser of a man who kept saying, in a heavy Russian accent, "Now we jump!" while I held on to the sides of the open door looking down, terrified, wanting to be anywhere but where I was, which was having to face the prospect of hurling myself out into the sky. But I could see the little huddle of all my family and friends below, waiting to see me jump, and I could imagine what they'd think of me if I backed out.

So I jumped. I wish I could say I had been motivated by the desire to experience the airy freedom that comes from floating down to earth. No way. It was the pure fear of being exposed as a loudmouth that gave me the courage to let go of the door and hold on to my airborne partner. But guess what? It worked. It got me to carry through with what I said I was going to do.

In my work with families, fear has a place as well. If you're really afraid that your family is going to fall apart if you don't do something, you will try anything. A woman contacts me because she really doesn't want to divorce, she doesn't want her children to be raised in a single-parent household. A husband e-mails me because he is on his second marriage, which is going down in flames just like his first, and he'll do anything to keep it from happening again. Fear can be a powerful motivator. There's no reason to be ashamed if fear is what got you here.

Your own deep unhappiness with the status quo is another strong motivator for change. People come to me often and say, "I just can't take it anymore." You want to repair the hurts in yourself so you don't feel so wounded and alone.

And it's so bad that you are willing to reach out to someone like me, tell me the most private things in your life that you often haven't told anyone about, and hope I'll be able to help you fix what's broken in your relationship so that you can feel better.

I'm very grateful when someone is brave enough to contact me because I know that for everyone who asks for help in a troubled relationship, there are hundreds who never try. You are unique in reaching out for help, and I honor you for taking action.

Motivation to help yourself is crucial when trying to make changes and is an important tool to keep yourself moving forward. By itself, however, while it is a great and necessary beginning, self-help usually isn't powerful enough to keep you on the course when you are trying to fix your relationship. Despite the popularity of the idea that self-fulfillment is the goal to which we all should aspire for the best life, and the one which makes us the happiest, I've found that, by itself, trying to make yourself happier is not a long or high enough ramp to get you through the process of changing your behavior and making lasting changes in your relationship. It's not enough to support you in forgiving what has happened in the past or in switching your family's behavior from hostility to love. Self-fulfillment is just not powerful enough to ensure lasting change.

Believe me, I welcome motivation from almost any source and for almost any reason—it is the gasoline in the fuel tank on this journey. But what I've found time and time again in my work is that the most powerful motivational force that repairs families is the love for others. Some of the greatest changes people are able to make in their lives are made in large part because of the love for other people in their lives.

Right now you might be thinking to yourself, "Well, *that's* never going to happen. The last thing I feel for my husband right now is *love.*"

That's okay. I'm not asking you to do anything that you're not comfortable with (not yet anyway), but I want to alert you that as you go forward with this program, things are going to happen to you that will surprise you and change you in remarkable ways. And one of them is likely to be discovering that under all your pain and/or indifference, you *still* care very much for the others in your family.

The Ramp

I have a tool called "the Ramp" to help you set up the motivations you need to sustain change. Most people really want to change. Their will is strong, at least at first. But they haven't thought through all the steps it will take to get to the finish line. It's like building a house without a plan. You want a house with four upstairs bedrooms, but you forget to put in a staircase.

People also don't plan for the inevitable setbacks that always come. You know if you're building a house that one day the plumber isn't going to show up when he promised, or the bathroom tile you ordered will be out of stock. It's the same with changing your behavior. There will be setbacks. No one is perfect. But if you think *ahead* of time in a very specific way what it's going to take for you to get to your goal, you're helping yourself a lot. That's what the Ramp does.

I named the tool after the daredevil Evel Knievel. If you're in your forties or older, you know who I'm talking about. He was the closest thing to a real-life superhero I have ever known, famous for jumping his motorcycle over unbelievable things—school buses, buildings, even canyons. In 1967, he attempted a jump over the fountains in front of Caesar's Palace, but crashed horribly and was unconscious in the hospital for a month. Yet he recovered and continued to defy gravity in his spectacular events, sometimes succeeding and sometimes failing to get to the other side. But he never stopped trying.

When Knievel crashed, experts analyzing his failure usually blamed one of two things: that the motorcycle engine didn't give him enough power and speed, or that his takeoff ramp was too short to carry him up and over to the other side. Every time he jumped, he worked to improve both.

In my mind, you are taking a similar huge leap in your life right now, and like Evel Knievel, you need both the initial motivation to take a chance with your family life and enough power and lift to make it happen. When you make a decision to change, what I call a "life jump," building your Ramp and checking your power is as important as the jump itself if you want to succeed. Rebuilding your family will need a powerful engine and a Ramp long and high enough so you will succeed in what you set out to do.

Before we start, I'd like you to get a notebook that you can use exclusively for the Ramp tool and write the date on the first page. Now, let's proceed.

Set Up Your Own Ramp

Let's help you discover your own deep desires, so that you can name them and use them to harness your will power, self-discipline, and energy in pursuit of long-lasting change.

The next couple of sections pose some questions that are designed to help you identify what your most powerful motivators might be. Remember the Ramp—you will need a motivation long and high enough to carry you over the garbage dump of pain and anguish you've been living with. Half-hearted measures aren't going to do it. Wanting to get your partner to admit all his evil ways, for example, isn't productive motivation for change—it's looking for payback or validation for your perspective on the relationship.

What's Driving Your Desire to Try Again?

Why do you want to change? Do you truly believe that there's a chance for you and your partner to fix things? Do you remember when your relationship was strong, and do you want to return to those years? If your answer is no, think again, because I suggest that if you're reading this book, your heart may be saying yes.

How important is it to you to keep your family together? Why? Is it for yourself? Are you afraid of the image of your partner walking out the door, leaving you alone? Do you see the lives of friends who are divorced and don't want that for yourself? Alternately, do you know long-married couples who have weathered many storms and admire their intimacy and the pleasure they take in each other's company? How they seem to respect and care for each other, even though they've been together for years? Would you like to emulate them in your own relationship?

What about your children? Do you want to keep the family together for them? Are you a product of divorce, remembering how horrible it was for you as a child and don't want that loneliness and unhappiness for them? Do you instead want to raise your sons and daughters in a loving and supportive home, so that they will model that in their own lives and be productive and fulfilled?

What about your partner? Can you imagine him as a willing partner in this journey to find each other again? If he wouldn't join you now, do you think that if you change your behavior, he might follow? Do you still hold on, deep inside, a sense of the love you felt for him when you first met?

Why Do You Want Change Now?

If you've been unhappy for years, sliding into trouble, why suddenly do you want to take steps to change now? Has something happened recently that spurred your motivation? If you can't explain *why now,* and all you know is that you are sick and tired of the way things have been and you are ready to make things better, I'll accept that answer too! But there could be dozens of specific reasons why you've been moved to make changes in your life and relationship.

Did close friends announce their separation? Are you considering having an affair, which scares you or makes you feel guilty so that you want to work on your relationship? Have you or your partner actually *had* an affair and are dealing with the fallout, deciding whether or not to stay together, overwhelmed to discover how serious your problems are? Did you recently lose a parent, and now are thinking how unhappy your parents were in their marriage and don't want to spend the rest of your own relationship in the same way? Did your daughter ask you if you loved her father? Have you noticed that your kids are acting out the negative behaviors they witness at home? These can all be significant events, and you can use their force to help you focus on your desire to change with special attention and urgency.

In your notebook and/or below, write down as many reasons as you can *why* you want to commit yourself to change. Really, really think about these statements; they will become your motivations for transforming your relationship. They are absolutely necessary to embrace as we move forward.

Note: If you're having trouble tapping into a deep, deep desire to motivate you to change—if you are so angry and bitter toward your partner right now that you're completely unable to think about committing yourself to improving things between you—don't despair. Give yourself a little time to imagine a positive outcome for the two of you. Try to shut out your current unhappiness and ponder the possibilities that could open up for you if you changed your perspective and gave your relationship another chance. Remember what you loved in the beginning. Despite how you or your partner may feel at this moment, you were once attracted to each other, shared laughs and intimacy, moments of joy. Now ask yourself if you would like those feelings back. You don't have to know *how* to get them back—just wanting them back is enough for you and I to be able to move forward.

Writing Your Ramp

In the notebook, or below, I'd like you to write down *why* you want to change. Above I've outlined many common reasons people choose to change. What are your personal, most pressing reasons?

I really want to change because:

_____

_____

_____

_____

_____

_____

Describing these desires will be crucial to your success. Take your time and make them as personal and specific as possible—*what* prompted your desire to think about change; *why* do you think your relationship is worth saving. What you write will help you clarify your thoughts. Allow the words to really sink in. You will need to refer back to them often as you go forward. Imprint them in your mind and heart, revisit them often as you work through this book, say them to yourself at night before you go to bed and in the morning when you are starting your day.

What Will Happen If You *Do* Change?

After identifying your deep motivating desires, I'd like you to imagine the successful outcome if you work to achieve your desire. Think about the good things that will happen if you stick to your plan. Think about how much more content you will be. Think about the loving atmosphere that can return to your home, the renewed warmth and pleasure that you and your partner will feel toward each other. Reflect on this in as much detail as possible. What would it be like to sit at the dinner table when everyone is eager to talk to each other and share their day? How would it feel to have your husband grab your hand when you walk down the street? How will your children react when there is no longer so much tension in the house? What would it be like to feel renewed warmth and love for your spouse so that you could think of taking a romantic trip together? Then write these thoughts down in your notebook or below.

When I *do* change, I will feel/my partner and I will feel:

_____

_____

_____

_____

_____

_____

These wishes are the second part of the Ramp that will keep you moving forward. Imagining a good outcome to the changes you're about to undertake is as important as your reasons for wanting to change. They will be the reward for your hard work. And the more rewards you can identify that will come when you accomplish your goals, and the more vividly you describe them, the better they will guide you to success. You will need to refer to them in the months ahead, and they will help you stay on course.

Together, the answers to the two questions—why you want to change now, and what will happen after you do change—will be a big part of what gets you to your goal. They are both very, *very* important.

Track Your Progress

Your next step is to keep track of your progress in the notebook. This means writing down what you have accomplished so that you can see that you're making an honest effort and moving forward. Ideally you should do this every day, but if that's not possible, aim for at least twice a week.

Your notations don't have to be dramatic—in fact, just the opposite. It's the buildup of small, behavioral changes, step by step, that produces change. So when you refrain from fighting with your spouse in front of your children at dinner, write it down! When your husband empties the dishwasher without being asked and you thank him instead of saying, "What, did you run out of beer glasses?" write it down! As you read through the next section of the book about all the toxic ways couples behave and start changing your own behavior to avoid these traps, write everything down! (Note: Do not use the notebook as a catalog of your or your partner's failures—only good news here!)

Why write everything down?

Because you need to constantly congratulate yourself to keep you motivated for the long haul. Staying focused on change is relatively easy at first because you're excited by the possibility of change and committed to working at it. But inevitably, as you begin working through your problems, your enthusiasm may start to wane. You have a terrible argument with your partner and are so angry that you don't want to bother working on your relationship. You find it *really* hard to let go of your resentments—it seems impossible to forgive your husband or wife for a cruel insult or selfish behavior. Your husband responds sarcastically to a suggestion you make and all your good intentions go out the window—you answer back with your own sarcastic rebuttal and flip him the bird for good measure.

At times like these, you may regret that you even started this process.

This is when you need to retreat to a quiet place, take a deep breath, and review what you've written. Read over what you wrote about why you chose to begin this movement toward change. Allow yourself to remember the feelings that motivated you to begin this journey. Then read what you imagine will happen when change takes place.

Next, read through your progress reports and recognize all the hard work you've already put in on this project. All the small kindnesses, nasty words not said, and fights avoided are there in your notebook. This will allow you to see how far you've come and give you the courage to continue.

Documenting your progress can be the powerful tool you need to keep you on track. You will be surprised how empowering and motivating it can be to see your achievements noted on the written page, reminding you of your goals and giving you hope to continue. When you recognize your progress, no matter how small, you will feel very good about yourself. Even if your partner is reluctant or slow to respond to change, you will gain confidence in yourself and muster enough strength to continue forward.

Give Your Partner a Chance

Aiming for change is energizing and optimistic. Honor yourself for your courage! There are many people who will not or simply cannot take this step. But please also honor your partner's potential willingness to change. I say this because it's been my experience that while most people think *they* are capable of change, they have a hard time believing that *other* people can do the same.

Someone will tell me about her partner's stubborn behavior, shrug at my suggestions of what she could ask him to think about, and say, "He'll never change," or "You can't teach an old dog new tricks." What so odd is that these comments often follow their own reports that they've lost weight, or stopped drinking, or gotten a new job. So *they* are able to change, but their partner? No way.

Don't buy into this double standard or you will slam the door on the potential for improving your relationship. It's not fair to give yourself all kinds of credit for your capacity for change but refuse to believe that your partner can take the same strides himself. You could be understandably furious at him for all the problems in the relationship, but do you really think it's *impossible* that he could ever really do the work necessary to change things? Consider for a moment just how unfair that viewpoint is, and take a moment to open your mind to the notion that yes, the other person is capable of change, just like you are. If, in fact, he can't or won't be a part of the journey toward a new, happier relationship, that's a problem you'll face down the road. But for now, give him the opportunity to embrace change just as you are doing.

Speaking of Your Partner . . .

But wait, some of you will say. I've already tried to reach out to him, but he refuses to try. He doesn't listen, he doesn't look at me, and sometimes he just walks out of the room. What's the point?

I ask you to be patient, because most often, when one person in a relationship initiates change in the way I'm going to describe in the next chapters—which is reasoned, nonthreatening, and incremental—the response is usually positive. It often takes a while for it to sink in that things are different around the house, but if you've toned down your hostility and *keep* it toned down, your partner will begin to trust your new behavior and respond in kind.

There are exceptions. There will be some partners who, for whatever reason, do not want to engage in change. In that case, I say that you can still work on this program yourself. There will be rewards for you, regardless of your partner's lack of involvement. You will gain self-confidence and a sense of accomplishment and will learn a lot about yourself. If the final result of the program is that your relationship cannot be rescued, you will still emerge with the skill set to take better care of yourself, no matter what happens.

But for many couples, when one person starts removing the roadblocks in an unhealthy relationship—roadblocks that we'll discuss in the next chapters—he or she opens up an entirely new way of communicating, making for a far less volatile exchange. And it is catching. Who wouldn't rather see a shy smile across the kitchen counter in the morning before work instead of a tense glare that challenges the target to make a snide remark? It's these little gestures that begin to turn relationships around.

Get Used to Constant Change

There are many other aspects to change that are crucial to the LCA Plan, and we will discuss them throughout the book.

I'm super excited to help you along the way, because I believe you can create a wonderful new life for yourself and your partner. Think of all the time, years maybe, that you've gone to bed, silent and angry, hoping that the next day will be better, that you and your husband will stop fighting, that he will listen to you, that he will stop putting you down in front of your friends, that he will help around the house without asking, that you could enjoy an evening together the way you did when you were first together.

And now you're going to do something about it. I've learned through all the work I've done with so many couples that hope doesn't change things—*change* changes things. And that's what you're going to do.

Love: The Most Powerful Motivator

One of the most dramatic examples of the power of strong motivation involved a man I'll call Brett, who wrote me a heartbreaking letter asking me for help in reuniting with someone from his recent past. Unlike most requests I received for help on *The Locator*, which were searches for parents, siblings, old friends, etc., this man was asking for my help in reuniting with . . . his wife. And it wasn't his ex-wife. They were still married. Further, he didn't need me to locate her, as he knew exactly where she was—staying with her sister, where she had been since the day she walked out six months earlier after discovering he was cheating on her.

Bret wrote that he had seen how I had talked to people on my television show, had read about my loving relationship with my wife, and just knew I could "talk some sense into her."

What?!? He cheated on his wife, and now he was asking me to talk some sense into *her*? This infuriated me as a man and as a faithful husband. I decided to call this man then and there. He was a bit surprised that I responded to his letter with a personal phone call, and more surprised when I started by saying, "Per your request, I am calling to talk some sense into you." He was clearly puzzled and said, "I didn't ask you to talk sense into me. I said my wife." I replied, "Your letter stated you cheated on the woman you love and cannot live without. So it seems to me that you're the one who needs some sense, not your wife." He didn't say a word for a few awkward seconds, then muttered, "Go on."

I began by explaining I was not a therapist, and all I could do was share my own experiences and opinions about marriage, relationships, forgiveness, and change. I then talked to him about motivation.

I asked him what motivated him to cheat on his wife, and he gave me a long, drawn-out explanation about how it was no big deal, that he didn't love the other woman, that it was just a physical thing, that his wife overreacted, and that all men do it. I then said, my voice rising, "I don't. Never have. Don't use me or other men to rationalize your selfish impulses and lack of self-control. The bottom line is you abused your wife and she correctly left your butt."

He then got quite angry and dropped a few f-bombs on me as he stated he had never, ever laid a hand on his wife and thinks men who do so are losers. When he finally finished his rant, he was talking rapidly, breathing hard, and clearly upset with me. I let a beat of silence fill the moment so he could calm down and we could return the conversation to a slower pace.

After a moment or two I said, "Brett, if a man walked up to your wife and slapped her, would that upset you?" He quickly replied, "I would kick his ass." I then said, "What's your wife's name?"

"Kelly," he said.

"Okay, so what if a guy just walked up to Kelly, never touched her, but said, 'Lady, you are the ugliest woman I have ever seen. You are undesirable, and I'll bet your husband is repulsed by the very sight of you.' Would you be okay with that guy saying that to your wife, Brett?"

His response was, "Hell, no."

"So you would consider that abusive even though he didn't touch her?" Brett replied, "Yeah, but I've never, ever said anything like that to Kelly."

I waited for several moments and then said, "Brett, brother, I have some terrible news for you. You *did* say that to Kelly. But instead of

Family: The Good F-Word

69

words, you used actions. By choosing to violate your marital vows and turning to another woman sexually, you basically said all of those things to Kelly."

Now I had his attention, so I went on: "I'm sure hearing those words from a stranger would be painful enough, but having the man she loves and has dedicated her life to say that to her by what he does? That's catastrophic. It is the worst beating you can possibly give someone. Brett, whether you want to admit it or not, I'm here to tell you, by sleeping with another woman, you beat your wife severely, and she is at her sister's being nursed back to health."

The sounds of Brett beginning to weep filled the phone. It began as sniffles but quickly turned into the cry of a man who has realized how much pain his wife was in—and worse, that he was the source of that pain. After at least three or four minutes of continuous sobbing, he slowly regained composure, caught his breath, and said in a very soft voice, "Thank you."

I then asked, "So what happens next?"

He said, "I fix it."

And for him, that's when it happened. He had the motivation, the Ramp, to make a huge life jump. His motivation was driven by the love he had for his wife and the desire to be the source of her happiness instead of the source of her pain.

Six years later, I received a Christmas card at the office from Brett and Kelly. It contained some very heartfelt thanks and went into great detail about how amazing their marriage was and how different things were in their family now. Brett had found the motivation he needed to not just make that tremendous life jump, but to make it last year after year. He wrote me, initially, because of his own pain and suffering, but it was his love for his wife and fear of causing her any similar pain in the future that he used to create a Ramp big enough to carry him back to a happy marriage.

Your story may be completely different from Brett's, but, like him, you can be open to embracing the power of your love for your partner. It is a very powerful motivator.

Life-Changing Action Plan: Step 3
Tear Down the Roadblocks!

Even the most loving marriage can occasionally stumble, falling into bad behavior patterns that undermine intimacy and affection. And when the behavior becomes ingrained in a relationship, like deepening ruts in a road, it blocks the love that flows between a couple. Roadblocks are thrown up. The road is closed.

We're going to talk about these roadblocks in the next 10 chapters. These negative behaviors can eat away at any relationship. Why? Because they are so tempting! It is much easier to blame someone else for something you did, think that you're right all the time instead of listening to another point of view, or brush things under the rug instead of taking the time to talk through a problem. These self-indulgent behaviors—and they are self-indulgent—can make you feel good for a short time, but they don't resolve conflicts; they create new and more damaging problems.

The roadblocks we will be discussing are all very common. Like invasive weeds, they creep up on you and your family, choking out all the oxygen and nutrients, spreading everywhere and smothering the healthy ways a good family functions. And that's not all. The more you practice them, the more you slowly come to believe that the sarcastic, negative, and nasty ways you and your partner communicate represent the real truth of your feelings for each other. It's as if you've lost the recipe for creating the loving and kind relationship you pledged to each other when you met or married. You've forgotten what a good meal tastes like.

Couples in sound relationships know this and have learned to steer clear of the seductive power of these roadblocks, but if you're not in a good place in your relationship, it's very tempting to resort to them when you're angry or hurt. Call them bad habits, muscle memory, whatever. I call them destructive, and we must work to change them.

You may recognize some, if not all of these traps in your own behavior with your partner. Good! That means you are being honest with yourself. I don't worry that someone in a troubled relationship is struggling with these issues; I worry when someone believes they aren't! Denial is the first step to destruction. Be aware, and take action to get rid of them. When you do, the results are dramatic. So let's call out these roadblocks and banish them forever. Then you can choose better, healthier ways to communicate and behave toward your spouse. You can have your cake and eat it, too! Consider this your course in Relationship Traps 101.

Life-Changing Action Plan: Step 3
Tear Down the Roadblocks!

Even the most loving marriage can occasionally stumble, falling into bad behavior patterns that undermine intimacy and affection. And when the behavior becomes ingrained in a relationship, like deepening ruts in a road, it blocks the love that flows between a couple. Roadblocks are thrown up. The road is closed.

We're going to talk about these roadblocks in the next 10 chapters. These negative behaviors can eat away at any relationship. Why? Because they are so tempting! It is much easier to blame someone else for something you did, think that you're right all the time instead of listening to another point of view, or brush things under the rug instead of taking the time to talk through a problem. These self-indulgent behaviors—and they are self-indulgent—can make you feel good for a short time, but they don't resolve conflicts; they create new and more damaging problems.

The roadblocks we will be discussing are all very common. Like invasive weeds, they creep up on you and your family, choking out all the oxygen and nutrients, spreading everywhere and smothering the healthy ways a good family functions. And that's not all. The more you practice them, the more you slowly come to believe that the sarcastic, negative, and nasty ways you and your partner communicate represent the real truth of your feelings for each other. It's as if you've lost the recipe for creating the loving and kind relationship you pledged to each other when you met or married. You've forgotten what a good meal tastes like.

Couples in sound relationships know this and have learned to steer clear of the seductive power of these roadblocks, but if you're not in a good place in your relationship, it's very tempting to resort to them when you're angry or hurt. Call them bad habits, muscle memory, whatever. I call them destructive, and we must work to change them.

You may recognize some, if not all of these traps in your own behavior with your partner. Good! That means you are being honest with yourself. I don't worry that someone in a troubled relationship is struggling with these issues; I worry when someone believes they aren't! Denial is the first step to destruction. Be aware, and take action to get rid of them. When you do, the results are dramatic. So let's call out these roadblocks and banish them forever. Then you can choose better, healthier ways to communicate and behave toward your spouse. You can have your cake and eat it, too! Consider this your course in Relationship Traps 101.

Relationship Roadblock #1: Blame

5

Blame is often a desperate attempt
to escape responsibility.

—Troy Dunn

"It's *your* fault we don't talk anymore, because every time I open my mouth you criticize me."

"It's *your* fault our daughter is so out of control, because you never put your foot down."

"It's *your* fault I'm stuck in this job, because you spend too much money."

"It's *your* fault we never have people over, because you won't help clean up the house."

Does any of this sound familiar?

Blaming plays a big part in troubled relationships. It is one of the most common roadblocks to open communication in marriages because it is provocative and hurtful, and it creates enormous hostility and anger between couples. And it solves nothing. When your partner blames you for everything wrong in his life, do you say, "Oh, I never noticed that before. You're right!" Hardly. If you're like most people, your reaction is to shut down and return the favor with your own blaming. Blaming is one of the immature communication weapons children use and are supposed to grow out of, right along with name-calling and pouting. And yet we grown-ups do it all the time because it's easy, feels good (at least in the short term), and let's you completely off the hook when something goes wrong.

But if you want to improve your relationship, blaming is a very bad habit you *have* to break.

Breaking Down the Blame Machine

Blaming is like going into a fun house filled with distorting mirrors. You look around and can get completely confused in trying to figure out what's true and what's not. For instance:

1. It's a *fact* that sometimes those who get blamed are absolutely guilty of what they have been accused of. (Your wife *did* stay out late without calling.)

2. It's also a *fact* that sometimes those who get blamed are innocent of any wrongdoing. (Your wife *did* try to call but you had your phone turned off.)
3. It's a *fact* that the one who is doing the blaming may truly believe he has been wronged by the person he's blaming. ("I was *really* worried when you didn't call because I thought you'd been in a car accident. Remember what happened to that guy from work?")

4. And finally, it's a *fact* that sometimes the blamer has an ulterior motive in shifting the responsibility from himself to another person. ("You're always on me for not calling you when I'm going to be late; you do the *same* thing.")

Sorting out the blame game is hard, and unlike a fun house, it's not a lot of laughs. So why do people play the game at all? That's easy. Because it's the easiest—and laziest—way out of a disagreement.

If you turn every fight on its head so that it's always your partner's fault, then everything that happens becomes his fault. It's his problem, not yours.

But blaming usually backfires, because it ends up hurting you as much as your partner. It creates lots of hostility, pain, and anger in your relationship. Let's look more closely at what's really going on between the two of you when you spend so much energy blaming each other. I want you to see how blaming robs you of the ability to communicate in positive ways.

In my work with families, I refer to issues of blaming as a "blame event." There are two types of blame events: Past Blames and Future Blames. A Past Blame refers to a past event that, though it could have happened days, weeks, even years before, still resonates as if it happened five minutes ago. Holding on to a Past Blame is one of the most destructive things you can do to a relationship—it delays healing and keeps families apart for far too long.

Past Blames

A Past Blame can be anything: your husband didn't clean out the garage when he said he would; he forgot your wedding anniversary last year; he didn't stand up to his mother when she insisted on having Christmas at her house the first year of your marriage; you put a dent in your husband's car a week ago; you refused to let his friends come over to watch a football game last fall, just because it was inconvenient for you. It's basically any time you point the finger of responsibility at someone else after a negative event or conversation and *keep* pointing it—in fact, stabbing the air with it! And while this might make you feel like you're the better, nicer, fairer, more thoughtful person, it makes your partner feel like you are rigid, critical, and unforgiving. And it certainly doesn't do a *thing* for your relationship except create ongoing resentment and acrimony.

Assigning blame has no place in a healthy marriage. If you want to clean up your neglected relationship, you must start by throwing out the old issues and hurt feelings. Some people hold on tenaciously to anger and simply cannot throw it away! They keep every memory, every hurtful word on a mental hard drive and replay it frequently. Like a hoarder on a television reality show, they accumulate and embrace hurt feelings like precious possessions.

When asked to clean house and throw out the piles of useless emotions and old grudges, these people make weak attempts at rationalizing why they still need to keep all of the old crap! "It's unresolved," they tell me, or "He hasn't properly apologized to me," or "I can never forgive her for what she did," and so on. These are nothing more than lazy excuses for holding on to Past Blame. Far better would be to do the hard, necessary work to release old, simmering resentments or, for more recent problems, talk them through with your partner and forgive each other.

What about you? Does reading this remind you of yourself and the Past Blames you may be holding against your spouse?

Please write down one Past Blaming episode that is fresh in your mind, either on your part or your partner's. Just mention the issue and who blamed whom. (For example, "My husband blamed me for not paying the mortgage on time," or "I blamed my husband for spending too much time watching sports on TV.")

_____

_____

Now, answer a few questions for me:

1. When was the blame mentioned?
   Immediately   Eventually

2. Regardless of whether the blamer was you or your spouse, what was the tone of voice when the blame was assigned?
   Calm   Annoyed   Sarcastic   Angry   Rage

3. How did the one being blamed respond?
   A. Silence
   B. Admission and apology
   C. Cast blame back
   D. Walked away angry

4. What was the outcome of the blaming episode?
   A. The issue was resolved to my satisfaction.
   B. The issue was not resolved and will likely repeat itself.
   C. We are both acting as if it never happened, and no progress has been made.
   D. The blame episode has left lingering anger and resentment, and we are still not back to normal.

5. Was the blame worth the price you paid?
   Yes   No

Take a moment to review the answers you circled above. Are you surprised to see what your blaming incident looks like when you break it down? If you did the blaming, was the temporary elation you felt at getting the upper hand worth the fact that you and your spouse are now on the outs? If your spouse blamed you and is still carrying a grudge, how does that make you feel? Are you chastised, angry, wanting to get back at him, or are you willing to reach out to him? Really think about this. Honestly evaluate your communication style. This is an opportunity to step back and ask yourself if you could improve the way you handle disagreements between you and your partner.

Please, if you are reviewing your answers to the questions and are now defending how you behaved and/or minimizing the feelings of your spouse, *stop*. You don't want to step down the path of blaming anymore.

Instead, just review what you have circled, think about it, and think, too, about taking ownership where it is needed. Maybe you did forget to mail the mortgage payment and now have to own up to the fact that you've incurred a penalty. Or you were tired from work when you screamed at your son. Doing this simple task is a positive step forward and counts as making things better for you and your family.

Get *Past* Past Blame!

An extreme and very sad example of a Past Blame for me was the story of a woman who wanted my help reuniting her son with his father. She described a very intense experience from years before when her then seventeen-year-old son and her husband got into a heated argument that resulted in the son storming angrily out of the house, never to return. Now, fifteen years later, the woman blamed the loss of their son on her husband for losing his temper. She believed he hurt their son's feelings, which caused him to leave their home and their lives.

She had embraced this interpretation of the incident as the truth, causing a rift in the marriage.

But, as I learned in talking further with her, the fight between father and son was about the son's constant use of drugs in their home and the bad effect it was having on their younger children. That night, the husband had practiced some tough love by saying, "If you choose to continue using drugs, you may not live here." That set off their son, who blew up and slammed the door behind him as he barreled out of the house.

It seemed to me, as the story unfolded, that there was enough blame to go around. The son was obviously endangering his siblings as well as himself by his drug use. The father had drawn a line in the sand, but apparently had never revisited his decision or tried to reach out again to his son. But his wife had spent far too many years blaming her husband without trying to resolve anything. She had wasted a large chunk of her marriage holding on to her blame. For what? Nothing. All that happened in those years was that she, her husband, and her son grew older and lost years. They missed countless birthdays, fishing trips, Thanksgiving gatherings, vacations, and memories—all because they were too stuck, stubborn, and proud to sit down and work through their problems in a timely manner. Past Blame cost them dearly.

Thankfully, this woman, by coming to me, signaled that she was open to change. After she told me her story, I asked, "What is most important to you right now?"

"That Tony [her son] come back into our lives," she answered.

"And what is the second most important thing?" I asked.

Although she'd answered the first question easily, this time she paused. She even looked a bit puzzled as she muttered the question back to me, almost as if talking to herself. "What is the second most important thing?"

I waited while she stared intently at the floor, as if perhaps the answer was hiding somewhere in the carpeting. Eventually, she lifted her head and said, "I guess what is second most important is that he knows we love him, and we can find a way to rebuild our relationship."

I smiled and said, "Excellent, because that is doable."

We then cast aside the issue of blame and set out to make a connection with Tony where his parents could make it clear that they loved him, they missed him, and they wanted to see him. There was no need to discuss drugs, house rules, or expectations. Those issues were clearly implied by events of the past, and if they were still an issue in Tony's life, the topic would naturally surface soon enough. For the moment, we were able to focus on what was most important and second most important to his mother.

Blaming her son or husband was no longer relevant when she began to fight to save her family. Blame is the first thing to get thrown out as families move toward forgiveness. It has no place in a healthy relationship.

Future Blames

In the same way Past Blames corrode relationships, Future Blames can prevent the forgiveness you need to repair your relationship. A Future Blame is when your feelings about your partner are based on how you *think* he or she will act or react rather than something he or she actually *did*. It sounds nuts that you would blame a loved one for something that hasn't even happened yet, but it happens all the time and, like Past Blames, there is usually enough truth in the blame to make it tempting to hold on to.

As a young man in my twenties, I'm embarrassed to report that I was a walking (or should I say driving) example of road rage. It made me crazy with anger when drivers flipped their middle fingers at me or drove recklessly, endangering the lives of others, including mine! As a former college and semipro football player, I tended to let my aggression get the best of me, which I "blamed" on too many years of football. When a rude driver did something offensive, I would usually chase him (it was always a guy) down and give him a piece of my mind, sometimes worse. I take no pride in admitting this and have never spoken of it publicly before, but I want to be totally open and honest with you here. After I beat up a few of these bad drivers, my very upset wife gave me a "talking to," as my grandma used to call it. Jennifer expressed her disappointment in my loss (or total lack) of control and said that one day I was going to approach a vehicle in anger and the driver was going to shoot me, leaving her a widow. Unfortunately, her pleas fell on deaf ears.

But one day, driving to work, I was stuck dead still in bumper-to-bumper traffic. Suddenly, I saw in my rearview mirror that a car was driving along the shoulder of the road trying to bypass all of us who were in line! To stop him, I inched my car over the edge of the road so that he couldn't pass. As he neared my car, he began honking his horn aggressively, which in those days used to make my blood boil. I threw the gear into park, barreled out of my car, and marched back to the driver's window of this honking maniac. His window was rolled down and I was prepared to reach in and . . . do something. But I looked at him and saw that he was crying. Sobbing, actually. He told me that there had been an accident at home involving his little girl, and he was trying to get home to her and pleaded with me to please move my car out of the way.

It's hard to express what I felt at that moment, but within a microsecond, my heart shattered, my mind was altered, and my anger was replaced by humility and shame. I realized that I had no idea what was going on in somebody else's life at any given moment. Here I was, drawing my own assumptions about a man's behavior without any information as to what was causing that behavior. The experience of seeing that man so frightened about his daughter really changed me and ended my road rage forever.

Jennifer, understandably, was surprised at the dramatic change in my driving habits. For a while she still got in the car with me braced for drama, anticipating an incident that would trigger my anger. But as time went by, she realized that I had truly changed my behavior and she relaxed.

But what if she hadn't been open to me changing? What if years later she was still tense in the car, gritting her teeth every time someone cut us off on the freeway? I would be extremely resentful that she was still holding a grudge against me for something I'd worked hard to change. Her lack of trust and refusal to accept my growth would drive a wedge between us. That is what Future Blame can do to a relationship.

Do not anticipate and therefore blame people for things you expect them to do in the future just because they've made mistakes in the past. That is stagnant thinking. People do change. Be aware and protect yourself, but leave room for others to grow.

Are you and/or your spouse carrying around Future Blame? Did you have a bad period in your life when you regularly ran up your credit card bills, but now, even though it's been several years and you pay your bills in full, your spouse is always "just checking" to make sure you're not overspending this month? Did your husband once have trouble at work, slacking off and getting fired, and now, even though he's got a new job and is working hard and successfully, you find yourself holding your breath when he complains about something at work and ask him if he's gotten in trouble?

If Future Blaming is a part of your relationship, I'd like you to write down some examples of the Future Blames held by either you or your spouse. Ask yourself the same set of questions outlined above in the Past Blame section. Think how discouraged and hurt you feel when your spouse always seems to be expecting you to revert to your past behavior and blames you when you haven't done anything! Then realize that he feels exactly the same when you judge him by *his* past actions.

In your marriage, or even when parenting your children, if you want to strive to grow and empower others to grow, it's important to leave room for growth. When I was a young boy, my mom bought my shoes a half size too big so I had room to grow. So it must be in our relationships.

I Can't Ever Blame Anybody for Anything?

Does all this mean that nobody should ever blame anybody and nobody should ever get blamed, no matter how wrong/stupid/annoying/mean/dangerous the event or conversation was? Well, I don't like the words "ever" and "never" so I'll say my answer is "generally speaking, yes!" I would be very happy to banish the word "blame" to a toxic dump.

Because the other side of blame is *accountability* and *responsibility*. Holding someone accountable for an event asks him to take responsibility for an action, which can include acknowledging a mistake he made or explaining what led to a bad outcome. It opens the door to fixing what's wrong without the judgment, accusations, and anger that blame *always* carries with it.

Let's say you're going to bed earlier than your husband, and you ask him to finish cleaning up the kitchen before he comes to bed. You get up the next morning and there are all the pots and pans still sitting in the sink, caked with grease and gunk, which you have to wash before you can start breakfast. If you're in a blaming mode, you automatically assume your partner is lazy, selfish, and has no respect for you—after all, you cooked him a nice dinner and he can't even follow through on this *one* chore to help you out! And this isn't the first time—he did the same thing the week before. In fact, now that you think about it, he hardly *ever* helps in the kitchen. You start slamming around the pots and pans so that by the time he shows up in the kitchen, you're furious and ready to kill him.

But what if, instead of going into blaming mode, you hold him accountable. When he comes into the kitchen, you tell him you were really upset to find all the dishes still in the sink and ask him what happened. Then, listen to his response. Whatever he says—he forgot, he was too tired himself, he got distracted because he got a text from work and became worried about something—will involve him taking responsibility for what he did. If you can refrain from jumping in with judgment or blame ("How could you *forget*? You can't get out of the kitchen without walking right by the bleeping sink!"), it's likely that he will own up to what he did and even apologize. You may still be fuming, but at least you've opened the door to compromise by holding him accountable instead of blaming him. Instead of both of you retreating to your corners and staying angry, you've increased your chances of more cooperation the next time you ask something of him.

My wife and I have a couple of rental properties. When a tenant is late with his rent, I don't stand in his driveway pointing at him and shouting, "It's your fault your rent is late!" That would be casting blame.

My accusation may be inaccurate, and it's certainly unproductive. What if he was robbed on the way home and the thief stole the man's wallet and with it the rent money! That would mean my tenant is not the cause of the late rent; the thief is to blame, if blame was being assigned. But instead of blaming anyone, I simply stay true to my relationship with the tenant, which is to hold him responsible. He is not to blame for the late rent, but he is responsible for making sure the rent ultimately gets paid. Blaming him gets me nowhere. Responsibility is what is important. There is a difference.

Turn Down the Blame Flame

I'm sure your spouse or partner has blamed you for things plenty of times. Some of those times you knew you were in the wrong; other times you're equally sure you were being unfairly blamed. But there are a lot of occasions when the situation is fuzzy about who's right and who's wrong, and your instinct may be to "get to the bottom of it." My advice? *Don't try!*

In these borderline situations, the objective is not to determine if you are right or wrong; it's to manage the way you act and react, whether you are right *or* wrong. Modifying your behavior in this way will reap great rewards. I've seen this happen in the families I've helped.

When the blame flame flares up, take a deep breath and blow it out. By that I mean, calm down. Think about what has happened. If appropriate, take your part of the responsibility for an event or conversation that has caused friction. See what happens. If you speak with sincerity, I bet you'll be surprised by the productive response it will elicit from your spouse. Maybe not always, and maybe not immediately, but it will, especially the more you do your part to extinguish the blame flame before it rages out of control.

Peace will come not only from what your partner says in response, but also from the knowledge that you have acted appropriately. Believe me, it will feel much better than the sick feelings you get after raging and tossing out angry words and cruel accusations. Blaming each other only delays the process of resolving conflict and moving forward. It's like falling off a boat when a sudden wave causes you to lose your balance. You can flail around in the water, blaming the waves, the boat's skipper, the weather—or you can swim back to the boat.

Relationship Roadblock #2: Scorekeeping

6

Relationship Roadblock #2: Scorekeeping

6

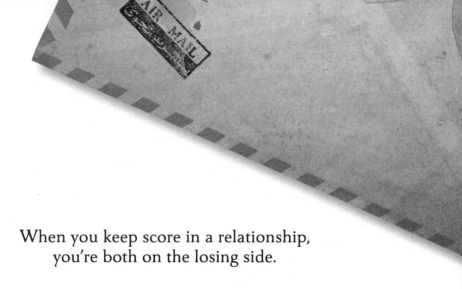

When you keep score in a relationship,
you're both on the losing side.

—Troy Dunn

Is there a large, virtual scoreboard lit up in your brain that keeps track of
everything you and your partner do and say, so that one of you is always
the winner and the other always the loser? Instead of working together in
your relationship, you are on opposing teams? Then it's very likely that
you're a scorekeeper! Scorekeeping is one of the most common roadblocks
there is in preventing healthy communication between couples.

Think about some of the ways you might be keeping score within your
relationship. You take the recyclables out to the garage on the way to work,
not because it's a task you can easily fit into your morning but because your
partner said he was going to do it last night and didn't, so now you've got
something *on* him. Score one point for you! Or, your spouse answers the
phone one evening and it's your mother. He's overly friendly and chatty
with her before he hands off the phone, not because he's naturally kind
and respectful to his mother-in-law but to get back at you because you
were short and impatient with *his* mother when she called last. Slam dunk,
one point for him! Or your partner loses his temper with your son after he
talked back to him and you step in to calm things down, not to ease the
conflict between them but to show that you're a more patient, better parent than your partner. *Ding*, another score!

Here's another possibility: you may not be having royal battles in your
household on a regular basis, but you just may be very competitive people, used to seeing the world like a sports event in which you're either the
winner or loser. Without really thinking about it, you may treat your rela-

tionship the same way and not think there's anything wrong with a little healthy competition.

Do any of these scenarios sound familiar? If they do, you're not alone. Scorekeeping is very common when relationships and marriages aren't on an even keel. It means that somewhere along the line, instead of handling the normal conflicts that surface in your day-to-day lives together by simply talking them through as a couple—or, for this scenario, a "team"— you've begun engaging in one-upmanship to "prove" that one or the other of you is "right," or is the "better" person. But you haven't actually discussed anything! In place of working things out between you, you're both ignoring each other and performing in your daily lives as if there is an invisible judge who will "decide" in your favor.

If you've had a long history of anger, misunderstanding, and hurt in your relationship, if you're not listening to each other anymore, score-keeping can feel like the only way you can stand up for yourself and make yourself heard, even if it's only in your head. But believe me, if your relationship has been reduced to scorekeeping behavior, you are going down a dangerous and destructive path—one in which *nobody* wins.

When you got married or committed to this relationship, you promised to love, honor, and respect each other, not to compete and score points off each other's mistakes and foibles. This is your partner, not your opponent! You're on the same team, and you can only win if you play with, not against, each other. Holding each other's shortcomings over the other's head forces both of you to always be on the defense, ready for the next attack. No one can endure that forever. No one should have to.

And many couples don't, so they get divorced.

It doesn't have to be that way. Let's talk about how to throw out that scorecard and help you both win by strengthening instead of weakening your bond.

When Did the Scoreboard Show Up?

Why do you think you and your spouse do this to each other, and how did you fall into the scorekeeping trap? Well, it could be that you're both modeling the behavior you experienced when growing up. Were either of your sets of parents guilty of keeping score? Do you have memories of your mom claiming credit for being the better parent, or your dad professing that he was calm under fire while your mom flipped out over even the smallest problem? Did they tear each other down rather than build each other up? Maybe they still do! If you grew up with this kind of hostility and regularly witnessed their resentments, or if you were asked to take sides or pick the parent who was "right," you were the victim of scorekeeping. That experience could have imprinted upon your psyche a belief that spouses are meant to be opponents, not teammates, and your current behavior is merely a reflection of that embedded belief.

If this describes your experience, then it only makes sense that when pressures mount in your own marriage, you fall back to keeping score yourself. Let's imagine for a moment that your husband comes home and announces that he's just been in a car accident. Do you think, "Thank goodness he wasn't hurt?" Or worry that he must be shaken up and really upset that his car is now out of commission? Not if you're a scorekeeper. Instead, you might think, "I always tell him I'm a better driver than he is, and this just proves it! *I've* certainly never been in an accident." What kind of logic is that? Using your husband's car crash as a way to "one-up" him? Does that sound even remotely like healthy behavior? But if it's what you know, if it's what you've learned through experience in your own upbringing, you've got to acknowledge where it's coming from and decide to change it.

Don't kid yourself about the severity of the scorekeeping problem. Even when it seems perfectly harmless on its surface, it is truly poisonous thinking, and the more you allow yourself to indulge in it, the faster it can suck the life out of your relationship.

So, what makes scorekeeping so powerful? After day in and day out of being verbally battered by your partner, accused of not being good enough, of being incompetent, of having every one of your motives questioned, you start to put up walls to protect yourself. And you know what? Your partner feels exactly the same way. No matter how strong he might appear on the outside, your scorekeeping words do damage. At a certain point, you're both feeling so hurt, dejected, and defensive that every conversation becomes just another opportunity to pick each other apart. And then the cycle becomes self-perpetuating, and before you know it, all communication breaks down.

Once the scorekeeping cycle really takes root, it seeps into all areas of your relationship, and you become conditioned to measure every con-

Family: The Good F-Word

versation and event by who wins and who loses. Words begin to automatically fly out of your mouth without you even having to think about the verbal jabs you're throwing. It's exhausting always playing defense. So often, couples get so caught up in this struggle that they can't untangle themselves, even when they desperately want to.

And if you have children, let me raise a big red flag for you here. Just as you absorbed the behavior of your own family, your own kids are watching everything you do and learning from you how to act in their future relationships. We shield our children's eyes when something scary or inappropriate pops up on TV because we don't want them to have those images in their heads. But when you're keeping score, you're bringing ugly, cruel behavior right into your home and into their lives. When children are raised in an unhealthy environment and start acting out as a direct result, I call this "broken by association." I know you don't want to do that to your kids.

I want to point out one final and devastating outcome of keeping score. When you continue this behavior, you're burying the love in your marriage. All the passion, respect, kindness, and tenderness that you once had for each other (and still may have) gets buried so deeply under piles of cruelty and competition that you forget the reason you fell in love. And then you realize your suffocating relationship is on life support. And maybe one (or both) of you is tempted to pull the plug.

Take Down the Scoreboard

Okay, so you're ready to call a truce. Good! That's an important first step. The fact that you want to change, the fact that you want to stop this madness of keeping score against each other, shows me that you are ready to do what it takes to turn your life and marriage around. And here's the really exciting part: you can make an abrupt change right now. I'm talking about immediate, "stop the presses" kind of change.

It starts by you and your spouse admitting to each other the terrible damage you've been doing to yourselves (not to mention your kids) by keeping score and constantly trying to "get" each other instead of working together. This opens the door for both of you to begin to let your walls down, to trust each other again, and open yourself to improved communication, collaboration, and the power of each other's genuine love.

Even if you're reading this book by yourself, it is possible to stop the scorekeeping in your household. Start by making changes in your own behavior and soon your partner will notice the difference, even if he doesn't say anything. You've heard the old saying, "Kill him with kindness"? Well, I say, "Guide him with kindness!" Your spouse may be unsettled by the new way you act, and he might even try to goad you back into your usual way of communicating, but the longer you stick with the plan below, the less satisfaction he will get from his one-way attacks. He will notice and appreciate your change, and thus you'll be guiding both of you into calmer waters.

If even a flicker of its original warmth remains, your relationship could begin to spark with new life as he responds in ways that surprise and hearten you. If he simply can't respond in a positive way, at least you will know in your heart that you tried your best, that you did your part.

Setting the Stage to Eject the Scorekeeping

Take a moment to do some introspection and circle the appropriate answers to the questions below. They will help you analyze if you're a scorekeeper and how far you and your partner have traveled down the path of scorekeeping. This will give you a clearer understanding of what it's going to take to climb back to healthier communication.

1. Is keeping score a common way you communicate with your partner?
   Yes   No

2. How often do you find yourself keeping score of your behavior and your partner's behavior?
   A. Once or twice daily
   B. Once or twice weekly
   C. Once or twice monthly
   D. Rarely
   E. Never

3. When you engage in scorekeeping, is your tone:
   A. Joking and friendly
   B. Hostile and sarcastic
   C. You never verbalize the scorekeeping

4. Do your children witness your scorekeeping battles:
   A. Always
   B. Often
   C. Sometimes
   D. Never

5. If they do, do you involve them or manipulate them into taking sides:
   A. Always
   B. Often
   C. Sometimes
   D. Never

6. Describe a recent win-loss event you had with your partner. If scorekeeping is common in your relationship, it won't take long to think of one, as it likely happens in almost every conversation the two of you engage in. It could have been a small issue, like whether or not it was you who had the TV remote last, or something more significant, like which of you is wasting money on the things you buy or, even more volatile, who is the most giving in the relationship.

   The topic of our most recent win-loss event was: _____

   _____

   _____

   _____

   _____

   _____

As I result, I feel:

   I won   I lost

7. **If you asked my spouse the same question about this particular event, he would say:**
   He won   He lost

Now, let's break down the above incident a little further. What did you hope the outcome would be when you engaged in scorekeeping? That he would apologize? That you would "win"? Did you predict your spouse would see the outcome the same as you or differently? Is it possible you and your spouse define a win and a loss differently? Is it possible that if you two continue to fight against each other, you will always define victory and defeat differently? Did anything improve as a result of the win-loss event? Was a situation resolved that won't happen again? Do you feel you have a clearer understanding of the problem between you?

Write your reactions and thoughts to the above questions here:

———————————————————————————————————
———————————————————————————————————
———————————————————————————————————
———————————————————————————————————
———————————————————————————————————

Steps to Change

If you answered the above questions honestly, my guess is that you figured out that scorekeeping didn't help you solve your disagreement and, in fact, most likely made you both angrier at each other. So I'd like to help you permanently kick the habit of toxic scorekeeping. I want you to take a deep breath and commit yourself to taking the steps below, not just once or twice, but over a consistent period. At first, this will feel like dental surgery with no anesthetic. But if you really want to change the dynamic between you and your partner, it's worth the initial pain because these steps work. You have to be consistent and stick to your new behavior, even when you get nothing in return. Depending on how entrenched keeping score is in your relationship, you will need a lot of willpower and self-discipline. A lot. Sometimes you'll have to just grit your teeth and wait for the scorekeeping urge to pass. But it will pass.

If you feel comfortable telling your partner your game plan, then do so. But if you're not up to that, then just dive into these steps on your own.

1. **Clean up the way you talk to your partner, both in what you say and how you say it.**

   Your words *and* your tone are equally important. One change doesn't work without the other. Starting right now, decide that you are putting an end to the sarcasm and snide remarks that feel oh-so-good in the moment but leave a trail of destruction in their wake. When a zinger comes to mind, squelch it. This may not be easy to do in the beginning, because your ingrained instinct will be to let those remarks fly from your mouth. Replace those knee-jerk thoughts with reminders of your new goal, which is to salvage this relationship. If you simply can't bring yourself to say something kind, just keep your conversation neutral. He forgot that you had a dinner date at your parents' house? Don't say, with your usual sarcasm, "I remember *your* mother's birthday, wedding anniversary, and her g**d*** dress size, and you can't even write down the night *my* mother's going to cook us dinner?" Instead, try: "I'd appreciate it if you could change your plans, because they're really looking forward to this," spoken without hostility or anger.

   The first time you do this, you will probably be as astounded as your partner—you, because you're not used to speaking to your partner in this manner, and him, because he will be processing how foreign these words sound coming out of your mouth. But it will get easier and less jarring if you continue to communicate in this new way. It's almost like learning a new language. It's awkward at first, but the more you speak it, the more fluent you will become.

2. **Assume that your partner's motives are good, even when you believe in your heart he's trying to score points.**

   This will go against all your self-protective instincts, but it is crucial if you are both going to shift the ways you treat each other. When he takes the outdoor furniture out of the basement, rinses it off, and puts it on the patio without being asked, you might immediately assume this gesture is just his form of nasty payback for something you forgot to do. Zig Ziglar, the father of all self-help motivational speakers, would call that sort of thought pattern "stinkin' thinkin'," and I would agree with him. Rather than assume the worst about his motives, decide to look at it through a positive lens. Thank him for getting the household ready for spring, and believe that he did it because he's looking forward to spending some family time enjoying the backyard. This will feel extremely hard to do if you're used to constant negative judgment, but remember that there was most likely a time early in your relationship when you *did* do such helpful things for each other. Convince yourself that this is one of those times.

3. **Force yourself to do something thoughtful for your partner that's not connected to payback.**

When you're using his car, fill it up with gas. Pick up his dry cleaning. Let him sleep in one weekend morning. Don't overdo this, because you could quickly slide back into resentment if he doesn't respond the way you think he should. And be aware: if you're doing this without your partner's knowledge, he will likely be suspicious of your motives. But if you are able to make one or two kind gestures in a week, consciously not expecting recognition, and do so casually, acting as if it's not a big deal, you will open up new ways of behaving toward each other without the dreaded scoreboard in your head.

4. **Exercise humility.**

Decide to set aside your ego and begin to exercise humility with your partner. How do you do this? When he loses his temper and tries to one-up you, just remember all the times you've done something similar—or worse! He's not perfect, but news flash: neither are you! The quicker you can accept the fact that you aren't perfect, the better.

Next, focus on good memories of your partner. This will help you embrace humility by softening your perception that you have more good traits than he does. Think about the time he quickly bundled you into the car to take you to the emergency room when you nearly sliced off your thumb cutting up a cucumber. No matter how far back in your memory you have to go, find good thoughts, feelings, and traits about your partner to focus on and paint that picture of him in your mind. It is difficult to practice humility if you've spent years trying to prove that you're right, but when you open the door to its power, you will find yourself transformed. Humility is not weakness; quite the opposite, actually. It is a sign of great strength. Embrace it and change your life and relationship.

5. **Let the change unfold.**

    If you concentrate just on what you are doing—following the above recommendations—it will keep you from trying to micromanage the results. While there is some level of predictability in the outcome you're aiming for—just like putting up an umbrella in a rainstorm will keep you from getting soaked—you can't know how your partner will respond. So don't dwell on your partner's response but rather on knowing that you are acting on your own intense desire to change the way you and your partner behave toward each other. When you set up the coffee machine at night for your partner, even though he usually does it, don't let yourself anticipate his response. If he thanks you, that's great. But don't do it purely for the gratitude; that's just another form of keeping score. If he doesn't seem to notice, that's okay. Just keep doing what you're doing for your own sake. See what happens, not after one day but after several weeks of consistent change.

6. **Honor your courage.**

    Every step of the way, give yourself credit for trying to shift your behavior. This is hard work. Pat yourself on the back as you accomplish small goals, like holding your tongue when your partner snaps at you, or noticing the first time your partner refrains from doing the same. These are *real* victories, whether anyone else knows them or not. Celebrate them in your mind and heart. This will give you confidence and make you feel good about yourself, and it will inspire even further change as you continue to grow as an individual. If these changes save your relationship, that will be wonderful. But if they do not have the hoped-for changes in your partner, they are still valuable skills for you to have mastered.

Scorekeeping . . . and Not Scorekeeping

Read the following two scenarios. Each describe the same domestic chaos at the end of a typical day, but the first describes how events unfold when the couple is locked into keeping score, and the second when two partners enjoy a healthier relationship. Which story most closely resembles your own? Which story would you like to live?

He is on the way home, exhausted from a punishing day at work that included losing a big client in his contracting business. He drove three miles out of his normal route to pick up their son, only to discover that the boy got a ride from someone else and nobody told him. He got stuck in horrendous traffic in that part of town—and the A/C in his car isn't working! Bad day is an understatement.

Her workday was also a disaster. Her office computer's hard drive failed, erasing this month's sales data from the store where she manages the books. She walked in the door from a trip to an overcrowded grocery store and was instantly hit with the smell of vomit: the dog threw up all over the place after getting into the trash that no one took out. She is on the floor scrubbing the vomit stain out of the carpet as her husband walks in the door, hot, tired, and mad. The house reeks, the kids are screaming, and there are no signs of dinner. Bad day just got worse.

He purposely slams the door in frustration as a signal to let her know he's irritated. She gets up and shouts, "Don't slam the door at me! Look at this mess I have to clean up because you forgot to take out the garbage. And why are you so late?"

He quickly bites back, "Because no one told me that Scott had another ride home and I spent a half hour sitting in traffic. You think I have nothing to do all day but drive around? Let's face it, I'm a little busier than you at work."

She glares at him, holding the soggy, smelly paper towels in her hands.

"So my job isn't as important as yours?" she says, waving the paper towels at him. "Tell that to the bank! Without my salary, we would have never gotten a mortgage."

Then she begins to reel off the list of all the errands and household chores she's had to do today in addition to her job, while he "just sat at

Family: The Good F-Word

99

work." He responds with equal sarcasm, telling her that all that exercise hasn't helped much with her weight, which makes her cry.

"You know what? You disgust me," she hisses at him, and heads upstairs to the bedroom, slamming the door loudly enough for him to hear in the kitchen.

He feels a smug sense of satisfaction that he successfully got under her skin and chuckles to himself. Their kids have long since vacated the room, hiding in their bedrooms so they don't have to listen to their parents' fight.

There's no dinner, so he pulls some chicken nuggets out of the freezer and zaps them in the microwave for the kids. He pours himself a beer, grabs a bag of chips, and goes into the den to watch a football game on TV and forget about his day. He and his wife don't speak for the rest of the night. She's in bed, seemingly asleep when he goes to bed after midnight, exhausted, with a headache from the beer. He's still really worried about losing his business client, resenting that his wife doesn't care about his work. She is not asleep, lying stiffly on her side of the bed, angry, hurt, and hating her husband.

Now let's take a look at the same scenario when a couple responds to the day's troubles as a loving couple who isn't keeping score. We'll pick it up from when the husband gets home from the same awful day and finds his wife in the same situation described above . . .

When he comes through the door and sees his wife on her hands and knees, he puts his bag down on the counter and asks what happened. She explains, and he realizes he's the one who forgot to take out the garbage. He apologizes and offers to finish cleaning the stain in the carpet. Sure she's tempted to say something sarcastic, like "It's a little late for that," after her own bad day at work, but his apology is really sincere. She can tell he feels badly seeing her having to deal with the mess, so she says it's okay and instead asks him to get the chicken out of the fridge, fire up the grill, and get the kids ready for dinner.

While he starts on that, she asks him why he was late and he explains about the ride mix-up, and she reprimands her son for not waiting for his father just because he wanted to ride with his friend. The boy apologizes to his father. They all sit down to eat, and their daughter reports that her Spanish teacher complimented her on her accent and asked her to recite a poem in class, and her father and mother make a big deal of it because she's been struggling with her schoolwork.

She mentions the computer catastrophe at work, but now it doesn't seem so horrible. It may take a little extra work, but she realizes she can re-create the missing sales figures. It's not until after dinner that he tells her about losing the client. Since he's talked about this guy a lot, she knows this is a big deal for him and she says she's really sorry. He explains what happened with the guy, laments about what a bad break it is and what a hit his business is going to take, and she nods. It'll be okay, she says. He looks over at her, meets her eyes and thanks her, sits for a moment, and then says he's going to watch the football game to take his mind off the day. She gets it, says fine, and he and the kids clear the table before he goes into the den and the kids go upstairs to do their homework.

She's happy to have a little time to herself. She throws a load of laundry in the wash, makes herself a cup of coffee, and sits down to do the crossword. After a while she goes into the den, sits with her husband for a few minutes, then tells him she's going up to bed. She checks on the kids, spends time getting them organized for bed, and eventually gets in bed herself. She's reading when he comes upstairs, and they talk while he changes and climbs into bed beside her. He thanks her again for listening to him go on about the client. He asks if she wants to talk about her computer glitch, but she's over that. They give each other a good-night kiss—no sex tonight because they're both tired—and turn out the light.

Looking at these two scenarios illustrates how the normal ups and downs that occur in every life can be filtered so differently by a family, depending on whether or not the two partners keep score.

In the first family, everything that happens becomes grist for scoring points. The result? The husband celebrates the fact that he can make his wife cry, but what does that get him? A night with the TV and his beer, unhappy children, and an angry wife. His wife also gets her jabs in, venting her anger and disgust at her partner, but she goes to bed in misery.

In the second family, the day's problems are shared, which softens their impact, and the couple use their feelings for each other to support each other. Their household is calmer, more productive, and the children are happier. Wouldn't you rather live in a household like that?

You can if you stop keeping score.

Relationship Roadblock #3: The Silent Killer . . . Silence!

7

Relationship Roadblock #3: The Silent Killer . . . Silence!

7

If you don't have anything nice to say . . . dig deeper.

—Troy Dunn

Occasionally I talk with a husband and wife who have been married for several decades and they say, proudly, something like, "We have never had a single disagreement." To that I reply, "Either senility is setting in and you are losing your memory, *or* you two never talk, *or* one of you is suppressing your true thoughts and feelings."

The fact is that silence is *not* golden when it comes to a healthy relationship. Many couples have bought into the idea that arguing indicates a lack of love or appreciation for another person and should be avoided at all costs. But just the opposite is true.

Success in a marriage is not defined by never disagreeing, but by the quality and tone and outcome of the arguments you and your partner *do* have. You and your spouse are not always going to agree. You are two different people with different perceptions, opinions, backgrounds, and outlooks, so of course you're not always going to see eye to eye. This is a good thing! It's part of the natural dynamic of two people living together. Otherwise you'd marry yourself! In a healthy relationship, couples use disagreements to resolve small problems before they become big ones, learn more about each other, understand each other better, and continually reset the balance in their marriage. It's how a relationship grows and enriches itself.

So when partners don't speak up when something bothers them, they lose out big time. When they choose not to air their differences in honest, productive ways, they are left with simmering silences that are filled with misunderstanding, resentments, and anger toward each other. They shut down the natural progression of getting to know each other better and loving each other more.

And it's not like keeping a lid on your feelings helps anything. It's just the opposite. While it may feel like you're avoiding trouble by not telling your husband that you resent all the time he spends watching football with his friends, you're not doing either of you any favors. First of all, by not bringing it up, you give him no chance to change his behavior, or at least try to explain to you why time with his friends is so important to him. Secondly, your resentment doesn't disappear; it just settles in and increases a little more each time he goes off to watch more football. Gradually, it becomes a bigger and bigger obstacle between you. You end up feeling more hurt, more betrayed, and more miserable. If this goes on long enough, you stop wanting to share *anything* with your partner, even good times.

It's Too Quiet in Here!

There are lots of understandable reasons why couples refuse to speak up. Sometimes you and/or your partner believe deep down that fighting within a marriage means you're on the road to divorce. Or, you keep quiet because you're so afraid of losing your partner that you'd rather hide your true feelings than face a potentially ugly confrontation. Many times, the "silent treatment" is the only way you know how to disagree, because you or your partner grew up with parents who acted in this way—the dysfunction has been handed down to a new generation. Finally, very often you and your partner *have* tried to resolve your differences, but it didn't work. Past arguments have led to nasty name-calling, endless back-and-forth accusations, and shouting matches, where not only is nothing resolved but you're both angrier than ever. So eventually, you're just worn out from these abrasive confrontations and give up. You've pushed away and hidden your true feelings, pretending they don't exist.

But to enjoy a mutually satisfying relationship, both parties must feel—and actually *be*—heard. You both have to be able to share your beliefs, opinions, and principles, even if they are not always in line with the other person's. If you allow silence to prevail, you begin to feel invisible. It's as if your partner doesn't see *you* anymore. Sure, he looks across the room and sees what you look like, what you're wearing, and he might even notice the expression on your face, but it seems as if what you think doesn't matter.

Amplifiers and Fadeouts

Someone who feels invisible usually reacts in one of two ways. He or she becomes either an Amplifier or a Fadeout.

Imagine for a moment that you actually *are* invisible, like a sci-fi movie, where nobody can visually see you even though you are standing right there in front of them. As a young boy, I used to imagine how cool it would be to be able to move from place to place without ever being seen. But in a relationship, there's nothing cool about feeling like the person you love can no longer see you.

Feeling this way triggers some people to try even harder to become noticed, which is why I call them "Amplifiers." They realize they aren't being seen, so they work extra hard to be heard. Unfortunately, these attempts to amplify one's self can be quite extreme and too often destructive. As parents, we can see this sort of behavior in our children, can't we? Our baby, Trevin, has been told over and over not to touch the electric outlets (which have safety covers on them, by the way), yet he will occasionally still crawl over to an outlet and reach out for it while looking directly at us! We are amazed at how brazen he is, but he is simply saying, "I'm here!" When adults turn into Amplifiers, they are often overreacting to feeling invisible. They look for any way to get a rise out of their partner, such as drinking one too many at a family gathering and causing a scene. If you tend to always draw attention to yourself, to the point where those around you call you out on your behavior, you might be an Amplifier.

Alternately, others react to feeling invisible by simply fading away. They are the "Fadeouts." If you feel like no one sees you at all and have felt this way for a long time, you may come to the conclusion you are always going to be invisible, never to be seen by people ever again. What might be a "natural" reaction to this acceptance? For starters, you may decide it's a waste of time to spend any energy on how you look or what you wear. Why bother to do your hair, put on makeup, and pull an outfit together? Nobody will notice because nobody can see you anyway. You may even abandon the most basic social interaction, like direct eye contact, smiling, or showing looks of interest, compassion, or love. Why make the effort? Nobody can see your face anyway. Do you see how that could seem logical if you were invisible?

Sadly, there are many people who have been made to feel so invisible in their own lives and relationships that they do just that—stop taking care of themselves, stop any kind of social activity. They fade out as much as possible, which has a disastrous effect on their self-worth and bleeds into every area of their lives, from relationships to employment, sometimes even affecting their will to live.

It is dangerous indeed to feel invisible or to lead others to feel invisible.

It's a terrible feeling to be ignored for who you are. And guess what? Your partner may feel exactly the same way.

But you can stop now. If you and your partner have too often pushed the mute button on your arguments, nursing grudges and drifting further and further apart, take heart. You *can* repair this part of your relationship.

And it will be far more rewarding than you imagine. For one, the process of learning to really "hear" each other is very validating—it strengthens you both as individuals. Allowing your partner to express his opinion is a sign of respect. Notice I didn't say "agreeing" with him or her is a sign of respect. You don't have to agree with someone to respect him. But listening to him talk and honestly express himself, without interruption and sarcasm, is a really cool way to say, "I love you!"

You also actually might learn something. Your opinion is based on your own knowledge and life experiences. But when you hear another's opinion, which is based on his or her knowledge and experiences, who knows? You may grow a little! Be open to it.

There is also the happy-ending factor to a successful argument. When two people disagree, then hear each other out and either come to a compromise or agree to disagree, they feel a new intimacy and warmth for each other. There is a reason why make-up sex is so popular!

Disagreement 101

Setting the scene: Mark and Amy are newlyweds, and they have quickly realized that they operate on two different timelines. She believes in being right on time—if you're invited to someone's house for 7:00 p.m., that's when you should show up. He disagrees and doesn't like to be rushed into getting out the door. So every time they go out, Amy ends up downstairs, car keys in hand, purse on her shoulder, tapping her foot, while Mark is still searching for his socks. By the time he shows up, she's furious. She says he should have started changing earlier, now they're going to be late, and so on, and he shrugs and tells her she should take a chill pill. They both slam the doors as they get into the car, don't talk, and set off on a rocky start to what could have been a nice evening together. Again.

If they never sit down and really discuss their different feelings about being "on time," they will repeat this scenario every time they go out. They will both get more and more locked into their separate points of view, become increasingly resentful of each other, and begin to dread what should be nice nights out together.

But let's consider the alternative: What if they *do* calmly discuss it? They could come to the realization that there is no right or wrong here; they are just "wired differently." Since they both hate the constant and predictable fighting every time they're going out, they find a solution.

They have two cars, so perhaps they decide on two departure times. If Mark wants to arrive at their destination with Amy, he makes sure to be ready when she is. But if he's running late, Amy's okay with leaving on her own and having him join her a bit later. If Amy feels really strongly about a certain event, she alerts Mark ahead of time that she'd really like him to be ready to go with her. Mark does the same. Or they split the difference in their preferred timetables, sometimes leaving when Amy wants to and other times when Mark is ready. In fact, any number of solutions can be feasible—but only once Amy and Mark have decided to listen to each other's opinions in a calm and respectful manner. A possible roadblock in the new marriage is nipped early!

So Let's Talk . . . Disagreements Wanted

Have you stifled disagreements with your spouse? Instead of discussing something that bothers you, do you brush it under the rug to avoid an unpleasant conversation? Do you lie to yourself and try to convince yourself that something that happened between the two of you is no big deal, but in your gut you know it really is?

I'd like you to write down the last time you disagreed with something your spouse said or did. It could be anything. Maybe it was him not giving you a heads-up that he was going to be late from work. Or maybe you're constantly frustrated and feel disrespected by his lack of tidiness or disregard for cleaning up after himself. Perhaps he gave your son permission to go to a friend's house without asking you, or he's casual about paying bills so that you often have to pay a late fee. Whatever it is, no matter how big or small it might seem, write it down here:

_____

_____

_____

Now, think about your response. What did you do? Say nothing? Go "nuclear" and scream and holler? Ask him why he did it? Tell him not to do it again? Make the time to talk about it when you could do it calmly? No matter how you feel about your actions, be honest and write down how you responded when you felt "wronged" in some way by your spouse:

_____

_____

_____

_____

_____

_____

I want you to now think about why you responded in that way. It might take a little digging, but every action (or lack of action) has a reason behind it. Did you keep it to yourself because you were afraid of a confrontation? Did you scream because you thought it would be the only way to get through to him? Did you ignore it because you figured he wouldn't listen anyway, so why waste your breath? Think hard about this one, and write down your reasons for your reactions here:

_____

_____

_____

_____

_____

_____

Finally, what was the outcome? If you filed your frustration away, is that anger still brewing under the surface? If you yelled, did it escalate into an all-out fight? If you tried talking calmly, did he consider your feelings and agree to change?

_____

_____

_____

_____

If you've been in the habit of keeping silent, congratulations on speaking out! These are hard questions to ask yourself, and you deserve kudos for your honesty and efforts to break down your style of arguing (or not arguing!).

How to Disagree

You might feel hopeless about changing your communication style with your partner. If you've spent a lot of time in your relationship *avoiding* conflict, it seems kind of crazy to *invite* it! But I'm not suggesting that you put on boxing gloves and get into the ring with your partner—far from it. What I'm suggesting below are some practical, nonconfrontational steps to help you air your differences with your partner, so that you resolve them and move on without all the hurt feelings and resentments that probably color your disagreements now.

There have been countless books written about the proper ways to communicate, argue, disagree, etc. Most of them contain useful information, but too many of them have too much information. They are written as if they want you to become a professional counselor on communication, when all you really want to do is *argue less and get along more.*

So I am going to give you a set of 11 guidelines for having a disagreement, which I call "Resolution Talk."

When you and your partner disagree, following these steps will increase your odds of a successful conclusion. The more unusual or "weird" you think this method is, the more you probably need it! So don't critique it, just embrace it. It is designed to build up your relationship by guiding you to resolving your conflicts in a productive way.

It is best if you and your partner can read these steps aloud together before starting your discussion. This will introduce you both to what may be a very different way of communicating and clarify the structure and boundaries of what you're going to do. If you don't feel comfortable asking your partner to read along, or he refuses to be a part of this, don't give up. You can still introduce these steps yourself the next time you see a conflict looming, and very likely your partner or spouse will take notice and change his own responses.

Family: The Good F-Word

111

1. **Agree on a time to discuss whatever is bothering you.**

   If at all possible, this should be a time other than the instant when the disagreement arises, a time when you can have some privacy, and when there is sufficient time available to discuss it without being rushed. Try not to do this late at night, when one or both of you are exhausted after a long day of work, kids, and "life."

2. **Sit face to face within five feet of each other.**

   This amount of space limits the ability to be overly dramatic, stops either of you from walking around (or walking away), and removes the possibility of nervous pacing. It is an intimate amount of space that allows for lowered voices and smaller physical gestures.

3. **Maintain direct eye contact.**

   Speak all of your words into the face and eyes of the person sitting in front of you. No looking toward the floor or ceiling. The eyes really communicate numerous nonverbal messages, and you need to each be able to receive one another's true feelings.

4. **Start by thanking your partner for taking this time to talk through this.**

   Hopefully he or she will return the thank-you. This starts the conversation with a baseline level of respect and appreciation, which is a healthy and wonderful way to begin an argument. When you act like adults, you can communicate like adults.

5. **State your position about the cause of the disagreement factually and slowly.**

   Use short sentences and *no* inflammatory adjectives, verbs, or figures of speech. Just the facts, ma'am. For example, begin by saying, "I would like to discuss the way you spoke to Cindy when she came over last night." Don't say, "I'd like to discuss what a total a**h*** you were to Cindy when she came over last night." (Even if—heck, *especially* if—that's the way you feel!) You want to set a framework for conciliation, not provocation, judgment, and blame. Otherwise you'll be right back where you started, locking horns or retreating to your corners. Then, give a brief account of the incident that has caused the disagreement. Sticking to simple summaries of the facts, without "decorating" your statements with drama, will help you stay on course. After you state your position, your partner should repeat what you've said back to you to confirm he understands what you're talking about. If need be, repeat this step to make sure you're both clear and agree on what's been said.

6. **Let your spouse state his/her position as outlined above.**
    Now it's your spouse's turn to discuss his or her perception of the disagreement. After that, you will have introduced the topic you want to discuss, and you both will understand where you each stand.

7. **Explain *why* you are bothered by the incident that caused the disagreement.**
    Again, no adjectives, no increased volume, and no increased speed of speaking. Rapid speaking is often a signal of anger. So speak slowly and in a normal voice. Keep your sentences short and your explanation as brief as possible. State each point once, and don't tag on a drawn-out story to each point. Do not repeat yourself.

8. **Let your spouse or partner do exactly the same thing.**
    There is no interrupting each other ever, ever, ever, and absolutely no sarcastic, dramatic, or condescending facial expressions or gestures of any kind. When listening to each other, the listener should have their hands resting in their lap and eyes on the speaker at all times.

9. **Throughout this whole process, take your time.**
    Pause. Embrace that word, because it is part of the secret to the success of this technique. Again, pause! When your partner is speaking, *stop* thinking about what you're going to say next. Instead, listen very carefully to every word your

partner says. Be quiet and don't interrupt. After he completes his statement, *pause* to take in his words and process what he said. Then, with control and calmness, respond to what has been said using the rules outlined above. It will be your spouse's turn to sit quietly, without interrupting, and listen intently to your viewpoint.

The power is in the pause. Taking lots of time to let your communication unfold allows you both to breathe in each other's opinions and feelings, to really understand what you're both trying to say. It is important that these pauses be silent. As your partner pauses, don't fill the silence with more banter. Sit still and wait for him or her to reply. This single step in the process will keep arguments from escalating the way they used to in the past. (By past, I mean yesterday or even this morning!)

10. Propose a solution.

Now it's your turn to resolve the disagreement. Begin by saying, "Based on what I have heard you say, I'd like to propose the following compromise . . ." You then show some effort to resolve this issue by making a step toward resolution. You may have to step outside your comfort zone here, but it's important to be as open-minded and generous as possible to make it clear that your intent is to resolve this conflict with compassion and love, and not win in anger. Once you have suggested a compromise, ask your partner how he or she feels about what you've said, and then be prepared and open if your partner suggests an alternative to some or all of your proposal. Pause and consider what he says without getting defensive. Keep your eye and feelings on the goal, which is to both resolve the problem you're having now *and* to create a new, better way of communicating. Keep talking and negotiating until you settle on the final version of a compromise.

11. When a compromise is reached, end it the way you began.

Thank your spouse for taking the time to discuss the disagreement with you.

Bam! It's resolved and over. If you are used to fighting at fever pitch or stomping away from arguments without speaking, you will feel a strange new calm after a Resolution Talk. It might be a bit scary, and you might wonder if all the old feelings will soon come rushing back in and send you back to your old behavior, but take a deep breath and savor what you've done. This is the way many happy couples communicate and resolve conflict. Now you can join their ranks!

Further, after you've had some time to absorb the lessons in the Resolution Talk, I suggest you think about the disagreement you described earlier in the chapter. Think about what made you angry; what you thought, did, and said; and the outcome. Then play back the scene as if you had handled it with a Resolution Talk. It might be helpful to write down how you would resolve it, step by step, using a Resolution Talk. Would the outcome have been more satisfactory?

If your partner or spouse is on board with you, congratulations to you both. You can make the decision to try a Resolution Talk the next time either one of you wants to work through a disagreement. The more you do this, the easier it becomes. Eventually, the steps in the Resolution Talk become the normal way you and your partner talk about your differences, and the whole tone of your relationship will improve.

If you've read this by yourself, you can still refer to a Resolution Talk the next time you want to try to communicate with your partner in a healthier way. By carefully sticking to the steps as best you can, you might find your partner more responsive than you think. He, too, might deep down be tired of all that's not discussed between you, especially if he can see that your method eases the conflict between you.

Resolving disagreements this way takes discipline, concentration, and effort, especially if your track record of resolving conflict is either nonexistent or filled with acrimony. Some issues will be easier to resolve then others, but there is *no* issue that can't be better handled using a Resolution Talk.

Talking is Golden

By agreeing to disagree in a respectful and caring way, you are giving yourself and your partner a great gift. When you are able to talk more freely with each other, trusting that you will be fair and listen to each other, the whole block of negative behavior and energy that has taken up a huge amount of space in your relationship will gradually disappear. Remember that in a healthy relationship, where continuous conversations are flowing like a river after a rainstorm, the occasional disagreements and misunderstandings and miscommunications that occur simply float to the surface and are discussed, attended to quickly, and then washed away. So it will be for you. All the silent resentments and dark thoughts that once filled your heart and mind will slip away, making room for a flood of affection and love for each other.

You will discover in a new way that talking is a form of intimacy. Maybe when you think of the word "intimacy," a nice chat on the couch isn't the first thing that comes to mind. But when you are able to share your deepest desires, your strong opinions, your rough days at work, your bad dreams, even your bad hair days with your partner, you will experience a wonderful rush.

Communication, even just the run-of-the-mill "How was your day?" kind of communication, is the glue that builds a bond between you and your spouse. It heightens and enriches your life with your spouse or partner in every way. It has the power to dramatically increase the pleasure you share in the simplest things, like a child's good report card, a movie you saw, even gossiping about people you know! Simultaneously, you have a strong, loving, and supportive ally when things go terribly wrong—when you lose your job, or when a parent dies.

Even the best of marriages and relationships can lose their footing because of the lack of good, quality talk time. So by talking, disagreeing, agreeing, challenging each other's thinking, you will be open to the idea that you are not always right and you don't know everything. That truth, when embraced and ingested, will stop 50 percent of your future arguments from ever happening.

So let *me* pause for a second and direct your focus to what has happened. I don't want it to pass by you unnoticed. In the course of the past few pages, you have just changed the course and therefore the destination of your marriage and family! Even if it is all still feeling new, like a pair of shoes you haven't really broken in yet, you are doing it. You are slowly, steadily undoing what might have been suffocating your relationship to death. Heck, you might have just reversed generations of dysfunctional family communications!

Do you realize what this means? Your children are likely going to have better, stronger relationships because of what you are now embracing as your new normal. If I were standing next to you, this would be a great time for a fist bump or a hug or a happy dance even. (I actually do have a "happy dance"—shhh.) Well done, my friend!

The Pause Button: Slow Reactions Lead to Positive Actions

The pauses that are so important to the success of Resolution Talk are very useful in *all* areas of your life. They are a great way to slow down your thought processes so that you resist that urge to pounce and spew out the first thoughts (angry or otherwise) that come to your mind. This can be an extremely damaging habit, especially when your family is in trouble.

When something bothers you—a flippant or insulting comment, one of your kids behaving badly, a frustrating meeting with your boss—don't react right away. Imagine there is a big red Pause Button on a table in front of you and push it. Stop for a moment. Breathe. Let your initial reaction subside. Slow everything down—your breathing, your thoughts, your physical movements—everything. Shift into slow motion and allow your mind and your heart and your gut to synchronize. This takes a moment; sometimes two or three moments. Try to give yourself all the time you need to just think about what happened and why you are feeling angry about it.

Hitting your internal Pause Button will give you time to discern whether the situation is as it appears or if you are taking something out of context. Did your husband really mean what you think he meant? Do you have all the information you need to form an opinion about something, or are you filling in the pieces yourself, pieces which may or may not be true? Asking yourself these questions will clarify your thoughts and may keep you from saying something you will regret, something that could trigger a reaction in the person on the receiving end of your knee-jerk response.

The time to discipline your child is not at the exact moment when you are enraged by the window he broke or the black eye he gave his brother. If you do it then, you are likely to beat him like a piñata! Use the Pause Button, send him to his room, let things *really* slow down. Then, when you have gathered yourself back together, take a stroll to his bedroom, ease the door open, and then—and *only* then—engage him in a calm voice. You can still discipline him, but instead of overreacting and saying and doing things that leave you feeling guilty and abusive, and leaves your son feeling even worse, the punishment will actually fit the crime because you took the time to think things through.

The great thing about the Pause Button is that if it turns out that your instincts are right and a situation is as bad as it appeared to be in the beginning, you are still able to take action to fix it. But now you can feel confident you are doing it calmly and from a healthy place. You're not making a decision when your adrenaline is pumping, your heart is pounding, and your mind is possibly creating thoughts that are inaccurate. Things are not always what they seem. By using your Pause Button regularly (as the father of eight kids, my Pause Button is *worn out* from being pushed!), you can better determine the facts before you put your foot in your mouth. And in those times when things turn out to be exactly as they seem, your Pause Button will allow you to offer your controlled reaction without doing long-term and possibly permanent damage to your family.

Relationship Roadblock #4: Don't Believe Everything You Think

8

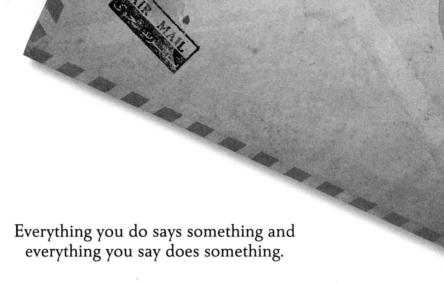

Everything you do says something and
everything you say does something.

—Troy Dunn

When I was 10 years old, I had a sleepover at my house with my friend Jeffrey. We decided to play one of our favorite games, silent hide-and-seek, which was similar to regular hide-and-seek except that we played it in the middle of the night while everyone else in the house was asleep. The rule was you could only hide in a room where someone was sleeping. This required deadly quiet and stealth and was very risky. What if we woke up my parents? We would get into big trouble—which was why we loved it!

So I counted to 50 while Jeffrey snuck off to hide. After some room-to-room searching, I crept into the darkness of my little sister's room and saw, in the soft glow of the night-light, that he had curled up underneath a blanket left on her floor. Judging by the shape of the blanket, I could tell he was lying in the fetal position, so I decided to sneak up and kick him in the butt. And I did.

Imagine my shock when he let out a scream like a girl! Not at all part of the rules of silent hide-and-seek! Then, in one of the most horrifying moments of my young life, the blanket flew off and I discovered it wasn't Jeffrey at all—it was my sister's friend who had slept over with her! As my panic-stricken brain was trying to comprehend what I had just done, I also realized I'd been wrong about the shape of the blanket. I didn't kick her butt; I'd kicked her in the face. There sat this little six-year-old girl, crying loudly, her hand on her bloody lip, as my parents came barreling into the room, half asleep, and yelling frantically, "What happened? What's going on?"

The bleeding girl pointed right at me and said, "He kicked me in the face while I was sleeping!"

The next few minutes were not the most pleasant for me, nor was the next morning, when I had to explain to the girl's parents what I had done so they understood why she was going home with a fat lip.

But what really shocked me when I relived the awful incident was how right I thought I was. At no point did I ever consider the possibility that the lump under the blanket was not my friend Jeffrey. And at no point did I even hesitate to believe what my eyes told me about the position "he" was in under the blanket. I was wrong on so many levels.

The Lying Eye

Too often in families, people jump to conclusions based on what they *think* they know. I have learned a very important principle from my own life, as well as through the lives of those I have reunited with loved ones: *don't believe everything you think.*

In the words of my business partner and close friend, T. J. Hoisington, author of the book *If You Think You Can*, people can too often make important life decisions based on what he calls "false evidence." In his book, he explains that people are constantly sifting through their life experiences and feelings to make choices about what they think and the actions they take. With his permission I quote him:

> The challenge is that people often lock onto perceived realities and beliefs that may not be accurate or useful in the first place. Or maybe the accepted "reality" is useful for the short-term, but has few long-term benefits. They find false evidence that may not be grounded in reality but believe it to be true. And once we accept something as "truth and reality," we continually find evidence to support it— making the belief ever stronger.
>
> For example, it's common when two people who were once deeply in love find themselves at odds with each other. In many cases, such circumstances didn't change, but their perceptions did. Rather than focusing on the positive attributes that had originally brought them together, they began focusing on negative attributes that repel them.

I've found this "false belief" a big problem when working to reunite families who haven't seen each other for many years. Truths and lies get passed around and rearranged so much that the real story often disappears completely. In one of my more dramatic cases on *The Locator*, a woman asked me to find her twin sons. She had been 16 when, pregnant with twins, she'd married a man more than 25 years her senior. They divorced when the boys were 14 months old because her husband was abusive. Because she was so young and had no means to support them, she moved back to her father's house in another state to get her life back together while her ex-husband took custody of the children. Every summer she returned to see her sons for a six-week visitation. But soon after one of the visits, her ex-husband, without her knowledge, put the boys up for adoption and they disappeared from her life.

I found them living with their adoptive parents. The couple who had adopted them had believed the father when he told them the boys' birth mother had abandoned them. They were shocked to learn that, far from abandoning them, the mother had been searching for them for years.

This was a story overflowing with lies. The boys, who had also believed that their mother had abandoned them, were thrilled to learn that she was looking for them and were thrilled to meet her. Their adoptive mother felt both guilty and afraid that she would lose her sons' affections to their birth mother. And their birth mother had to wrestle with her terrible sadness at missing her sons' childhood, her anger at her ex-husband, and her ignorance about the illegal adoption, which had taken place 23 years earlier. It took a long time for all these people to let go of what they *thought* was true and embrace the real truth, which was that the twins' mother had agonized over losing her sons and never stopped thinking about them.

But the same blind spots exist in families who live under the same roof. Maybe it's not so dramatic as the situation above, but we all have a tendency to see things through the narrow lens of our own feelings, needs, and biases at the expense of the true circumstances.

I saw this in a husband and wife who came to me because they were deeply unhappy, especially the wife. Stephanie complained that her husband, George, was inattentive to her and did pretty much what he wanted to do without ever consulting her. Every action seemed to show that he didn't love her, from not asking about her day after she asks about his to hunkering down in front of the television every night after dinner. But when I asked George, he said that no matter what he did to try to please Stephanie, it was never good enough for her. According to him, *of course* he loved her, but he resented that she didn't get it and was fed up with the animosity between them.

Then Stephanie happened to mention that her father was the same way—distant, not interested in what she did, and that her main job growing up had been to please him. This sent up a red flag for me, because I've seen over and over again how the patterns of a given family can be deeply embedded in their children. When I mentioned this similarity to Stephanie, she jumped on it.

"Of course. I chose someone just like my father!" she said with a note of triumph in her voice, satisfied that she'd successfully spun my observation to her favor.

But as we talked, I learned that George really did support her in meaningful ways she had failed to notice. He'd agreed with her decision to go back to school at night and helped out at home so she could study. He admired how she raised their sons and respected her common sense and advice. He clearly loved her deeply but had never expressed it in ways she recognized because he wasn't particularly demonstrative. As he and I spoke, I could tell by the look on her face that she was hearing these expressions of genuine love and respect from her husband for the very first time. She was quite moved by his words, however clumsy they may have felt to him.

I told her that all these actions seemed just the opposite of a distant and uncaring spouse.

"George doesn't really sound much like your father at all," I said.

She looked stunned as she took this in.

"I think you're right," she said after a long silence. "I've sort of made him into my father, and he's really not like that."

This was a big "aha" moment for this couple. Stephanie had been doing two destructive things for most of their 15-year marriage. First of all, she had been wrongly projecting her own dislike of her father onto her husband, and secondly, she had not recognized her husband's way of expressing his love since it was different from her own. George, understandably, wasn't thrilled that he hadn't gotten any credit for being the good husband he was trying to be, but he also realized he could have been better at telling his wife how he felt about her, instead of assuming she would figure it out from what he did rather than said. They both were then able to step outside of their own "truths," understand each other better, and begin to repair their relationship.

Keep Your Eyes On the "In Between"

There's nothing wrong with having your own, personal take on every situation—that's what makes you *you*—but it's important to understand that everyone else, even your partner, has *his* viewpoint too, and it might be very different from yours. In fact, there are *three* sides to every encounter or situation: yours, your partner's, and what's in between. And it's usually in the "in between" where you find the real story.

Say your father offers to lend you the money so you and your partner can buy a bigger house. You are amazed and touched by his generosity, as this way you'll have room to start a family, but your husband refuses to accept the money. You completely don't get this! You're hurt that he's rejecting your dad's thoughtful gesture, frustrated because it's a great location in a good school district, and angry at him because he doesn't seem to care that you love the house.

But your husband sees your father's offer in a completely different way. To him, it's a sign that his father-in-law is trying to control your lives, that maybe he thinks that his son-in-law isn't a good provider, and he's also suspicious that there will be strings attached to the offer. And he doesn't like it one bit that you seem to be taking your father's side against him. He would much rather wait and buy a new house when you can afford one on your own.

Somewhere in the middle of these two opinions is the reality. Maybe your father *is* trying to throw his weight around, but maybe he also genuinely cares for both you and his son-in-law and would like to help you out since he can. "What else is money for?" he thinks. Maybe it would be nice to have a bigger house right now, but the fact is that your place isn't a shack and can certainly fit a baby. Maybe it's a true that you're a bit of a daddy's girl, and it might be a good idea to put a little distance between the two of you. On the other hand, maybe it *is* really a good time to buy the house—mortgage rates are low—and you know you could sell your present home in a heartbeat. Maybe your husband is being a bit too sensitive to your dad's offer because he knows his own father would never be as generous.

The point is that the more you and your partner hear and understand each other's points of view, the less conflict you'll have between you. When you get stuck in your own narrow viewpoints, believing your opinion is always the *right* and *only* opinion, you keep yourself from seeing the full picture and making the best decisions.

Relationship Roadblock #5: Misdirected Healing

9

Relationship Roadblock #5: Misdirected Healing

9

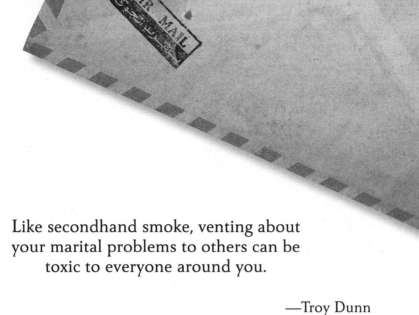

> Like secondhand smoke, venting about your marital problems to others can be toxic to everyone around you.
>
> —Troy Dunn

Another common problem that comes up between couples is that they turn to others for comfort when they're having trouble at home rather than talking to their partners when a problem comes up. There are lots of reasons this happens, including the fact that it makes you feel a whole lot better to unload on a friend about your selfish/nasty/thoughtless partner (and who will most likely absolve you of any part in a disagreement) than to actually get down to the uncomfortable business of sorting through a serious conflict with your partner.

Let's say you have a big fight with your partner. He slams the door, you hear the car pull out of the driveway, and he's gone, the car tires screeching down the street. You call your sister, mother, or best friend, sobbing into the phone so much that you can barely get out the words, telling her the whole sordid tale—the names he called you, the way he banged around the kitchen, broke the utensil drawer, refused to listen to your side of the story, that you can't stand his terrible temper, and so on. Whoever you call will be alarmed on your behalf and sympathetic to your obvious pain.

If your confidant is sensible, she'll calm you down, say, "This, too, will pass," and tell you that you need to talk to your partner. If she's not sensible, she's likely to inflame your anger by taking your side, agreeing with your rants that your partner is a louse and a loser. Either way, you're in the same place you were before you called in the cavalry. You and your husband are still at loggerheads, and nothing between you has been fixed.

This is called "misdirected healing," and it's way too common among quarreling couples.

On the face of things, there's absolutely nothing wrong with reaching out to friends or your mother when you're in trouble. That's what intimate friendships are for, and if you can't call your own mother when you need her, well, what's the point of having a support system outside your nuclear family?

The point is that as good as it feels to get some welcome sympathy when you and your spouse are fighting, it can seriously undermine the work you need to do with your partner if you really want to repair your relationship. I can think of five reasons why this isn't a good idea . . .

Number one—If what your partner said to you left you hurt and in pain, *he's* the one you should tell, because *he's* the one who can apologize, make amends, and get the message not to do it again. No friend or family member can do that for you. And the worse the fight, the more hurt you feel, the more important it is for your partner, not your mother or your friend, to know how really wounded you are.

Number two—When you spill all your feelings to a friend after an upsetting fight, you get a false sense of resolution. You've calmed down, you feel back in control, and you are less likely to want to open up all those wounds again to talk to your partner. It's much easier to just pretend the fight didn't happen and hope it doesn't happen again. The opportunity to try to talk things through with him is lost.

Number three—The advice you get from friends and other family members, while comforting, can't be 100 percent reliable because they're only hearing your side of the story. What they recommend might seem logical, may even *be* logical, but since they weren't in the kitchen when the pots were flying and the insults were being hurled, they can't know what the best solution might be for you and your partner.

Number four—When you unload the details of your intimate fights on a close friend or other family member, you're sharing things that you might later regret exposing to others. Do you really want to put it out there for the world to know that your partner can act like a two-year-old, has a mean-spirited side, or can't stand your mother? All this can come back to bite you.

And number five—Your partner is probably doing the same thing you are. He's at *his* friend's place, having a beer, getting his anger off his chest, telling his side of the story at your expense, detailing how uncaring and demanding you are, the names you called *him*, etc. Does the thought of that make you happy? Both of you are acting out instead of acting together.

There can be logical reasons why you might not want to engage your husband after you've had a fight. Most often, you and your partner may not know *how* to fight in a way that resolves issues, so it's too discouraging to even try to work things out afterward given the toxic nature of your relationship. But if you are reading this book, you're learning that there are many *good* ways to argue that get results, and it's really important to keep the lines of communication open with your spouse, even after a big fight. Otherwise, your marriage will suffer.

The bottom line is that your husband is the one you signed up with for life. And even if "for life" sounds more like a prison sentence than a marriage right now, and even if he just called you a you-know-what in front of the children and stormed out of the house when you gave it right back to him, *he's* the guy you need to sit down with. Not your friend, not your mother, and not your children. He's the one you've made a lifelong commitment to, and you owe it to yourselves to try as hard as you can to make your relationship work.

I've worked with many families who've found how much it helps to keep fights "in house" when rebuilding their fractured relationship. It's really hard to do at first, especially when you're used to venting to your friends and family, but they learned: venting is denting. In restraining the urge to vent, though, they were able to strengthen their relationships and feel the security, trust, and enormous sense of well-being that come from believing in a lifelong, committed relationship. You can do this, too.

So while it may be tempting to pick up your cell after an argument or go out to lunch with a friend and share your unhappiness about your partner, please don't. Your friend may make you feel better temporarily, but it's like spray-painting over that rust spot on your car. It looks okay, but the problem is still there and is growing worse by the day underneath that blanket of paint you covered it up with. Similarly, your unresolved disagreement with your husband will come back to haunt you when you fight again.

Instead, the next time there's a blowup, try something different in its aftermath. If your partner slams out of the house, take a deep breath, take a walk, do *anything* but pick up the phone to call someone for sympathy. When you calm down, you'll be able to think more clearly and put your fight in perspective without the drama that comes from reliving it with a friend. (And as a side note, know that some "friends" take secret pleasure in the relationship problems of others, and their enthusiastic agreement that your mate is a no-good this-and-that may very well be their attempt to fan the flames of your discontent for their own entertainment.)

Ask yourself, what triggered the fight? How did it escalate? What could you or your partner have done differently to resolve what happened instead of leaping into a full-blown confrontation? Perhaps not blame each other, not try to score points, not bring up old fights, not make snide, sarcastic remarks? All the above? Asking yourself these questions puts you on the road to solving things with your partner so that you can stop the fights that cause you both so much unhappiness. Remember that, most likely, he's just as upset as you are about what happened, hard as that may be to believe.

Once you have some clear ideas about what happened, you can think about how to fix things. This book is filled with information about the toxic ways couples fight, as well as strategies to change your behavior, so read through the sections that apply to you and your partner and figure how to make them work in your particular situation. This way, at the end of the day, you can look across the table at the guy you signed up with and know he'll be there in the morning, the next day, and every day afterward. Yes, your mother will always be there for you. But make sure your partner is, too.

Relationship Roadblock #6: Deal Breakers

10

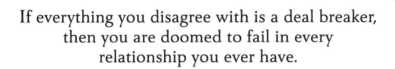

> If everything you disagree with is a deal breaker,
> then you are doomed to fail in every
> relationship you ever have.

—Troy Dunn

I hear this phrase a lot from angry couples. Spending so much time on his boat is a deal breaker. Wasting money on too many clothes is a deal breaker. Having your mother come to stay for three whole weeks is a deal breaker. For couples in trouble, deal breakers are everywhere, littering a family's life like the orange cones that mark highway construction.

A deal breaker is when one person says to another, "This is a non-negotiable boundary for me."

And there certainly are those in a marriage—drug abuse, infidelity, and violence are what I would call real deal breakers, all violating the basic foundations of the commitment two people make to each other. But unhappy husbands and wives often set up all sorts of so-called deal breakers that really have no use in their relationship except to create more problems. They set up a rack of bowling pins, daring their spouses to knock them over. It is a myth to believe that setting up these deal breakers is the way to stand up for yourself in your marriage.

I support your right to have certain boundaries, or deal breakers if you want to call them that. But be careful how many you put into your relationship, and make sure they are really important to you. Not emptying the dishwasher should not be on any list of deal breakers. Requesting privacy—that no one read your e-mails, for instance—would be more reasonable. But don't let the idea of stepping over boundaries automatically default to, "We are done here."

Your partner needs to understand that if he does cross a boundary, he will need to help you understand how it won't occur again and make you feel safe in knowing that is true. But don't treat your relationship as a disposable item. You have invested in your marriage on way too many levels to toss it aside like spoiled milk.

When your boundaries are crossed, some sort of action or repercussion will occur, but keep things in perspective. Don't look back and wonder if you overreacted and cost yourself something good.

Four Myths That Make Marriage Miserable

11

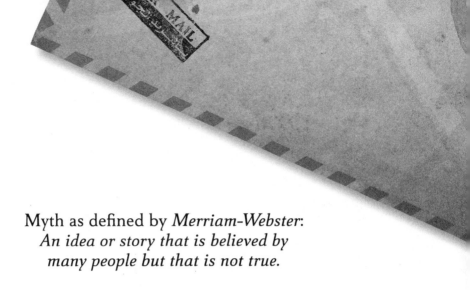

Myth as defined by *Merriam-Webster*:
*An idea or story that is believed by
many people but that is not true.*

Myth according to Troy Dunn:
False beliefs that can destroy your marriage and family.

Just because somebody says it, doesn't make it true. What am I talking about? False myths. There are all sorts of false truths floating around society that some people grab on to and use to make important, life decisions. There are many of them, but the ones that follow are those I believe cause the most damage in relationships. You may be rattled to learn that some of these long-heralded "truisms" are not at all true. Ready for a truth check?

Myth #1: People Just Drift Apart

It drives me crazy when a couple tells me they're considering divorce because they've "drifted apart." They speak of it as if it's almost inevitable that two people in any relationship that lasts beyond the honeymoon phase will eventually drift apart! They announce this with regret, as if it is destiny and they have no power to fight it.

What are you, a fishing boat? Drifting is what happens if a boat loses power, when intentional effort ceases and the watercraft submits to the currents and the storms. If you have felt you and your partner have "drifted" apart, one or both of you has stopped swimming!

To help couples step out of this destructive myth, I ask them to imagine themselves on a boat when the engine conks out, and they are left bobbing and weaving in the waves. Would they just settle back and say, "Oh, well, that's that," and look out at the water, watching the shoreline disappear as they await their fate? Hardly. They would get to work trying to get the motor started again so they could get into port. They would radio for help, prepare life jackets, and inflate a dinghy if they needed to. They would take action to avoid catastrophe.

So it should be in a marriage that runs into trouble. But in our culture, drifting apart is an acceptable reason for not working on a marriage. In divorce court, documents refer to it as "irreconcilable differences" or "insupportability." Whatever the lawyers and courts decide to call it, I call it a cop-out. To me, it is not acceptable to wash your hands of responsibility for your relationship under the guise of this myth.

Sara and Mike, a couple I worked with, had bought into this passive way of thinking about their marriage. They had been married for seven years, had three young children, and Mike was working two jobs to allow Sara to stay home until the kids were school age. They had agreed to this plan together and were committed to their family. But both parents had long, tiring days and often crawled into bed too exhausted to talk, let alone make love. With no real conversation, they had no understanding of each other's days or empathy for each other's sacrifices. Sara gradually began to feel ignored, Mike to think he was only being used for a paycheck. Since they both made the decision to fall fast asleep each night, neither blamed the other for the lack of intimacy. They didn't even recognize that this disconnect between them was a large part of the problem. They were just going along, hoping things would get better, but they were doing nothing to make that happen.

Hope doesn't change things, however. Change changes things.

I told them the boat story and they perked up, eager to be able to take action and make plans to carve out some time together. They were an easy couple to work with because they were very fond of each other and, luckily, hadn't "drifted" too far apart. Their mistake was that they had bought into the myth in the first place, that drifting apart just happened between couples and was unfixable.

Once they realized they could change things, they went for it. They began by setting up a date night every other week and used their time together to rekindle their affection for each other and remember why they'd gotten together in the first place. Then they both made a point, each day, of thanking each other for the things they did for the sake of the family. Even if dinner was reheated chicken from a meal that wasn't so great in the first place, Mike thanked Sara. And even when she was so tired from chasing after their children all day that she was cross-eyed with fatigue, she forced herself, when Mike came home, to ask him about his day and listened to what he said. At first their exchanges were awkward, as they'd both carried around their hurt feelings like badges of honor, but slowly, their new behavior toward each other became the norm. They began to share more about their lives, just the way they had before they had kids. They learned that a long-term relationship could get better and better, more intimate and more sustaining. Just the opposite of drifting apart.

If you are like Mike and Sara, please don't assume that drifting apart is the evitable outcome of a long relationship. Do as they did. Leave the drifting where it belongs in nature, amid snowdrifts and lazy rivers. It has no place in your marriage.

If you have drifted *far* apart, into dangerous waters of deep resentment, anger, and hurt feelings, refer back to the previous chapters to clear away any relationship roadblocks you may have set up for yourselves. Work on repairing the way you communicate. Then continue reading ahead to the next step of the LCA Plan for more help in creating a newer, closer relationship.

Myth #2: Actions Speak Louder Than Words

Not true. Actions *and* words both speak volumes, and you should pay attention to what's being said in your relationship as much as what actions take place.

Action is very important, no doubt. Quitting smoking is better than *saying* you're going to quit smoking. Pulling a drowning person from the river is better than yelling, "Get out of the water!" I once sat with a father who had abandoned his children, and after hearing him list off all his good intentions when, the truth was, he'd never once so much as sent his son a birthday card, and I told him, "Your actions speak so loudly, I can hardly hear a word you're saying."

I spend a good part of my time helping people take action to repair their relationships.

But make no mistake: words are *just as important* in relationships. Don't dismiss their formidable power both to inflict terrible hurt and to create new harmony. The wrong words spat at you in anger can feel as painful as a slap across the face, and the right words said at the right time by the right person can lift you higher than the moon.

Over the years, when I'm trying to help reunite two separated people, the first thing I want to know is what damaging things have already been said. Has someone threatened divorce? Has either partner shouted, whispered, texted, e-mailed, or hinted at his intense hatred for the other person? Does the couple indulge in nasty sarcasm when they talk to each other? Do they regularly denigrate each other with dismissive comments or cruel comparisons to past loves? This extremely toxic way of communicating is like throwing hand grenades at your marriage. It is terrible verbal abuse.

Depending on what they reveal, I can lower the temperature of the couple's anger and hostility by coaching them on how to speak to each other. I guide them to lower their speaking tones and avoid sarcasm, name-calling, and threats. Believe it or not, sometimes just asking someone to stop saying certain words and start saying other words can almost instantly begin to resolve a decades-old conflict. If a spouse regularly calls his wife a b****, for instance, persuading him to cut that word out of any arguments can have a dramatic effect on her. She might be able to actually listen to what he's saying instead of completely shutting down and tuning out when she hears that lethal word. Ditto when a wife calls her spouse a b******. Name-calling, especially using swear words to describe your partner, will quickly put the brakes on any reconciliation between a couple.

"Always" and "never" are two other needlessly inflammatory words. They are generally significant exaggerations and rarely reflect the reality of any situation. If your spouse says to you, "You *never* want to make love," he has just negated the times when you have, in fact, wanted to make love. Your past efforts have been reduced to insignificance, if not completely erased. Then you begin to ask, "Why should I even try?" That's when things go from bad to worse.

Erasing the words "always" and "never" from your disagreements reframes the problem away from such extreme positions and introduces some reality into the conversation so that you can at least entertain the possibility that you can resolve things.

Always Remember Never to Use "Always" and "Never"

I suggest you become hyperaware of the words "always" and "never," no matter where you are and no matter who is using them. It could be a teacher at your child's school or the dentist who is chatting you up during your visit. As soon as you hear someone include the word "always" or "never" in a sentence, ask yourself, "Was that use of the word truly accurate, or was it an exaggeration simply to make a point?" I believe you will find that more often than not, those two words are used incorrectly simply in an attempt to overstate a point. Rarely is something "always" or "never" the case. Once you realize this, you'll have some clarity the next time your spouse uses either word. Not to excuse your partner's word choice, but he's most likely using it to boost his side of the argument rather than because it's true. And if you're honest with yourself, you might realize you do exactly the same thing. So banish those ridiculous words from your vocabulary or, at the very least, from your arguments.

But enough about the destructive words that cause so much harm and shut down communication. I want to turn your attention to the awesome words you can *add* to your vocabulary—the ones that heal broken hearts and save relationships.

At the risk of oversimplifying the complicated world of relationships, there are a series of words and phrases that can improve the way a couple communicates. You'll recognize them right away, because it's likely they are words and phrases that you would love to hear from your spouse. When spoken sincerely and frequently, these words can work wonders for a relationship.

"I'm sorry."

This is when you take ownership for something you did, and that's an important thing to do when you have wronged someone. When you say you're sorry, it's because you have thought about what you've done and

Family: The Good F-Word

143

sincerely regret your actions or words. You have put yourself in another's shoes, realized how you've wronged that person, and want to let him or her know that you recognize your mistake and understand why he or she is upset. A sincere "I'm sorry" can change a couple's dynamic in a heartbeat. Your partner will appreciate being heard and be grateful that you are willing to take responsibility for something that hurt him. You will reap the rewards of owning up to your behavior. It feels good to act like a grown-up. (We'll talk more about taking responsibility for your actions in chapter 15.)

In the world of saying "I'm sorry," however, are some too-common fake apologies that defeat the whole purpose of apologizing in the first place. The first is using the word "but." If you follow the "I'm sorry" with "but," as in, "I'm sorry *but* if you hadn't blah blah blah, then I wouldn't be forced to blah, blah, blah," you're not saying you're sorry at all. You're blaming the *other* person for what *you* did.

The same applies to use of the word "if." Saying "I'm sorry *if* you are hurt that I spend time with my friends, but I need some 'me' time" is the same thing as saying, "I'm going to spend time with my friends, so deal with it." That's not an apology; it's a statement representing the opposite of an apology. You are not acknowledging your spouse's feelings, nor are you showing any understanding or compassion for her point of view.

A third fake "I'm sorry" is when you say, "I'm sorry that you feel that way." What does that mean? It means you're telling your partner that it's too bad she feels the way she does, but that's her problem because *you* didn't do anything wrong.

Authentic apologies are different because the person who apologizes sincerely means what he or she says. And this leads us to another, unspoken phrase embedded inside the words "I'm sorry," and that is, "I won't do it again." Those words shouldn't need to be said aloud because when you apologize, you are also promising not to repeat the behavior that has caused so much harm. It is expected that when you are acknowledging a mistake, you are vowing not to do it again. And when someone tells you they are sorry, you are allowed to assume the same thing: they will not do it again. Anything less is not an authentic apology. Hold yourself and others to this higher standard of apologizing.

Imagine for a moment that your son has wandered into the kitchen to discover the batch of cookies you've just made for a party you're going to. You've left a big sign by the cookies that says, "DO NOT EAT. These are for the party." But your son can't help himself—they look and smell too,

too good—so he pushes the note aside and grabs a cookie. You come back into the kitchen and catch him, mid-chew, and point to the note.

"I'm really sorry, Mom," he says, then grabs two more cookies as he runs out of the room. His words do not match his actions. His apology meant nothing because he continued the action for which he was apologizing. But then, he's eight years old and we're talking about cookies.

When *you* apologize for something or your partner apologizes to you, you have to back up your words, which isn't always easy. Your wife has called you out for spending too much time playing golf on the weekends and not enough time with your children. You realize she's right, so you say you're sorry. But that's not enough. You then have to work out a mutually acceptable arrangement with her so you're both okay with your golf schedule, and stick to it. An empty "I'm sorry" is the same, and in many ways worse, than no apology at all.

Love means having to say you're sorry . . . and mean it. And when you *do* mean it, your partner knows right away and the healing can begin. Both your hearts feel lighter, and you begin to trust and enjoy each other again.

"Please forgive me."

People rarely say this to each other, even when they apologize, but it carries a very strong message. If you say it after saying "I'm sorry," you are empowering your spouse with the opportunity to actively forgive you, which is a great way to clean the slate. When a couple in conflict both decide to seek and forgive, these words are enormously soothing. (See chapter 16 to learn why it's so very important to ask for forgiveness.)

"I love you."

This simple, three-word sentence seems the most obvious, but you would be shocked to know how many people long to hear it from the people they love. And don't. But when it is said sincerely—and sincerity is absolutely necessary—it can create a huge new opening for you and your partner. How do we say it with sincerity? Well, I have come to the conclusion that sincerity is more art than science. If it was a straightforward, step-by-step process, someone would have patented it by now. But there is no rulebook. There are as many ways to say, "I love you," as there are people who need to hear it.

Your job is to get your message across to your partner in a way that he or she will not only hear it, but embrace it and know it's heartfelt. For that, you have to know your partner. What's the best way to say, "I love you"? Is he or she someone to whom direct eye contact is important when you speak to her? Would she respond better to physical contact—touching her hand, stroking her shoulder while saying your words of love? Or would she like the written word—loving, sincere words in a little note taped to the bathroom mirror or slipped inside a briefcase. Or all the above? It's not enough to just be sincere. You need to make certain your spouse knows you mean it. That is an art. It is also one of the secrets to successful relationships in all areas of life.

Tongue Tied

A word here about men who can't say, "I love you." Their excuses are familiar:

"I don't need to say it. She knows it."

"I'm saying 'I love you' every time I get up and go to work for this family and every time I mow the lawn."

Men like this often feel that their actions speak for them, and they most likely have little experience with saying "I love you" aloud. He doesn't get it that his wife is thinking, "Well, he'd have to go to work and mow the lawn even if he wasn't my husband—big deal." But if a guy shows his love by working for the family and mowing the lawn *and* also telling his wife how much he loves her, he will create a very powerful bond in their marriage.

If your partner is one of those silent types who would rather eat nails than talk about his feelings (which is most men!), and if you are someone who really needs a verbal sign of his love, you're going to have to ask for it. In a calm moment, when both of you are relaxed, you can say, "You know how I tell you out loud that I love you?" He will nod, warily. "Well, I just need you to do the same thing. I know you love me, but I really need to hear you say the words out loud." He may protest that it's not the way he works, he's never been that way, you shouldn't need to hear it when you know he loves you, etc. "I just do," you respond. And if you're calm and persistent, he'll come around. And when he does, you smile and hug him and give him a kiss, and then another one, and he might realize he's got a good thing going and say it again.

While on the topic of saying, "I love you," I want to point out that it's not just your spouse who needs to hear those words. Your children need to hear them just as much, perhaps more, than your spouse. Remember, you are not just one of the relationships in your child's life—you are the first relationship, the primary relationship, and the one that most of your child's future relationships will be modeled after! No matter how silly or cheesy your child may think some of your expressions of love might be, like the little love note in her lunchbox or tucked into his cleats, it will have a powerful, long-term impact, beyond what you might imagine. It is a level of security children need. It is a visual aid of the depth of love you have for them. It is an action that reinforces the words, which is a form of sincerity.

Regardless of their age, your children will be lifted by these simple words—not just your adorable three-year-old but your teenage son whose voice is changing and who is nursing the stubble on his chin. And because you taught them well, when the day comes they will tell *their* children how much they love them, and the tradition of speaking of love will be carried on.

The right words can touch the heart and initiate change in as dramatic a way as any action. Take advantage of words as a means to mend your marriage. Actions don't speak louder than words; they speak louder *with* words.

Myth #3: Never Go To Bed Angry

Where did this half-baked myth come from? It's one of those pearls of wisdom that sounds sweet when you write it in the little white "advice" notebook being passed around at your friend's wedding, like "Love is Never Having to Say You're Sorry," but it puts silly and unnecessary pressure on a couple trying to sort out their disagreements. And, by the way, it doesn't work.

Imagine this: Donna and Ted are out to dinner with friends, and Donna shares the hilarious story of how Ted recently backed the car into the new power mower (oops) and now—surprise—Ted has successfully gotten out of mowing the lawn. Everyone cracks up at Ted's expense, including Ted, who feels compelled to chuckle despite the fact that he's boiling inside. Ted is sensitive about the subject of his incredible clumsiness, which is only made worse by the fact that now his friends (the gossipy types) will surely regale all of their other friends with the story of his stupidity. "That Ted," they'll say. "What a klutz!" So Ted is mad at Donna.

He tells her on the way home that he really wishes she hadn't told their friends about his little accident, and she laughs it off, saying that everyone does stupid things and that no one will remember it anyway. "And besides that, Ted, you're way too sensitive."

Well, that really sets Ted off, especially because Donna has an epic meltdown if you dare criticize her deadbeat brother, who happens to be the one who borrowed and broke the old mower, which is why Ted had to buy a new one in the first place! Ted uses that as ammunition against Donna's attack.

Donna then fires back: "I'm sick and tired of you *always* criticizing my brother! Hey, he can't help it that he lost his job—and if you'll remember, he offered to pay for a new mower when he gets employed again!" With a roll of his eyes, Ted quietly but purposely retorts, "I won't be holding my breath for that to happen."

You get the drift. Ted and Donna are on a runaway train to nowhere town.

Now, if myth #3 held true, then the best course of action for them would be to sit down, tease out all the aspects of their argument, sort it all out, and still manage to catch a few refreshing zzz's. In their current frame of mind, the chances are slim to none of that actually occurring—the argument would only escalate. Going to bed mad is, in fact, a better option.

So what do you do instead? It's simple. Just say "3P please." By doing so, you're invoking the marriage-saving tool I call 3P. The sooner you and your partner know what 3P can do for you, the sooner you can each start to invoke it.

3P stands for Pause, Plan, and Proceed.

"Pause" simply represents the belief that this is not a good time to have this discussion. It's late, the kids are nearby, you're in a restaurant. Whatever the reason, one of you feels this conversation would be better happening at another time.

"Plan" means you agree to select another time to continue the discussion. You could even suggest a more appropriate time by saying something specific like, "3P until after the kids go to school tomorrow, okay?"

The final P is "Proceed," which means you will pick up where you left off when that agreed-upon future time is decided. This third P is very important and the easiest of the three to neglect. When you wake up in the morning, you may be calmer, which is good, but you also may not want to revisit the fight because it was painful and unpleasant. You might decide, "Why not just pretend it never happened and forget about it."

I'll add a fourth P here, which is, "Please don't do this"—don't let the argument go unresolved. Ted's feelings were hurt when Donna teased him in front of their friends, and they have very different feelings about Donna's brother, which obviously causes friction between them. If they push these problems under the rug, they won't go away. It will be just the opposite, because they'll return with a vengeance the next time Ted makes a snarky remark about Donna's brother, or Donna tells another story at her husband's expense. But if they sit down after tempers have cooled, air their differences, and set some new ground rules for how to behave with each other, their relationship will grow stronger. It may be that Donna and Ted together figure out a better way for dealing with her brother when he shows up to borrow the power saw, and that next time they're out with friends, Donna refrains from making a joke about Ted's clumsiness because she knows he's sensitive about it.

Calling for a 3P will allow you both to get some rest and revisit your disagreement at a better time. You will no longer be caught up in the moment of anger and, assuming neither of you is looking for a fight first thing in the morning, you will awaken with a fresh perspective and some rest, which may mean kinder communication.

No marriage failed because of a rescheduled argument. The opposite of "don't go to bed angry" usually ends up being "stay up and fight." Choose to sleep.

Myth #4: Timing Is Everything

I didn't even know this was a myth until I encountered it during my work on *The Locator*, when I found reunion after reunion being postponed or not happening at all because the "timing wasn't right." A mother whose birth daughter wanted to meet her refused because the "timing isn't right." I heard the same thing from the son of a man who wanted to reach out to his boy after abandoning him as a child. And when a sibling wouldn't meet the brother seeking her after 20 years of separation. These people all seemed convinced that good timing was the secret ingredient to success, that one day the stars would be aligned and *then* they would be ready for a reunion. "Timing is everything," they would tell me seriously. But now just wasn't the right time.

I realized that most of these people either didn't want to meet a loved one from their past or were afraid of the changes that might come from such a meeting. So they had bought into the myth that nothing could go forward if the timing wasn't right, that timing was everything. This myth became just an excuse to do nothing.

Timing may be everything when it comes to catching a train or being on time for your daughter's play or a dinner reservation. But when it comes to fixing your relationship, the time for change is *right now*. Don't buy into the false belief that there is some "better" time ahead for you to repair your marriage, some future date when everything will automatically click into place, as if fixing your relationship has to be timed like the spotting of a solar eclipse.

Commonly, someone will report to me that she is unhappy, feels alone and unloved in her relationship. She wants to tell her spouse but worries it will lead to conflict. "He doesn't need this right now," she'll say, or, "He's under so much pressure at work—this isn't a good time."

But as we talk, it becomes clear that time isn't the issue, but rather her fear of talking to her husband. How will he respond to her sadness about their lack of intimacy? Will he dismiss her concerns, even get angry at her for bringing them up? When we peel back the layers of self-deceit and denial for these reasons, she stops using time as the excuse for her reluctance, and we begin the work of helping her talk to her husband.

There are a few other big stumbling blocks couples buy into when believing in the timing myth. One is that they should decide to wait for a "more convenient time" to sort out their difficulties. Or, they reason if they "just let things go," everything will gradually improve. These are bad ideas. Firstly, there is no "*more* convenient time," because problem solving is never convenient; it is hard and sometimes scary work. Secondly, deciding to "just let it go" is just a fainthearted way to put off this necessary work. The longer people wait for the "perfect time" to magically appear, or the longer they push their problems under the rug, the more troubled their relationships become. There is too much time for further erosion of their feelings, further damage to their esteem, further resentment and animosity, further likelihood that they will be tempted to stray from their marriage, and so on.

This leads me to my most important point about timing and your relationship. When it comes to timing and marital problems, I ask you to live with a sense of urgency. Not a sense of panic, but a sense of absolute urgency. You must realize that you could be on a path to losing the one you love—or loved at one time. Please don't play the waiting game. It is urgent that you turn on the pump the minute your boat starts leaking. Don't wait until the water's up to your knees, then fills the cockpit and the boat finally starts to sink. In this sense, timing *is* everything.

Myths and mythmaking have been around forever, from the ancient Greeks right up to Cinderella, who lived happily ever after with her prince. But as comforting and as timeless as myths can be, false myths can cause trouble for you and your spouse. Buying into them can raise unrealistic expectations, guide you to behavior that undermines your relationship, and cause unnecessary misunderstandings that you have to unravel.

The ones I've described above are the most common I see, but you and your partner might have your own sets of false beliefs, usually handed down from your parents or grandparents, truisms that have become part of your thinking, whether you know it or not. And they might not be true after all, or at least not true for you and your spouse!

Some can be lighthearted—the argument over when presents are opened on a holiday. Others can be more serious—a persistent worry that there's never enough money. But there are always some deeply held beliefs in a relationship that, when looked at in the light of day, aren't immune to scrutiny and debunking.

Many of these myths are hard to tease out because they are so embedded in your mind that they seem absolutely true. But if you and your partner circle around the same disagreements over and over again and one of you thinks the other one is making no sense, it would be a good idea to step back, ask yourself why you believe the way you do, and look into the logic of your feelings. You could be driven by your own false truths.

Explore your past. Did your parents, grandparents, or other influential people in your life have strong feelings about what you and your partner are arguing about? What were the circumstances of those feelings compared to your own circumstances? Is there a possibility that what was true for them *isn't* true for you? This will help you untangle the past from your life today and guide you to getting rid of outdated false beliefs that cause unnecessary trouble for you and your partner. Leave the myths to the storybooks where they belong.

Master Your Money: Talk Dollars and Sense Back into Your Relationship

12

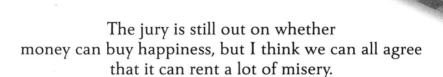

> The jury is still out on whether
> money can buy happiness, but I think we can all agree
> that it can rent a lot of misery.
>
> —Troy Dunn

If you look closely around your house, you will see them lurking in desk drawers, coat pockets, even in your purse. These men follow you to the gas station, the mall, and the grocery store. You may not have ever noticed them, but they are always there, waiting to inject themselves into your relationship.

Their names? George Washington, Abraham Lincoln, Alexander Hamilton, Andrew Jackson, Ulysses S. Grant, and Benjamin Franklin. As U.S. presidents and statesmen, they were once all great men in their own right, but once their faces were printed onto our money, they became the number-one home wreckers in America! If you know a couple who is having significant marital issues, chances are these green guys are lurking nearby.

Be the Master of Your Money

You've heard the saying that "money can't buy you happiness"? Well hold on a second because I believe, actually, that money *can* buy happiness when used *properly*. It can bless your life and the lives of others you love when you are prudent and take the time to manage your money.

Money is nothing to be afraid of. It is intended to be your servant. It has no wants, no needs. It's not some sort of mean, ugly monster with giant fangs, ready to pounce and make your life miserable. Instead, see money for what it truly is: a tool that enables you to access necessary, even nice things that would be out of your reach without it.

Unfortunately, I've seen how the fear of money, or the lack of it, has the power to create extreme misery in the lives of people who abuse it or hold it above all else in their lives. No matter how much money you have or don't have, fights about money are the *number-one* factor that tips the scales of an unhappy marriage into divorce. (See box.) I want to help you and your spouse take back your power over money, so that it is your servant and you are its masters.

The Big One: Money

Disagreements about money are the most serious threat to the stability of a relationship, according to a July 2013 study by a Kansas State University researcher. "Arguments about money are by far the top predictor of divorce," said Sonya Britt, assistant professor of family studies and human services and program director of personal financial planning. "It's not children, sex, in-laws, or anything else. It's money—for both men and women."

Further, she found that it doesn't matter how much or how little money a couple has.

"We controlled for income, debt, and net worth," Britt said. "Results revealed it didn't matter how much you made or how much you were worth. Arguments about money are the top predictor for divorce because it happens at all levels."

And, it takes longer to recover from money arguments than any other kind of argument, according to Britt, and such arguments are more intense. Couples often use harsher language with each other, and the arguments last longer.

The bottom line is that you should not handle money disagreements any differently than other issues that pop up in your relationship. Don't give money any more reverence than you do issues about sex, about household chores, parenting decisions, or even which movie to see when you go out. Poor people can be happily married and rich people can be happily married. So money doesn't deserve all the outsized attention it gets in marriages.

This chapter is not a detailed manual on how to dig yourself out of financial trouble, nor will I ply you with charts, diagrams, and specific instructions on rebuilding your financial world. Such advice would take up, and does fill up, many books, magazines, and websites dedicated to money management.

Rather, my job is to help you and your partner understand your attitudes toward money, the role money plays in your relationship, and, if you're not happy with how the two of you approach your finances, how to change your thinking so that the two of you work together, not against each other, when it comes to money.

But to do that, you have to do a bit of research on your own money meter.

Money—The Shadow That's Always Lurked

If you have money issues in your relationship, I want you to first step back and remember that money existed in your life before you became part of a couple. Handling money wasn't a new task that suddenly showed up when you entered into a committed relationship. You had an income, you had bills, and you had wants and needs long before your partner came on the scene. By the way, so did he (or she). So this isn't the first money rodeo for either of you.

How well did you manage money on your own? Did you pay your bills on time? Overspend, or watch your pennies? Did you set up a savings program, or did you just cross your fingers and hope that some day you would win the lottery?

Whatever your money "style," you brought it with you into your relationship, and it is still with you and still affects your feelings and actions now. And it is the same for your partner.

The difference is that now you and your spouse are sharing a household and all of the financial requirements that come with living as two—or more, if you have children. It's fun and exhilarating to start your new life together: picking a place to live, decorating your new home, making new friends as a couple, juggling the in-laws, planning holidays—there is a lot to be excited about.

But too often, couples don't talk about the hard stuff. A serious sit-down to talk about how the two of you handle money so that you can integrate your personal money methods and decide how to manage your new, joint fiscal responsibilities in a way that suits you both? It doesn't happen. Or, it doesn't happen until a money problem or issue arises. And then the trouble starts.

It might help to know this is the case with a lot of couples, and it's not that you're undisciplined, lazy, or "bad" with money in some way. It's more likely a combination of the fact that you're both busy and that money is really, really hard to talk about.

You and I both know that doing taxes ranks right up there with a root canal as a fun way to spend your time. And how tempting it is to leave monthly bill paying until the last possible minute. Equally so, the prospect of sitting down and going over your finances, making a budget, and learning each other's feelings and philosophies about money is not something people look forward to, to say the least.

Added to that is that a lot of people know very little about how to properly take care of their money. Sadly, "Money Management 101" is not required before you can get your "adult card." And because you don't feel experienced, educated, or prepared to manage finances, it feels like the right solution is just to skip the conversation, continue your old patterns, and pray that somehow everything will turn out all right.

But I promise that learning the basics of money management doesn't have to be scary or too hard. And if you and your partner take the time to learn to do this together, you will reap the rewards over and over again.

Clash of the Cash

When it comes to attitudes about money, there are two general camps: savers and spenders. Within those categories are a wide range of personalities, from coupon cutters and penny pinchers to impulse buyers and spendthrifts. Excepting the edges of the spectrum, when one person is completely unreliable about money or the other thrifty to the point of hoarding, there's nothing wrong with either attitude toward money. They're just different.

You should be able to discuss your feelings about money with your partner in the same way you discuss everything else. Then you compromise on how you will go forward together. If this is a problem for you and your partner, if you can't seem to agree on the "right" way to handle money, let alone get together to make important financial decisions, you might need to look into your own attitudes about money. My Money Confessional is a good place to start.

The Money Confessional

Honesty is the best policy here, even if it makes you uncomfortable to admit your spending habits.

1. **Are you more of a spender or a saver?**

   Rate yourself on a scale of 1 to 10, with 1 being a spender and 10 being a saver. A spender is generally somebody who makes purchases impulsively, who is first in line for discounts or sales regardless of what the item may be, and who tends to think of reasons to buy something rather than hold back. A spendthrift is the most extreme example of a spender, one whose constant buying depletes or negatively impacts the household finances, someone who lives beyond his means.

   A saver is the opposite. He looks for reasons not to spend money. He tends to think carefully before buying something, makes no purchase without knowing exactly where the money is coming from. At the far end of this tendency is someone who forgoes a needed purchase to avoid spending money, who never buys anything on impulse, who lives consistently beneath his means to the detriment of his family's happiness and sense of well-being.

2. **Do you tend to expect money to always just be there somehow, or are you more likely to worry that it's likely to disappear at any moment?**

   Rate yourself on a scale of 1 to 10, with 1 being someone who's unconcerned where money will come from and 10 being the person who's afraid money will evaporate.

3. **Do you wish that you didn't ever have to think about money?**

   Rate yourself on a scale of 1 to 10, with 1 being someone who hates to think about money and 10 being more comfortable with money issues.

4. Do you enjoy creating a budget and sticking to it?
Rate yourself on a scale of 1 to 10, with 1 being someone who doesn't like the idea of a budget and 10 being someone who's diligent about keeping track of spending.

Next, ask your partner the same questions, or if he or she isn't willing to participate yet, answer them on his or her behalf to the best of your ability.

How did that feel? Were you brave? Did you open up to yourself and admit to something that might be less than flattering? If so, congratulations. Doing so is yet another sign that you truly are seeking change in your life and are willing to start with yourself.

If you and your spouse have never before considered how you think about money, this exercise helps you both understand where you're coming from. Most people fall in the middle range when answering these questions, but if you identify with either end of the scale on any of them, it could mean you're bringing some deeply held (and not necessarily valid) beliefs about money into your present relationship.

Have you recently had a heated argument about money, or seem to have repeated arguments about the same thing? There may very well be a logical reason for your fights, but there also may not.

Let's say a money crisis hits. The boiler dies on a cold Friday night (it's always the beginning of a weekend). The repairman comes and tells you that he can fix it temporarily, but that you're going to need a new boiler, and sooner rather than later. This is bad news, as you've just had your hours reduced at your job, money is tight, and Christmas is coming.

You feel yourself sliding into panic. You're operating on a salary cut of 30 percent due to the lost hours, and now this? How are you going to find the money for a new boiler? What could happen next? It was a big mistake to buy this house, you think. You should have listened to your gut instead of your husband and made do in the smaller house in the old neighborhood, even if it wasn't as safe. Now you'll have to sell the house. You blurt this out to your husband.

He's furious that you're bringing up the purchase of the house, which was five years ago, and feels like you're blaming the broken boiler on him. He says you always look at the blackest side of anything that has to do with money. And, tit for tat, he points out that if you were still making the money you did before, this would be no big thing.

A huge fight takes place, which the kids watch, bug-eyed and worried, too, about whether there's enough money.

But what if you've figured out that your panic about money comes from your childhood, when there really *wasn't* enough money, and you really did have to move a lot because your father couldn't hold a job? And that both you and your husband are hardworking and pretty good about sticking with a budget? And that, even with less income, you've got the money to pay for a new boiler even if it means cutting back a bit on Christmas? Can you understand that what may have been true for you when you were growing up may no longer be so? That your panic may not be logical in your present circumstances?

These are the kinds of realizations that can come from the Money Confessional. Here's what you do next: Write down what you've learned about yourself and your history with money—the influences that had an effect on you, and what you remember about them. Let these memories sink in so that the next time a money crisis comes up, you'll be able to resist the old patterns and behaviors that no longer apply.

Next, bring yourself up to the present and decide if you want to make some changes in the way you spend or don't spend money today. For instance, you might note, "I have just realized I am too much of a spender." Now, write down a few little (or big) changes you are willing to make right now that will move you a little further from spender and a little closer to saver.

For starters, perhaps you will stop picking up coffee at the deli every single morning. Or maybe you'll start throwing away the flyers from your favorite department store offering points or discounts on clothing you know you don't really need. On the other side, if you tend to be stingy, you might change your ways as well. If you are in a restaurant with your family for a birthday celebration (a party you know you can afford), you'll keep yourself from complaining about the prices on the menu and relax and enjoy a special evening out with your loved ones. When your partner buys another fancy tool for his workshop, even though he doesn't strictly need it, you don't criticize him. These little changes might not seem like much, but they are very important because they are easy to incorporate into your life right away, you're likely to stick with them, and they help you change your behavior. Such small, conscious moves toward self-modification are a bigger step forward than you may know.

If your partner participates in the Money Confessional, you will probably find that there is less friction in your discussions about money—both due to the insights you will gain, and to the fact that you're both willing to honestly assess your attitudes about finances. But even if you do this on your own, you will gain a new sense of control about how you feel about money, and you will be empowered to be less afraid of or worried about money. Insights from the Money Confessional don't make financial problems disappear, but understanding how you each think about money and modifying your behavior where needed will make it a lot easier to talk your way to solutions without fighting. And changing your behavior is a gift to your children as well. They will learn by your example to treat money with less fear and more confidence. It is these small alterations in the way you think and live that change lives, and your marriage, your family, can become whole again. Well done!

Money and Trust Go Hand in Hand

If the idea of sharing finances with your spouse causes concern or doubt, then you may have a bigger issue—namely trust. Sharing your finances is a very significant sign of mutual trust, and I think it is a key to a couple's commitment to each other and to the relationship. If there isn't that bond between you, you should take a look at why.

Who marries someone they don't trust? Who wants to be married to someone who doesn't trust them? Not this guy! We aren't talking about a stranger or a new friend, right? We are talking about the person you let see you naked! If you have trust to that level but have trouble depositing a paycheck into a shared bank account, something is amiss.

If one partner doesn't fully trust the other or isn't quite fully vested in the relationship, it's cleaner to keep the money separate, just in case. There are sometimes practical reasons for this—if, for instance, one of the partners is completely unreliable about money, either as a spendthrift or a hoarder. But other times, partners feel that if the relationship doesn't pan out, there are no joint accounts to close, deeds with both partners' names on them, or other messy financial comingling to have to undo. You can just throw the dog in the backseat of your car and head for the hills.

If you feel this way, ask yourself some questions. Where does this mistrust come from? Is it based on fears or evidence? Is it something you have talked about calmly or argued about? Take a moment to ponder what has happened in the past to bring about this attitude. If it is something from your past, before this partner, then it's your issue to release. The same is true in reverse. If your spouse doesn't trust you because of something someone else did to him previously, then he needs to admit that and you should seek an opportunity to be trusted so the two of you can move forward.

You may dismiss this idea, thinking that people can handle money individually without wanting to leave a partner, that keeping things separate at the bank is okay. And it may be "okay." But a committed, long-term relationship is much more than "okay" when a couple is willing to work together on financial goals. You have a hand in each other's pockets, so to speak, and therefore share the rewards of putting your resources and ideas together to create a stable financial base.

Your aim should be to take the step to combine your finances. Doing so is a strong indicator that you're both in it for the long haul. And failure to do so may indicate the opposite. We will discuss this further later in the chapter.

The Five Ways to Kill Your Marriage with Money

No matter how much discord money has caused you over the course of your life, or how many past relationships it's wrecked, it doesn't have to be that way any longer. There's a way out, and no, it doesn't involve winning the lottery. If you are aware of the following five common money issues in relationships, and you take proactive steps to avoid the problems inherent in each, you will not only end the ugly cycle, but you'll pass down a sound, healthy relationship with money to your children.

1. Don't Play the Money Piñata

It's a tradition in our family to get a candy-stuffed piñata for birthday parties for the children. The idea is to blindfold the kids, hand them a stick and spin them around, then let them loose to try and swing the stick at the piñata. If they hit it, it breaks open and candy spills out, but if they swing and miss, they get nothing. To make it more interesting and fun, either my wife or I hold the rope and raise and lower the piñata, controlling its height so that it's harder or easier to hit. At some point, someone does break it open and all the children share in the bounty that spills out.

Unfortunately, there are some spouses who handle money like a piñata game and make their partner work hard to get it, sometimes relenting and handing him or her money, other times denying him or her by raising the requirements and putting the money out of reach. It's called a power grab.

You may have heard the old saying that the Golden Rule actually means, "He who has the gold makes the rules." There may be some truth to that in many areas of life, but in a marriage or committed relationship? No way. Money-centered power struggles are toxic to any relationship or marriage that is founded on love and trust between two people who have vowed to spend their lives together. If you and your partner have an agreement that one of you will earn the majority of the income while the other stays home and manages the household and/or children, that's fine as long as both partners feel good about the arrangement and sign on to it willingly. But it does not mean that the income earner has sole control of the purse strings. This also applies when one spouse earns more money than the other. The size of your paycheck doesn't dictate the percentage of authority you have in financial matters. Neither partner should be held hostage to money, under any circumstances.

That isn't to say it doesn't ever happen. It does happen. More than you think.

Dick and Beverly were so angry with each other when I met them that I had a hard time getting a word in edgewise. Truthfully, it was kind of hard not to laugh. Each time I started to speak, one of them would snipe at the other and then off they went into a verbal boxing match for a couple of minutes. It was so well timed to each attempt I made to speak, I almost felt it was a joke. But the fire in their eyes assured me this was no joke.

I finally started clapping in the middle of their argument. Just clapping away, like a monkey with cymbals in my hands. And believe me, I can clap loud, too! They both stopped mid-sentence and looked at me, with some level of frustration because I was clearly interrupting their very intense "conversation." As they stared at me, I continued to clap for another 30 or so seconds after they had gone silent. It was an odd moment for all of us, but I clapped away. Finally I stopped and said, "That's how you two sound to me. Just noise. Nothing uplifting or inspiring—just continuous noise." They got the point, and on we went with our conversation.

So here is what I gathered from combining their two versions of the truth: Dick wanted to buy a boat and Beverly did not. Dick earned a decent salary as a salesman and was apparently generous with his money to his family, but, without asking or telling his wife, he had put down a payment for a boat, saying he'd earned it and deserved it.

I didn't see anything wrong with a guy buying a boat if he wanted one and could afford it—but their fight wasn't really about the boat at all. Beverly resented that she had no idea how much money Dick had. That he could make such a big purchase floored her, and doing so without her input made her feel left out. Excluding Beverly from any knowledge of his finances was clearly a power play and a sign of disrespect for his wife.

"I don't even think I'm in this marriage," she said. "Don't I even get a say in our family making such a financial commitment?"

The answer, according to Dick, was no.

"What's her gripe?" he asked. "I work hard, give her anything she wants. Why can't I spend my money the way I like?"

"Your money?" I asked.

"Of course," he said. "She's not out every day, busting her chops, making cold calls, meeting customers—I am."

Dick didn't get it, and didn't *want* to get it. He and Beverly were supposed to be sharing their lives across the board, not just their house, children, bedroom, and cars, but the money he made to support the family.

I wanted to tell him, "Dick, the 1950s called. They want their mindset back." But I refrained.

He thought by being generous, he *was* sharing. But, in fact, he was wielding his money over her, holding his wife at arm's length when he didn't include her in his major financial decisions. She was hurt and angry, and it created a distance between them.

Do you have similar money/power problems in your relationship? Do you or your partner believe that the person who earns more money has the bigger right to call the shots as to how the money is spent? Does this result in fights, resentments, stony silences?

If so, you need a Power Talk. Here's how to do it:

1. **Assuming you're the partner on the short end of this imbalance, it's probably on you to set up a time to talk about it.**

   This will be more or less difficult depending on how long and how entrenched this behavior is in your relationship. The key for you is to get past all the emotion and resentment you may feel and prepare a reasoned case for a more equal sharing of your financial decisions.

2. **When you meet, start out by thanking your partner for the money he or she earns, and express how much you appreciate the commitment, hard work, and time it takes to earn money.**

    Further acknowledge that you know this work underpins a good deal of your lifestyle. If you're sincere, you will now have your partner's attention.

3. **Next, outline your own contributions to the family's bottom line—not only the money you earn in your job but the time you spend on family and household matters.**

    Demonstrate your equal investment in your marriage.

4. **Then explain how left out, unhappy, and marginalized you feel when you aren't consulted or included in decisions about how your money is spent.**

    Give a specific example of one of these decisions—the choice of where to go on vacation, for instance. Avoid judgmental words like "unfair," "selfish," or "greedy." (At least if you want results!)

5. **Ask for a specific change rather than a global rearrangement of the way you have been making financial decisions.**

    It could be about the vacation, that you sit down and decide together where to go. This allows your partner to focus on altering his behavior in a doable way.

6. **If he agrees, thank him and end the discussion.**

    This can be the first of several discussions, so that you and your partner gradually erase the imbalances that have caused so much friction between you.

If you are able to be calm and reasonable and specific in this discussion, your partner will likely listen to you. Of course, he may not (see Dick above). But even if this happens, don't lose heart. Stick to your guns and try again. By making your feelings known in a neutral and practical manner, your partner will be forced to think about his behavior in a new way. The payoff may be slow in coming, but your chances are good that he will realize the logic of your request and respond in kind.

2. Divide and Be Conquered

Separate bank accounts, dividing up who pays the bills, counting each other's pennies—all are fodder for arguments, blaming, power plays, and keeping score. Not only that, such divisions defy everything about a committed relationship. When you were single, you had your own home and your own food and your own bed. Now you and your partner share those things—the same home, rent or mortgage, life insurance policies, electric, water, and gas. You both watch the cable TV and eat food from the fridge. You drive the same cars, go on the same vacations. You have made all these decisions together as a united couple.

I disagree with those who suggest that you share all these things and yet keep separate checkbooks and finances, or that you divvy up the bills from your different paychecks. Why should one area—money—be treated separately in a relationship? Advocates of this approach believe it allows each person some autonomy in the relationship, but I think it's an unnecessary recipe for conflict.

Jen and I have close friends who are a couple, and we recently had a dinner date with them. But when we tried to call them to confirm the time, we couldn't get ahold of them on the phone. So we drove over to their house and asked why they weren't answering the phone. The wife rolled her eyes and looked over at her husband and said, "He pays the phone bill but he had some unexpected expenses with the washer and dryer, so the phone bill didn't get paid on time."

Baffled, I said, "But don't you use the phone too?"

"Yes," she replied, "but the phone bill isn't my responsibility. It's his. I pay the electric and you can see the lights are all on. This failure is on him."

Jen and I looked at each other. It seemed crazy to us to divide up the household this way, almost guaranteeing arguments. Life is tough enough! This idea of not merging your life together as a couple, and embracing all that comes from the combined resources of a couple, works against harmony and the intimacy that comes from shared goals.

It's not as if you can't have your own money. You can agree to each have an agreed-upon amount of individual "play money," if your finances allow for such luxuries. Simply agree on a specified amount that you both can spend with no accountability. But that money shouldn't be for life's necessities. The necessities should be something you *both agree* are handled from your collective finances. Take a second and reread that previous sentence. Do you see how I put emphasis on the words "both agree"? I have little patience for men and women who feel that because they earn the money, they control the money. (See the Power Talk above). That is short-sighted, small-minded, and not a characteristic of a loving, kind person. Marriage is a team sport, and as the old saying goes, there is no "I" in team!

Pointing fingers at each other so that a missed phone bill becomes a "got-cha" is negative energy in a relationship, and that's what can happen when shared expenses are split. It is a recipe for the types of financial disagreements that drive people apart. Stop it. Treat your money like you treat your groceries. Put it in the "fridge" (bank) and plan your "meals" (life) accordingly.

Here are three suggestions to set up the foundation for a healthy financial compartment in your relationship:

1. **Build a budget and stick to it.**

    This single act can eliminate a lot of money arguments. If you have never budgeted (and most couples who have financial battles don't budget), know that it is easier than you think. Type "household budget template" into your favorite search engine and lots of free tools will pop up. Grab one, answer the questions within it, and ***poof***—you two now have a budget!

2. **Have separate debit cards.**

    You can have a single checking account but still track and manage each other's spending patterns by simply having separate debit cards on the account. This will give you instant details online almost in real time as to how much is being spent and where. This makes the next suggestion more productive.

3. **Have a monthly money meeting.**

    In this meeting, you print out the statements from your account and review the month's expenditures. See how you, as a couple and as individuals, are doing with regards to your agreed-upon budget, get further clarification on certain expenditures, and just keep up with how the family money is being utilized. This meeting should be calm, non-emotional, and last 15 minutes or less.

3. Living Beyond Your Means

"YOLO—you only live once" and "you can't take it with you" are popular phrases encouraging us to relax a bit, enjoy life. Listen, I'm the first person to encourage people to make the most of their lives, but too many folks have (unwittingly or not) attached this "live for today" philosophy to their spending habits.

Is this a problem in your relationship? Does one or the other of you, or both of you, believe in YOLO even when you can't afford it? Have you been drooling over that beautiful new SUV your friend has but it's way outside the bounds of your budget? Eh, go ahead, lease it! Right? That's YOLO. Did you see a designer watch or pair of earrings in this month's edition of *Cosmo*? Hey, just put it on the credit card! YOLO. Did you opt for the McMansion instead of the bungalow, or did you join the high-end country club? Of course! Why not? YOLO.

It's true that you only go through life once. But do you want to build your one life on such unstable financial ground that you can't sleep at night? A life that means that you and your partner are constantly juggling which bills to pay, arguing about money, blaming each other for your extravagances? A lot of people who are living beyond their means are doing just this, and it is one of the biggest ways that money can torpedo relationships.

The idea of "get it now and we'll figure it out later" can be a disaster for a family, creating mounting debt and terrible stress for everyone in it, including your children. It also upends what makes a family strong by emphasizing material pleasures rather than the more intangible and longer lasting values of thrift, prudence, and—let's not forget—solvency!

A friend of ours, whose child is on our son's baseball team, called and asked if we could bring her boy home with us one day after practice because she had to work late. When she arrived later that evening to pick him up, she apologized, expressed her frustration over missing his baseball game, and noted it was the fourth one this season she has missed. But then, as if it was a reasonable explanation, she pointed back over her shoulder toward her very nice luxury vehicle and said, "But Mama's gotta work. They don't give those away for free, ya know."

She laughed and left with her son in tow after basically telling us that she works extra hours and misses her son's games so she can drive a nicer car. When someone says "I have no choice" about the type of job or the hours or the missed events in his child's life, I believe him. He may have dug a financial hole so deep he no longer does have a choice but to work long, hard hours. But at some point he did have a choice. Everyone has a choice in the way he or she manages money. They can choose a better quality of life with spouses and children over nicer clothes, a bigger house, fancier cars, lavish vacations, and so on.

Some of the choices we make in life create a string of domino choices that come with them. If you choose to amass piles of debt, you are choosing to spend more time at work than with your family. If you say yes to spending your hard-earned money on beer, cigarettes, and lottery tickets, you choose to have less money for your family's needs. You do have choices, and in many ways, you did choose the life you have right now. If you don't like it, you also have a choice to do something about it. In fact, if you don't make some important choices soon, guess what? Someone else will make them for you.

Let's say your house seemed affordable before the economy tanked or before you lost your job, but now you are drowning under mortgage payments. If you can't let go of the emotional attachment you have to the house and downsize, the bank will make your decision for you, at greater cost to you, by repossessing the house.

It's far better to bite the bullet and make big decisions for yourself than letting someone else make them for you. Spare yourself the humiliation of that experience. Dodge the marital friction that can come as a result of such a traumatic financial crisis. Take hold of your financial life and steer your own life toward the destination of your choice. It may feel daunting at first, but compared to the alternative, it's easy.

Start by making changes that have an immediate positive impact on your finances. I just gave you the extreme example of downsizing your house. But hopefully your situation isn't as dire. Smaller adjustments made today can slowly but surely lead you back to a more secure financial lifestyle. Less eating out, less-expensive (or no) cable TV plan, no more golf for a while—such small sacrifices can save the day.

I have helped several people through this process, and they have found it empowering, not only because their finances were no longer keeping them up at night, but because they felt a new sense of control over their lives. As tensions about finances eased, their marriages got better and their kids were more relaxed. Getting control of your world and guiding your own life is a fantastic experience, one I want you to have and to share with your spouse.

So sit down together with your partner and lay the math out in front of you. Spell out your income and then list where all the money goes. Then start making decisions about where you can save money, beginning with the least necessary expenses and working your way to the essentials. If you make enough bold decisions on the least crucial expenses you have—things like eating out less, cutting down on recreational activities, buying fewer clothes, no longer upgrading your television or computers regularly—you may not need to do anything significant with the essentials. As you look at each expenditure, do so through the prism of these two options, at least initially:

1. **Reduce.**

   Maybe you meet your friends for lunch every Friday and your husband golfs every weekend. It might be wise to reduce those luxury experiences to once a month rather than every week.

2. **Eliminate.**

   This is for when significant changes need to be made and need to be made now. Using the same example above, the two of you might both decide that for the time being, you will simply stop the lunches and golf altogether. It might seem like a big sacrifice, but when you compare it to losing your house or even just not being able to keep your daughter in dance lessons, it will be an easy choice.

Each time you label one of your expenses as "reduce" or "eliminate," give yourself a goal of when you hope to restart it again. Based on how long it may take you to get some debts paid off or get that next raise at work, you may agree that the lunches and Saturday golf games will begin again in nine months. It's great to have a goal like this. Just having it in place offers something to look forward to, some light at the end of the tunnel. You might discover, as some people have, that what you gave up to save money loses its luster after being out of your life for a time. Your priorities can shift as your heart and your mind come to like this feeling of not being financially strapped anymore. You may come to love how much better your relationship is with less debt hanging over your heads. Try it with your own budget regardless of your current financial situation. You may find you can shed a little debt weight and be a happier, fiscally healthier couple—and that's good for any family!

4. Separate Needs from Wants

Many families end up in financial distress because they have blurred the difference between a "want" and a "need." While the definition of a need has thankfully been expanded from the days of a lean-to, water, and a freshly killed buffalo to include more comfortable essentials like a home, heat, transportation, basic appliances, and the like, money can fly out the window based on perceived needs, that really are plain old wants.

One of the most productive ways to quickly start digging out of a financial disaster is to sit down with your partner, and then your children, and redefine what is a want versus what is a need. It's a most useful exercise even for someone who thinks he already knows this, and it is a very good concept for children to be taught to think about. The goal is to define where the dollars go *first* so that basic needs are met. Then comes the discussion of what to do with what's left, if there is any.

The word "need" is tricky in this country. Despite what economic challenges our country may face and regardless of whether the markets are up or down, we live in a very prosperous land. And we are quickly losing touch with that word—need. You need only to slip into the poorest areas of your city or pay a visit to some third world country to see how others define need.

I recently spent some time in Honduras, where my son was serving a church mission. It was a busy time for me to take off work and travel, but it was a trip I needed to make. I promised my staff I would stay in touch and, if anything urgent came up, to just e-mail me.

Within a few minutes of landing, I was in the car we had arranged to pick us up (you do not ever want to drive a car in Honduras because the roads are so bad you need a very, very experienced driver!) and I quickly realized I wasn't getting any cell signal. I didn't panic, as I was sure we would eventually be somewhere where I could get a little Wi-Fi or something. Nope. Not even close. In fact, we drove further and further away from civilization, until we eventually arrived in a community where the houses were simply sticks wrapped in sheets of plastic or made from scrap pieces of old billboards.

I spent two days with these good people and was touched by their generosity. In each home I entered, many of which had only dirt floors (cleanly swept, by the way), I was offered something to drink and a chair to sit in. Often the chair was the only one in the "house," and it was a simple plastic outdoor chair. I sat as the homeowner stood or squatted against a post in their home. To say it was humbling would be a massive understatement. At one point I wept privately—not for them, but for me. My family. Compared to these gracious, humble people, we really had no idea what the word "need" meant.

Most families don't. So let's begin to define the difference.

If you and your partner are locking horns in money matters, this idea of what's a need and what's a want could just become another excuse for arguing, so you might want to work alone on this at first. And the best way to start is to work up from nothing rather than to work down from everything. Nobody wants to give up anything that brings them joy and comfort, so it's more productive to agree that everything is officially cut off for this moment and then start to add back those things deemed a true need. Start with the absolute basics—food and shelter. From there, add back in other expenses until you reach the threshold of your family income, then cut it back a little so you have breathing room for the unexpected expenses such as a hospital stay, a car problem, or something else.

You might need some of the strategies outlined earlier in this book to have this conversation with your spouse in a neutral, non-blaming way, but it is a sound plan for clarifying how you will budget your money, forcing both of you to identify what is most important to you and your family.

When the two of you have outlined your own wants and needs, it's time to bring in the rest of the family.

When you sit down with your children to discuss needs, explain what you and your husband have done and ask them to do the same, starting from scratch and then putting things back. Talk about the difference between needs and wants. This doesn't have to be a threatening exercise, teaching your kids that they have to hoard money and be afraid of it. Rather, it's just a matter-of-fact discussion to teach them how to allocate money sensibly. They might find this hard to do at first. But when your son says he needs you to be sure and keep up the monthly service for Netflix, or your daughter will "die" if you cut off cable TV for a few months, I ask you to take a moment and share some simple experience from your own life when you realized what a need really is.

If you truly have some potentially spoiled kids who need to see how "the other half" lives in order to put their own situation in proper perspective, then that's exactly what you should do—show them how others who are less fortunate live their life. Volunteer your family for a night at a soup kitchen or handing out blankets at a shelter. Call the Ronald McDonald

House and offer to come in for a day to be with those who are in the midst of true crisis and tragedy. Not only is this a powerful experience for any family to experience together, it is a humbling realization for hard-hearted teens. Your teen may not acknowledge outwardly how impactful these experiences are, but I promise you, there will be impact.

And they will then have a better idea of what they've taken for granted and will be able to redefine "need." Not only that, it will give everyone some incentive to be part of the family's financial solution in the long run.

In the Dunn family, we recently announced that we were cutting off the Xbox Live monthly service (an obvious want, not a need). When our sons begged to know why, I explained that our electric bill had recently jumped up about $25 for no particular reason, so to offset the extra money I was paying in electric, I was cancelling the Xbox service. But I told them if the electric bill dropped back down the next month, I would consider resubscribing to the Xbox service. Well, the kids took it upon themselves to become the keepers of the electricity in our house. Lights were being flipped off, as were ceiling fans; they even adjusted the thermostat in their bedrooms! It seemed my kids were willing to live in hot, dark bedrooms if that's what it took!

Imagine my joyful surprise when the electric bill the next month was $68 lower! I showed it to the kids, congratulated them for their efforts, and told them I would reactivate their game service, but if the bill went back up again . . . they interrupted me exclaiming, "It won't, Dad, it won't!" I'm happy to report it went down even lower the following month.

5. Erase Entitlement, or "The World Owes Me a Living"

The word "entitlement" might be the hottest buzzword of the day right now. To me, it's always been an important word, because the problem of people thinking they are owed something they are not has always been around. Only now there seems to be more things to be entitled *to*.

If you, your partner, or both of you carry a sense of entitlement, you are working against your best financial interests. Why? Because first of all, a sense of entitlement is a false belief. The world, unfortunately, doesn't wake up every morning with the job of taking care of you to make sure your life is successful and satisfying. That's *your* job. Secondly, entitlement is a dangerous mindset that eats away at a family's financial health and happiness. Believing that you're not getting your "fair share" creates anger, bitterness, and resentment, just the emotions you *don't* need when you are trying to create a sound fiscal world for yourself and your family. Dwelling on what you "should" have, rather than actually doing something to get what you want, doesn't get you anywhere.

If you ask most people if they feel entitled to something, they will say of course not. But it's one of those seductive emotions that can creep up on you, thanks to comparing yourself to others and the slick marketing to which we're all exposed.

How many times do you see a cruise ship in a television advertisement, with all the happy people who look just like you, lounging on a deck, cruising down the Rhine or out on the Caribbean, and you begin to think, "Hey, *I've* never been on a cruise." Or you see a woman at work who's always so beautifully and expensively dressed that you're envious and decide you deserve at least a decent blouse like the one she's wearing.

Well, guess what?

Firstly, you have no idea how or why others are enjoying things that you're not. They may have worked their tails off and saved enough money to go on a cruise. They may choose to spend money on clothes rather than other things in their lives. Or, they may have just been born into wealth and don't have to think twice about how they spend their money. None of this has anything to do with you.

But most importantly, the *feeling* that you're somehow entitled to have what others have does nothing to guide you to the means to getting what you want for yourself.

The truth is that you are really entitled to very little. Want to take a second and answer a few questions to see if you might have a little (or a lot) of the entitlement mindset? These are just yes or no questions, and you can simply answer in your mind as you read them.

1. When you let a car into traffic or hold open a door for someone, do you expect a thank-you?

2. When there is a new position open at work, do you assume the job should be yours since you are older than your other coworkers?

3. Do you expect your adult children to take care of you when you're old?

4. When you donate to the police officers fund and put that little decal on your back window, do you expect to get a warning rather than a ticket next time you are pulled over?

5. When you slow down your car to let someone cross in the crosswalk, do you expect some sort of acknowledgment?

6. If you compliment someone, are you slightly offended when they don't compliment you back?

7. When you are contemplating a large purchase, do you justify it by saying you deserve it after all of your hard work?

8. As you board an airplane and find the overhead storage spaces are all full, do you feel as if someone needs to move their bag so yours will fit?

I could list a hundred of these little life moments that happen to us daily. The point being, if you answered "yes" to any single question above, you do have some sense of entitlement.

The fact is you aren't even entitled to live another day, so don't fall into the trap of thinking you're entitled to cruises, clothes, or houses you can't afford. When this thinking kicks in, you begin to justify all sorts of expenses that can drain your bank account. Good things come through planning, work, and discipline.

There are several ways to erase the feelings of entitlement that may be lurking in the dark, "poor me" corner of your mind. The first is to step back from the world of envy to catalog what you *do* have, things that you worked for, paid for, and enjoy from the fruits of your own labor. You have a home, furnishings, the clothes on your back, maybe a car, and hundreds of miscellaneous things that reflect your needs and interests, from working appliances to a favorite pair of running shoes. And you most likely have them because you earned the money to buy them. You decided on what you wanted, made a plan, did your research, figured out what it would cost, made sound financial decisions, and voilà—you closed the deal.

Extend this exercise to the rest of the family. Suggest that they each make a list of all that they have gained from their own planning and abilities, from skateboards to first cars. Then congratulate and honor yourselves for your achievements.

This works even if you are having financial troubles. There is always some item or idea you or any family member can point to that reflects your own hard work. Further, taking these steps will begin to clean up your thinking so that you dwell not on what's owed you, but rather on what you can do for yourself. Then you are better prepared to think about your own finances in a positive, can-do way.

Another way to erase entitlement envy is to concentrate on creating your own "entitlements." Set down what you would like to have and make a plan to get it.

This depends, of course, on the state of your finances. If you're having trouble paying bills, your "entitlement" might be to face your financial situation in a realistic way without panicking. Seek help, if need be, in setting up reasonable payment plans to do what you can to aim toward solvency. This may not sound very exciting or even like something you want to do, but by framing your situation in this way, you will have a better sense of control about your finances and your future. And you will feel more productive and confident.

For others in less dire money straits, the "entitlements" would be different, reflecting your interests and desires, but the philosophy remains the same. You are taking control of your own budget, finances, and lifestyle, all of which empower you. The sense of entitlement that can cripple you will disappear, and you will instead look forward to the much more satisfying mindset of setting a goal, reaching it, and enjoying its rewards on your own.

If the ideas and tools you and I have discussed in this chapter feel "right" to you, then I implore you to draw them into your own thinking and apply them to the choices you make each day. You will find not simply financial success but greater strength in your relationship, and you will have empowered your children to witness and experience wiser ways to live financially within a family. That's change that will impact your family for generations. Well done!

Sex: Bring It Back Where It Belongs

13

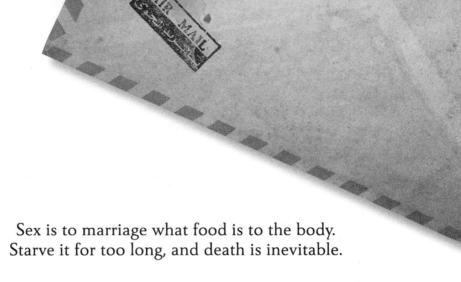

Sex is to marriage what food is to the body.
Starve it for too long, and death is inevitable.

—Troy Dunn

When I speak at marriage conferences, the topic that causes the most fid-
geting and awkward chuckles, and then the deepest silence when I begin
to talk, is sex. You can hear a pin drop after I say the word. Why? Because
while everyone is very familiar with the basics of sex, blasted at us from
every angle of our culture as it is, many are deeply disappointed in their
own sex lives. But they're not ready to give up. They're eager to learn how
to reconnect with their partners on an intimate level, despite how angry or
frustrated they might feel.

A couple used to have great sex, but now their sex lives are dead in the
water and they don't know how to restart things. Or one partner seems to
like sex more than the other. Or when they do make love, there's no spark—
it's boring. Is everyone but them having great sex? And what's up with all
the porn on the Internet? There are all these questions and no answers.

Healthy and fulfilling sex is an important ingredient in any intimate
relationship, including my own. I don't think good sex is all it takes to have
a happy marriage, but when partners aren't connecting in the bedroom,
it's never good. You're depriving yourselves of one of the most satisfying
experiences you can enjoy together—and it's free! Even more important,
you are denying yourselves the great power of sex to bring comfort and
healing. (For more about that, see chapter 15, where I talk about the good
news of sex.)

So, if you and your spouse are unhappy, confused, angry, frustrated,
about to give up on your sex lives, please give yourselves another chance.

Let me share with you some of the most common barriers to good sex, so you can take steps to get some spice back into your relationship.

Sex—Overrated?

Why is sex so important? Or is it? Can't you have a good marriage without so much emphasis on sex? Well, yes, there are some rare couples for whom sexual contact is seemingly unnecessary to their loving relationship. But most couples enjoy, or want to enjoy, full sexual lives with each other. The fuller the better! A warm, intimate sexual relationship gives you and your spouse tremendous pleasure in good times and supportive comfort through tough times. The act of making love builds trust between two people and strengthens the bonds of a relationship in a way nothing else can.

And, assuming you're in a monogamous relationship, it's the one joy you share with your partner and with no one else. That makes it very special. If you took the sex out of your relationship, you would be limiting its potential, reducing it to the level of friendship. While there's nothing wrong with friendship—I love to hear couples tell me that they are each other's best friends—a satisfying sex life means that you're enjoying all that can be yours in a committed marriage or relationship.

Most couples know, deep down, that what I'm saying here is true, which makes it hard to live with their own disappointing sex lives. The longer their troubles continue, the more they begin to doubt each other and themselves. They wonder what's wrong with them. And they don't know where to turn.

One place they certainly *shouldn't* turn to is pop culture. What do I mean? Think about all the ways in which we are constantly bombarded on TV, film, social media, the Internet, and so on by photographs and video of steamy sex scenes, provocatively dressed celebrities, and other messages about what our sex lives *should* look like. Magazine headlines in the grocery story promise "The Top 5 Things That Will Drive Your Man Crazy!" or "The Three Hot Spots on a Woman—They're Not Where You Think!" and "Take Our Sex Survey to See How You Rank," and when you read the results you feel like everyone in the world is having great sex . . . except you. And what about the reality shows where sex is discussed and takes place so freely and without feeling that it seems like it has replaced handshakes! What we imagined as being normal—sex as an act of intimacy and affection between two loving people—is made to seem abnormal. In this atmosphere, it is easy to start to feel inadequate, less than a real woman or man.

It helps to realize that the media uses sex to pursue its own agenda, which is making money. Ads and articles that highlight sexual innuendo, showcasing extraordinarily beautiful women and good-looking guys hooking up as regularly as you brush your teeth, are purely marketing tools media companies use to lure readers and viewers into picking up their magazines, watching their TV shows, or visiting their websites. They "shock" you to get your attention. The meaning of "shock" is something that is out of the ordinary. But it's all just a money grab, a way to get attention, because attention is how media companies create revenue.

Don't buy into any of it. What we are constantly exposed to in the media isn't a reflection of what is real. What's real is what happens between you and your partner. Your relationship is unique. Honor it, and don't compare it to unrealistic depictions of sex on the latest reality show or in make-believe advertising.

Okay, you say. Even discounting the crazy stuff on TV that passes for sexual intimacy, you're still in trouble, and you want to dig yourself out of the hole you're in. But it's awkward and you don't know where to start. Or you have tried and your partner doesn't seem interested. Or your lives are so busy you barely have time to sleep, let alone have sex.

When it comes to sexual intimacy, the odds are high that one of these two scenarios describes your current situation: either you and your spouse once enjoyed great intimacy in your early years together, don't know how you lost it, and yearn to have it back, or you two have never had a satisfactory sexual relationship (in your opinion) and would like to learn how to build one. Whichever one best describes your situation, and even if it's some combination of the two, I have good news—great news, actually. You *can* enjoy that intimacy in your relationship, just as you are hoping.

The "Second" Sex Talk

As kids, we feared the moment our parents (or health teachers, as the case may be) sat us down to have the proverbial sex talk. Now Jen and I are parents, and "the talk" is almost legendary in our home. Our younger children have been warned by their siblings and know it's coming. Jen and I get really geared up for it, have specific talking points and analogies, and no matter how many times we have sat down and had "the talk" with our children, we get a little anxious and nervous going into it. But it is an important talk to have, and leaving the topic untouched is a very dangerous—dare I say irresponsible—thing for a parent to do. Kids need information and guidance about sex from their parents as they step into adolescence. They need to talk to someone about their questions and concerns, and it's best if it starts with you.

But guess what? There is another sex talk that too many people skip over, and it is just as important as the one you have with your sons and daughters. It's the one you have with your spouse.

The first sex talk introduces the topic of sex to a child, but what I call the Second Sex Talk (let's call it the SST for short) introduces effective sex into an adult relationship. I know, just the words "effective sex" can be a total buzz kill. Like there aren't already enough (too many) expectations about sex, and now you're supposed to measure its effectiveness? Well, yes, you do. But the fact is that you already are measuring it even if you haven't named what you're doing. During sex, you and your spouse are likely watching for signs that you are effectively pleasuring each other, that he or she is enjoying the experience. Afterward, you draw conclusions. You know if you are satisfied or not, and, whether or not you say anything out loud, you probably want to ask your partner, "Was it good for you?"

While it sounds clinical and not very arousing to think about sex this way, these questions are exactly what's going on in both of your minds, and they're important questions. So since you're already trying to have effective sex, why not make it as good as you can? And the first step to more effective sex is having the Second Sex Talk.

"Forget it," you say. "I've already *tried* to talk to my spouse about sex and nothing has changed." Okay, I hear you. In many marriages, one spouse (not always, but most often the man) spends a lot of energy trying to convince his partner that sex is one of the most important ingredients in a happy marriage, and his partner (not always, but usually the woman) tries to get him to understand that she feels there are many other ways to express love besides sex. It's the sex tug-of-war that has gone on for centuries.

At the risk of being too agreeable, let me say that I agree with both of those "positions" (no pun intended). Sex absolutely is a very important part of a happy marriage and, just as importantly, there are a number of ways to express love in a marriage beyond sex. Happily, you can do both!

But less often discussed, or not discussed at all, is the lack of spark during sex, the resentments that keep couples from having sex at all, or the many pressures on a relationship that end up pushing good sex to the bottom of the list of priorities.

All these issues are very real and *very* sensitive. When you have sex or when you talk about your sex life, you are putting yourself in a very vulnerable place. Feelings get hurt and egos get bruised very easily. So it takes a lot of courage to speak up, even more so if you and your partner aren't used to talking about your most private fears and feelings.

But if improving your sex life is what you're after, you have to start somewhere, and talking to the person you want to sleep with is the most logical step to take.

Steps to a Successful SST

Let's face it: sex can be delicate territory, so you need to put a lot of thought into how you will initiate and carry out a successful SST with your spouse. Here are six steps to help you do just that.

1. **Be prepared.**

   Just like the first sex talk with your children, the SST with your spouse can be nerve wracking and anxiety inducing, so you should think ahead of time what you want to talk about and what you'd like to accomplish. Maybe, for now, you'd like to introduce the concept of talking at all, saying that you know it's awkward but that you really care about your partner and think it would be helpful to have a conversation about your lovemaking. Or you might be okay with talking about something specific that happened, or that you'd like to happen. Whatever it is, think ahead of time about how to introduce the topic in a neutral, nonjudgmental way. Be as positive as you can, as honest as you can, and as loving as you can.

2. **Select a good time.**

   It's your call when that best time is, but let me give you a few suggestions when *not* to do it. Don't attempt the SST as soon as your spouse walks in the door. Don't do it at the end of the day, when the two of you are both tired and short

on patience. Don't attempt it during or right after any disagreement of any kind. Don't try to have the talk while either
of you are feeling emotional or vulnerable. Don't attach it to
any other conversation, like discussing financial problems,
issues with the kids, or things needing repair around the
house. In fact, don't even bring up the SST if you are angry
or even mildly annoyed. The SST should be a tender conversation that happens when you are both relaxed and open,
and you have the time to spend a few minutes on a single
topic, with no place to go. I'm not suggesting you trap your
partner into a forced conversation; I'm suggesting you create
a captive audience.

3. **Tailor your words to your spouse.**

No one knows your partner better than you, so figure
out the best way to get his or her attention in a positive
way. Some possibilities:

- Catch your husband off guard with an opening line like,
  "I'd like us to have more sex," or, "I find myself craving
  more sex with you," or whatever else you feel will get his
  attention in a positive, nonthreatening way. Then go into
  your loving, gentle explanation.

- To your wife, perhaps something like, "I want to tell you
  how much I loved it when we used to _____ and I'd
  love to do that again," or, "I know sex has been at the
  bottom of the pile lately, and I'd like to see if we could
  talk about why," would work. And then say what's on your
  mind.

- Only use the word "you" in a positive reference, never
  negative. Say, "I love it when you _____" rather than,
  "I wish you would _____." When hinting at something
  that might be considered a negative, keep the focus on
  the word "I." Instead of saying, "I wish you would touch
  me more besides just during sex," try saying, "I love to be
  touched in the middle of the day."

- Avoid all uses of the words "always" and "never" in a negative reference (e.g., "You always fall asleep when we're

done," or "You never do such-and-such anymore").
This can shut down communication immediately.

- Sarcasm has absolutely no place in the SST.

4. **Be as clear as you can.**

Talking about sex is uncomfortable for most people, and it's easy to get vague about what you mean. Stay away from general comments like, "There's just something I don't like about the atmosphere when we make love." Instead, go with something more proactive like, "Can we turn the lights down in the bedroom?" Nothing drives someone crazy more than being informed there is a need for change but being left with no idea what changes are desired.

5. **Be ready for feedback.**

Once you have opened up the SST, your spouse may find it a safe time and place to share a few of his or her own thoughts and desires, so be welcoming to some good, two-way communication on this topic.

Jennifer's Secret to Successful Dialogue

At the risk of letting my wife discover I am on to her ways (smiling right now), I have learned that whenever Jennifer wants to have a productive conversation with me where she wants me at ease and vulnerable, it generally happens while she is sitting on my back giving me an amazing massage! It took me a few years to realize that those incredible massages usually came with a conversation, but once I did catch on, I didn't care. Her timing was great, and her words were healing. She effectively lowered my defenses, squeezed the stress from my day out of me, and gently expressed love while exploring a topic she felt we needed to address. Now when she asks, "Would you like a massage?" I will jokingly respond, "Oh great. What are we talking about today?" She just says, "Lie down and I'll tell you about it." I do.

6. Stop while you're ahead.

This is, hopefully, the first of many SSTs. Your goal now is to simply open the door to future conversations. Don't try and resolve every issue you may have in the bedroom. Plant a seed and then give it some time to grow. Don't seek full understanding, full resolution, and full implementation in your first SST. It's enough for your partner to know that you care enough to bring up this sensitive conversation, that you sincerely want to make things better between the two of you. So allow the SST to be a beginning, a conversation that can be continued later. Once you're both comfortable with communicating about sex, it becomes a natural way of improving your lovemaking. And as you grow and age, this topic and your sexual relationship will grow and change as well.

You might note that I've placed this chapter after we've talked about all the roadblocks to open and productive communication. All the tools we discussed in chapters 5 through 9 will help you better prepare for your SST, so you might want to review them. Or, if you aren't yet comfortable with those tools, just finish the rest of this chapter and continue on with the rest of the book. Come back to the SST when you feel it is a better time to do so. If you sense it isn't safe to have a sex talk with your partner without tremendous repercussions, then you probably have other, more pressing issues still to address anyway.

For those who feel ready to try to reintroduce satisfying sex into their relationships, below are some of the common sexual problems I've found that keep people from enjoying sex.

The Big Six of Sex

Below are six of the more common sexual issues that couples have revealed to me as reasons why their relationship is suffering sexually. If you and/or your partner have fallen into any of these traps, here are the ways out.

#1: Sex and (No) Money

This is a biggie. When financial problems come on the scene, sex often quickly exits stage left. You go to bed every night and wake up every morning sick with financial worry. The desperate, sometimes frantic search for a financial solution consumes your every waking moment, exhausting your body and soul. Sex is the last thing on your mind.

Well, the first thing you need to know is that you're not alone. Some men are so worried about finances that they become temporarily impotent. And it's been proven that, at times, the hormones associated with stress can reduce a woman's ability to reach orgasm. This is simple physiology and nearly always temporary, so there's no need to panic or overthink it.

Secondly, the effects of financial strain usually trickle (or flood) down into other areas of your relationship, not just sexual intimacy. You might find yourself arguing with your partner about things that normally don't register on your personal Richter scale. You might find your disagreements getting more intense, combative, or downright ugly compared to what they were before. Again, the elevated tension is usually temporary. This is something to take note of, but not something to overreact to.

In fact, when you connect the dots, you realize your problems are not a sign of your deteriorating relationship so much as a result of your deteriorating financial situation. There is good news and bad news here. Sure, it's a massive bummer that your financial situation is on life support, and the stress can feel unbearable. But I want you to harvest from that reality this reality—you and your partner still love each other. You are simply under a significant level of worry right now. Try to remember that as you work through your tough times. It does help.

The fact that stress due to financial challenges can negatively impact your sexual relationship may not be breaking news to you, but the fact that it can be reversed should be! For so many years, the only real advice or words of comfort provided to those in a financially stressed-out chapter of their lives, where sex had disappeared, was, "As soon as your financial situation turns around, so will your sex life."

But if you see no immediate end to your difficult circumstances, that's about as comforting as a cold shower. Heck, most people made vows when they married, which said something about loving each other "in good times and in bad." I interpret the "bad times" to include financial troubles, and I certainly translate the "loving" to include sex.

Another thing about the backward advice to "wait it out" is that improving your sex life could, in turn, improve your financial circumstances! As outlined in the list from WebMD (see box), sex has been shown to relieve stress, boost self-esteem, and get you more sleep. All of these things, emotional and physical, are some of the key ingredients to being able to think, work, and move forward in the fight to generate financial solutions. I'm not saying, "Have sex, earn more money" (not a profession I endorse), but rather I'm suggesting that taking your mind off stressful things by unwinding a little, connecting with your lover, and enjoying some balance in your emotional life can be a very good idea. When you feel calmer and happier, you can think more clearly, perhaps begin to come up with different ways to look at your problems, maybe even come up with new solutions. You might be surprised just how therapeutic and healing making love can be for other areas of your life.

If you are skeptical in reading this, or downright dismissive ("We could have wild sex every night this week, but there's still no money for the car payment"), I ask you to slow down and take one step at a time. This isn't a chapter about money; it's a chapter about how to improve intimacy with your spouse during rough times. There is great value here outside of dollars and cents.

Your relationship and your family do not have to become another example of how marriages fail due to money problems. You have a choice to make. You can choose to continue to argue and blame each other for your situation, or you can choose instead to acknowledge the issue and agree to provide comfort to each other.

If this makes sense to you, you can use the steps we outlined in the SST to talk to your partner about it. Maybe you both don't feel you can immediately drop everything and jump into bed, but you can certainly ease your burdens by realizing you can ride this roller coaster together. It may not be sex, at least at first, but it can still be an intimate encounter that brings the two of you closer together.

If you can decide, no matter how severe your financial problems, to relieve pressure wherever possible, breathe and hold on to each other, you will feel better. And when you do finally resolve your economic challenges, you will be closer as a couple and your celebration sex will be all the sweeter.

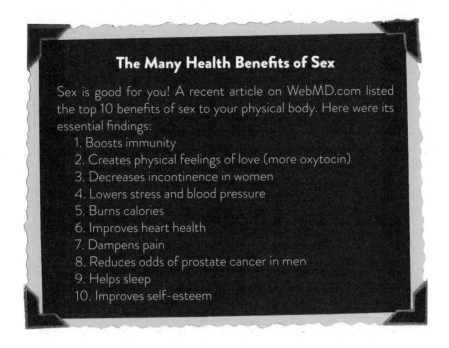

The Many Health Benefits of Sex

Sex is good for you! A recent article on WebMD.com listed the top 10 benefits of sex to your physical body. Here were its essential findings:
1. Boosts immunity
2. Creates physical feelings of love (more oxytocin)
3. Decreases incontinence in women
4. Lowers stress and blood pressure
5. Burns calories
6. Improves heart health
7. Dampens pain
8. Reduces odds of prostate cancer in men
9. Helps sleep
10. Improves self-esteem

#2: The Turndown

Rejection, in any form, is difficult to handle. Being told you aren't the right person for the job opening is painful. Not being asked to be a bridesmaid in your best friend's wedding can be a very difficult experience for some. But when rejection happens in the bedroom and it comes from the one person you love more than life itself, the impact can be devastating. And if you get rejected again and again, it's understandable that your self-esteem may drop like a stone, and you can begin to deeply resent your partner.

This goes both ways. Everyone laughs (sort of) that it's always the man who is clamoring for more sex, but women, too, are often turned down in their desire for sex. For either partner, repeatedly getting the cold shoulder is discouraging and sad.

There are lots of reasons why you or your partner might turn down an invitation for intimacy: fatigue, distraction, boredom, or serious problems like lack of trust. After all, it's tough to get "in the mood" when you're angry, hurt, or disconnected.

Now, there are plenty of times when one of you is feeling frisky and the other just wants to crawl under a rock. It happens! But when rejection and excuses become the routine, and one or both of you is feeling a general dissatisfaction with your level of sexual intimacy, something is not right. Eventually the rejected party will begin to wonder, "What's wrong with her?" or "What's wrong with me?"

What to do? First of all, compassion is key. Even if you're angry at your partner and can't imagine making love with her or him when asked, it is far better to temper any rejection with kindness and sincerity, so as to not discourage future advances or to hurt the feelings of the one you love. Rejection without compassion is simply using sex as a weapon, period.

Secondly, talk about it. One way to reject your spouse with minimal damage is to use the following formula, called the Gentle Rejection:

1. **Be thankful.**

   When your partner asks you playfully if "you've got some time, because I think I'm going to lie down," or pats your behind as he passes by you in the kitchen and nods his head toward the bedroom, express gratitude, even if you don't feel it, by smiling, touching him back, or whatever you normally do to express goodwill.

2. **Explain why you're saying no.**

   Make it clear it has nothing to do with him or her, but that you're too tired, too busy, worried about something at work, not feeling well. And keep your "no" brief. A long explanation only prolongs the rejection and makes it more awkward.

3. **Reschedule!**

   This is what pulls the stinger out of the rejection. If at all possible, let your spouse know that you would love to make love tomorrow after you get the kids to bed or at lunch in his office, or whatever other creative compromise you can muster up. When you reschedule, you're turning "no" into a "not now," which is far easier to cope with. It converts a rejection into a simple delay. Much less hurtful.

This gentle sort of rejection can soften feelings and sometimes lets in light on a quarreling couple. It might take real effort to change your behavior, but it will go a long way in lessening tension in an unhappy home.

If you are really furious with your partner, and there are some long-standing issues between you that make the thought of lovemaking feel like sleeping with the enemy, then it might seem impossible to tell him why you're rejecting him.

There might be very good reasons why you don't want to discuss deep-seated problems. But the more you say no to sex with no explanations, the more resentful your partner is going to become. Nothing is going to get better, that's for sure.

If this is your situation, then at the very least try to temper your rejection with kindness and compassion. Then, at another time, far from the bedroom, try the SST. If you follow the steps above—set up the right time to talk, keep your tone neutral and positive—and be as honest as you can, you may be able to release a logjam of resentments on both your sides and begin the process of reconciliation.

Or you may not. If your relationship is in serious trouble, trying to resolve your sexual problems could be putting the cart before the horse. Both of you are most likely feeling very vulnerable in this area, and you're better off referring to the earlier strategies in this book to address other issues between you. Then, when you are feeling closer in other areas of your relationship, sexual intimacy is more likely to return to your marriage.

Routine Sex Is Okay, Too

Let's be honest here. Sex isn't always a combustible explosion of desire between two people. Sometimes sex happens between two people in love only because one partner does not want to hurt the feelings of the other. That's okay. In fact, it's a wonderful expression of love to occasionally "take one for the team," as crass as that may sound. I'm, of course, not suggesting ever allowing yourself to be abused or forced to do something you disagree with. I'm talking about those times when one of the two of you may simply not feel up to it but in a tender act of love, you do so anyway rather than hurting your partner's feelings, or because you believe that in that moment, what he or she needs most is that physical connection or validation. Besides, such "generosity" toward your partner can very well bring its own rewards. I, for one, have always been grateful to be "on the team!"

#3: Sex as a Weapon or a Bribe

At marriage conferences, I ask for a raise of hands showing how many in the room have dangled the possibility of sex with their partners in exchange for something, or withheld sex as a way of punishing them. The room fills with nervous laughter, and a lot of women and some men raise their hands. Then I ask for a show of hands from those who feel that sex has been used as a weapon against them in their relationships, and up go the hands again, but with the balance of genders reversed.

I always bring this up because, even though using sex as a weapon or a bribe seems like a cliché, especially regarding women, it happens frequently enough in troubled relationships that I need to talk about it. Using sex in this way leads to bitterness, resentment, and sometimes a failed relationship.

While it's more often women who tend to use sex this way, at least in my experience with couples, it's important for both sexes to avoid this behavior.

Sexual intimacy as a carrot or a bludgeon to get your way or prove a point is a terrible perversion of lovemaking. Physical intimacy is, in its purest form, an act of expressing love. It is a pretty perfect way to share your feelings for each other, combining physical and emotional satisfaction to show your love. To abuse its power can be very destructive to a marriage.

The quickest clue to being aware when you're using sex as a weapon or bribe is when you wouldn't mind having sex yourself but turn your partner down anyway.

Let's say your spouse screwed up, didn't apologize, and you're angry at her. It's no surprise that when she cozies up to you, pretending nothing has happened, you don't respond. That's not using sex as a weapon—that's saying you're not in the mood because she's acted like a jerk. And you're really *not* in the mood to make love to her.

But what if she sincerely apologizes, and you know she means it. Enough time has passed that you've forgiven her, but then when she kisses you on the top of the head while you're reading the paper, suggesting you go upstairs, you tell her you're not interested. You actually wouldn't mind some sex but decide you just want to make sure she *really* knows she blew it. Now you're using sex as a weapon.

I could repeat this exact same story using a woman as the driver of the scene, where she withholds sex not because she wouldn't enjoy it but because she wants to teach her spouse a lesson. Pick your gender, but damage is done either way.

The bottom line is, please don't be someone who abuses the power of sex by using it for things that bring about negative emotions. That is the *anti*-love potion. Sex can be used to disrespect, abuse, and neglect. It is only "making love" when that is the intent of both participants. If you think of sex in that way, you can understand why promising it or withholding it is manipulating love in a cruel and cynical way.

#4: The Porn Ploy

There is so much pornography on the Internet now, much of it free and accessible to anyone and everyone 24/7, that it is a fact of life. A July 2013 Pew Internet and American Life Project survey found that the number of people downloading adult videos has doubled in six years, from 6 to 12 percent. Some 25 percent of men now report watching adult porn, and in a surprising jump, 8 percent of women reported watching adult videos, four times more than reported doing so only three years ago. Further, the researchers note that those statistics may be low, reflecting "a reluctance to report the behavior among some adults." All told, there are 68 million Internet requests for pornography every day, representing 25 percent of total Internet search requests, and 42 percent of Internet users view pornography.

I've seen the hurtful effects of the explosion of online porn in my work with families. It's mostly men who, hard as it may be to believe, have been watching so much porn that they think *that's* the way sex between a man and a woman really should be.

Let me give you a few brief scenarios. Imagine for a moment that a few nights a week, your husband is downloading adult videos. You're clueless about this, have no idea that he's even on the computer, but there he is, watching a video of a gorgeous woman—amazing body, perfect hair and makeup—who is lusting after her partner. She never talks (unless you count begging for more sex), she never asks anything of her partner, she's never cranky, has no PMS, seemingly no need for food or sleep. Heck, she never even goes to the bathroom. She has no job, no children, and no views on anything in life. Her only work is to wait for her partner to snap his fingers and then she comes to life, naked and ready to pleasure him. Afterward, she silently retreats, on call until he requests her again.

So when you approach him to make love, there is a part of him that is consciously or unconsciously comparing you to his "girlfriend," who may have just satisfied him earlier, unbeknownst to you. He rejects you as gently as he can because he is not in the mood. Why should he be? He has reduced sex to a simple physical act of release. Nothing emotional or intimate. So he turns you down.

You feel hurt, betrayed, maybe even ugly. You think it's you. You wonder if it's the weight you've gained or the fact that you are aging, or maybe it's that argument you had yesterday. But it's none of those things. It's him and his porn.

And if you are a man and your partner is dipping into porn? A 2012 Nielsen report that looked at the kinds of porn that men and women enjoy found that while men like straightforward photos and video of naked women who are submissive, women prefer stories and emotion. They turn to porn with plots, like the best-selling book trilogy *Fifty Shades of Grey*. They are aroused by romance novels where sexual tension and acts are played out, and where the men are handsome, amazingly well built, strong, silent, and able to perform remarkable bedroom feats. But these men are also sensitive to their partner's emotions.

Many women find reading these books makes them more interested in lovemaking and spicing up their sex lives with their spouses. For them, the books are titillating fun and no more. But if you and your wife don't have a good sexual relationship or are in a bad place in your marriage, you could look pretty bad compared to the guy in the book she's reading. So when you suggest lovemaking, she's thinking she'd rather read her book and tells you, with a sigh, that she's sorry but she's too tired.

So where does this leave the two of you? I'll tell you. In Nowhereland. You enter the bedroom to be with your husband, feeling perhaps a mix of self-confidence and self-consciousness, ready to "be with" your man and be his woman. And your time together ends up being highly disappointing, if not disastrous.

And if you're a woman, you can also get turned off. The hero of your novel is vulnerable, isn't afraid to talk about his feelings, and is amazing in bed—tender, sensitive, exquisitely adept at pleasuring his partner. Why bother with your partner? You roll over and go to sleep.

You may be reading this and thinking this is nuts. How could anyone compare these fantasies with real life?

The answer is: *a lot of people do.* Maybe even you. When men and women watch or read a lot of porn, they can convince themselves that these fantasies are real. I've spoken to far too many men who have secretly talked themselves into believing that what they see in their downloads is true, that the compliant women who are begging for more sex are the way most women behave. Except, of course, their own partners.

Women, too, though not nearly as many, do the same, yearning for a man who, unlike her partner, is a perfect combination of manliness and tenderness.

I work to remind these people that the porn *is not real.* The woman starring in a porn video is an actress. *Everything* she does is scripted, edited, and shot like a toothpaste commercial. She is pretending because that's what she's paid to do. In her day-to-day life, she argues with her partner, loses her temper, overeats, wishes she could move to a Caribbean island, complains about her bunions, and definitely is *not* on call for instant sex.

It's the same with the men in romantic novels. I'd like to say, as a man, that we're all sensitive, able to talk easily about our feelings, and perfect lovers. But, hey, get real. Mr. Perfect Six-Pack who has buckets of money, deep soulful eyes, and listens to every word you say doesn't exist. He's a fictional character.

Yet when a couple is having problems, they can retreat into this fake world and use it to hide from the reality of their own.

Do you find that your partner seems preoccupied, unresponsive to you, distancing him or herself? It could be the effects of pornography.

This is a tricky area to address. Your partner may or may not be honest with you. He may tell you that "every guy" watches porn and that you should relax. A wife may tell her husband, "It's just a book." But by alerting your partner that you think porn might be affecting your relationship and that to you it's a problem, you have raised a red flag.

Porn in any form can send your marriage off the rails. It's very tough to be on the receiving end of this mindset. Usually you have no idea what's going on and can feel intimidated and guilty, and then finally you get fed up with your partner's behavior.

The solution here is simple, but not always easy. If you believe that porn is a silent partner in your relationship, you can use the SST to speak to your partner. Talk to him right away. Don't be confrontational; be lov-

Family: The Good F-Word

197

ing, tender, patient. Chances are a guy feels a little dirty or creepy when viewing porn. To get through this conversation, it might help to imagine it is something other than porn. How would you react if your spouse was doing a strong illegal drug that was changing his personality, making him distant from you? What if the drug he was using caused him to have to sneak around, lie, battle with guilt?

Approach him with an expression of love for him and for your marriage. Then share with him your hurt, your humiliation. Be sincere, not dramatic, and keep anger out of this, because if either of you loses your temper, productive communication stops. Don't make ultimatums, not yet. Just express your hurt and plead with him to come back to you and leave his digital girlfriend behind. It is possible, if you have never truly expressed your sincere hurt, he may be surprised by how much it bothers you. In the world of guys, watching porn is a generally accepted practice and discussed amongst men openly as a normal activity. Not all men, of course, but many.

This advice goes both ways. If you are the one reading soft porn, you are in an equally sticky situation because your husband has likely never cracked open the cover of one of your novels and really has no idea what's in there. He doesn't know that for the space of 250 pages, you are swept up in the warmth and tenderness of another man who seems a lot more articulate and accomplished than your partner. So it's on you to make sure your paper lover doesn't replace your real partner in your mind and heart. Doing so will almost immediately pay dividends in your marriage.

#5: The Good Girl Syndrome

Another big stumbling block in relationships, especially if you or your spouse was raised in a religious home, is what I have titled the Good Girl Syndrome (GGS). Taught from an early age that sex is bad and wrong, and sometimes even that God would be angry if they had sex, these people, primarily women, often have a hard time enjoying physical intimacy when they are older.

They marry or enter into a close relationship and are expected to simply forget everything they have been repeatedly told about sex. It can be tough to break out of the deeply ingrained belief that "sex is bad."

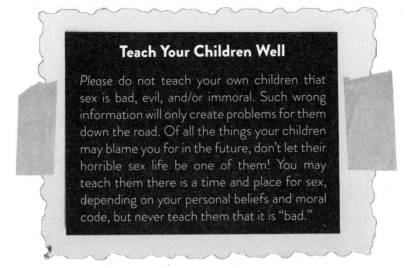

Teach Your Children Well

Please do not teach your own children that sex is bad, evil, and/or immoral. Such wrong information will only create problems for them down the road. Of all the things your children may blame you for in the future, don't let their horrible sex life be one of them! You may teach them there is a time and place for sex, depending on your personal beliefs and moral code, but never teach them that it is "bad."

Take this short quiz to see if you might indeed be suffering from GGS:

1. Do you feel guilty after making love with your spouse, like you did something dirty?

   Yes   No   Sometimes

2. Do you have moments when, rather than feeling sexy, as others do in intimate attire and situations, you instead feel slutty or otherwise uncomfortable?

   Yes   No   Sometimes

3. When naked in front of your spouse or when seeing your spouse naked, do you feel like you are going to somehow get in trouble for it or "get caught"?

   Yes   No   Sometimes

4. Are there any moments when your husband asks you to do or say something sexy but you hear the voice of your mother telling you, "It's not ladylike"?

   Yes   No   Sometimes

Answering "yes" or "sometimes" to any of these questions could suggest you may struggle with GGS. If you answered "yes" to all of them, I would say this is your issue.

So, how do you break through a mental barrier that was built brick by brick, year after year of your childhood? It can be very hard and take time. But the first thing you *can* do is to have an honest conversation with your spouse and tell him that this may be an issue for you. Then, ask him for his patience while you are working on it. Most likely he will be understanding, especially if he comes from a similar background.

In order to heal and move past these fixed beliefs, you need to make a plan. At first, set aside a quiet time at least twice a week to be alone with your thoughts. Then start thinking about all the well-meaning adults who taught you that sex was wrong, from your grandparents to your parents to your Sunday school teacher. Imagine them looking into your eyes and saying, "I'm sorry I told you sex was bad. I was wrong. Sex is wonderful and normal, and it is healthy for you to make love to your husband."

Let their words fill your mind until you can see their faces and hear their voices. You can also write their words down and repeat them to yourself. It was their mistake, not yours. Your mind is what has allowed these destructive feelings and ideas of guilt to linger, so it is your mind that you need to change. And you can retrain your brain by replacing all of those false, guilt-ridden statements from your youth with new, supportive statements that will steadily become your new mindset about sex. Think of the tender things that happen with your husband in your sexual life now. Even if you've felt inhibited in the past, you most likely have some happy memories of good sex. When childhood warnings about sex start to surface, make a conscious effort to push them away by thinking of your positive sexual experiences. Gradually, you will find that the new thoughts replace the old ones and you no longer have to spend as much time concentrating on the shift.

At the same time, if at all possible, make time to be alone before you and your husband make love so you can prepare yourself for a pleasurable time by reminding yourself over and over what a wonderful opportunity this is to connect with your spouse. Tell yourself repeatedly, "Making love is wonderful, it is good, and it is right." This phrase, or any similar message you create, will gradually ease you out of the fear and into the excitement and enthusiasm of building a deep and meaningful sexual connection with your spouse. You will find that with every lovemaking session, you and he are drawing closer and closer together. Sex is not an obligation, it is an opportunity, and one you can embrace freely and happily. Your partner will be thrilled with the change in your mindset. Go have some guilt-free fun!

#6: The Fire's Out

Have you essentially stopped having sex? Are you unsure just how you got here? Are you just going through the motions of your relationship?

There are a host of reasons why sex leaks out of a relationship. First are the practical demands of a busy life, where sex, once a big priority for you and your partner, somehow slips in importance when stacked up against work, kids, laundry, chores, and the bliss of a good night's sleep, so that making love ends up on the list somewhere between taking the garbage out and feeding the dog.

And there are the emotional components, harder to tease out, that keep you from each other. These include unresolved arguments that fester and cause resentments, and unproductive behaviors like blaming and keeping score that sap your affection for each other. And sometimes one or both partners have physical or personal problems that make them leery of sex. These can be anything from feeling fat and ugly, to worries about sexual performance, to low self-esteem.

But let's say you've been working hard on your relationship, perhaps from reading this book. You're communicating better, you've stopped keeping score with each other, there is less tension in your home and more pleasure.

And yet, when it comes to recharging your sex life, you've hit a brick wall. You're both awkward, discouraged, and perhaps thinking that the glory days of your sex life are gone forever. You look across the table from each other on your "date night," which is supposed to be your time to get together, in both the emotional and "biblical" sense, and what you feel for each other is . . . nada.

You're not alone. This can be a very common problem for couples who think that sexual desire for each other is either there or it isn't. Many reflect

Family: The Good F-Word

201

that it *was* there when you first met—it was probably part of your strong attraction to each other—but now it's gone and that's that.

This isn't so. Your sex life, especially when you've been working on your relationship so that you feel closer to each other, can be even richer than when you first met. But unlike the fairy tales, romance novels, and romantic comedies you read and watch, a new, improved sex life doesn't just *happen*.

But you can *make it* happen. I'm going to direct you to jump ahead here to chapter 17, where I discuss the steps to making love *right now*. Seems impossible, or at least unlikely? Not so. As you will learn, you can reintroduce sex into your relationship and experience the powerful healing and joy that comes with resuming your sex life. I urge you to go straight there.

Sex is one of the true blessings and joys in a committed relationship, uniting couples in shared pleasure, intimacy, and trust. If good sex has been lacking in your marriage because of any of the reasons outlined above, I hope you and your partner will together try to bring lovemaking back into your relationship. The payoff is enormous . . . and fun!

Welcome Your Children into Change: Listen, Love, and Guide Them

14

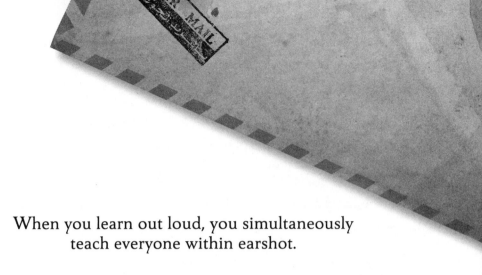

When you learn out loud, you simultaneously
teach everyone within earshot.

—Troy Dunn

If you have been repairing your relationship with your partner, you are probably hoping that the positive changes you've made are trickling down to your kids. Don't worry; they are! Even if they don't say anything, kids see everything. They are always alert to their parents' actions and slightest moods because you are their world—they take their cues from your behavior and model their own behavior on what they see at home.

Do they seem more relaxed around the house? Are they laughing more? Do they seem less distracted? Are they even misbehaving more? All these are signs that you have lowered the temperature in your home and that your children feel safer to be themselves. Even misbehaving is a good sign here because they're no longer cowering, afraid to make a wrong move and step on a familial land mine. They can be kids again.

If you are noticing these changes in your children, you must stop right now and give yourself a *huge* high-five. It is an enormous achievement to have brought about any one of these changes in your children by your own diligence and discipline in repairing your relationship. I really cannot congratulate you enough, as what you are doing will resonate throughout your children's lives and the lives of the families they found. These are changes you need to note in your Ramp notebook, because they are big accomplishments.

If you're still in the trenches, still struggling to work things out with your partner, hoping but not betting on change, it's okay. There are many ways you can improve your children's home environment despite your troubles with your partner.

If you are the good parent I assume you are or are trying to be, you likely already know that there are two things children need most from their parents. The first and foremost, of course, is to know that you love and cherish them. Secondly, they need consistency from their parents. They thrive on stability, predictability, and reliable behavior. They don't like surprises. The more boring, the better! That way they can feel safe, secure, loved, and free to grow and explore.

Even if they know you love them, it is really hard for them to come home after school and have no idea what they're walking into—a war zone of raging tempers, a stalemate of cold and wicked silent stares, a crossfire of cruel and sarcastic quips, or maybe just a huge bog of lonely and quiet nothingness. All this negativity pours down on them like acid rain, whether you realize it or not.

Now, you might be reading this and thinking, "Troy, cut me some slack. My relationship with my partner is far from perfect, but I do a fantastic job of shielding my kids from our unhappiness. My children know they are loved, and we take meticulously good care of them."

Hey, I get it! I believe you. You very well could be one of those well-meaning parents who is able to totally compartmentalize the bad parts of your relationship and maintain a semblance of normality in your home. But, I want to point out what may seem a harsh truth: even in the best of "bad" circumstances, if any part of your home life is unhappy, your children feel it in their bones. They see and feel everything going on at home, no matter how hard you attempt to hide their eyes from it. They are keenly, acutely aware if you and your partner are experiencing discord. And that, in turn, creates stress for them on three levels: their day-to-day lives at home with you and your partner and each other; their interactions with peers, teachers, and anyone else they know outside of the home; and, lastly, their future, because they will pattern what they see and feel at home when they set up their own families. You are creating a legacy for your children every day as their parent.

If your son invites a friend to sleep over but his parents won't let him because they've heard that you and your partner argue all the time, that might be a tough pill for you to swallow, but think for a moment about how this affects your son. His spirit is crushed. Or worse, if a friend does stay the night and all he and your son do is listen to you and your partner going at it like cats and dogs, his world feels topsy-turvy and his joy is quashed with humiliation.

Another common scenario you might relate to is when the kids have to constantly walk on eggshells, terrified they'll say something that will ignite another nuclear family blowout, ending in slammed doors, tears, and heartache. If your children are always on guard, watching their every move so as not to disrupt the calm, they are carrying too heavy a load and you risk stealing their childhood away from them.

Perhaps you are now a single parent, and your children have breathed a collective sigh of relief that the chaos at home and the toxic screaming matches between you and your ex have finally come to an end. You may have given them a calmer household, but you still need to monitor your behavior. Children are like little radar detectors, and if you are shooting out negative feelings about your ex, even if you aren't outwardly "bashing" him or her, your kids will pick up on that, and it will send their young minds right back to the hell they may have experienced before the split. They have battle wounds, just as you do, so it's your job to help them heal the wounds, not constantly reopen them. Furthermore, remember that your ex is still your child's other parent, and if you have contempt toward him or her, your children might easily make the leap and believe that you have the same contempt toward them. After all, that person makes up half of your child.

So, you're probably wondering, how do you ensure you are giving your children the best possible scenario in which they can grow into healthy, happy, productive adults, despite what you and your partner might be going through? Well, the first step is to discover and acknowledge any ways in which you might be negatively impacting your kids. The next step is to embrace several ways in which you can cushion and protect your children from here on out. So, let's get started.

Nine Steps to Achieving the Stability Your Child Needs

A stable marriage may be the single biggest factor in raising stable children, but sometimes, even in the best marriages, children go astray. Troubled homes only exacerbate the problem, because they undermine the stability that our young ones crave. No matter what your situation with your partner may be, it is still your solemn duty to provide proper examples and steady guidance to your kids. Here are nine steps to help you do just that.

1. Make disagreements invisible.

If you and your spouse both agree that you are very healthy arguers and you hope your children grow up to disagree exactly the same way you two do, then carrying out a healthy disagreement in front of your children isn't a bad idea from time to time. Go ahead and occasionally let your children witness an entire argument cycle, from the issue you disagree about, to the discussion from both sides, and then to the resolution. These "public disagreements" should, of course, be about simple matters that children can relate to on some level—it's not the time to bring up some deeply held resentments about your relationship.

Say you come home and find that your spouse has left the garage door open, despite the million times you've asked him to close it because the neighborhood cat always comes in and rips open the garbage. In fact, the cat *has* already been there, and this morning's leftover eggs and toast crusts are now spread over the cement floor like a breakfast collage. You are *not* happy. When you come into the kitchen, he's sitting at the table with your son, going over his homework.

In a perfect world, this is how your disagreement would play out so that your son can follow the flow of the argument, hear the tone, and witness the compromise.

You (controlling your temper): "Hey, honey, I hate to bring up a sore subject from the past, but I see the garage door was left open again. Didn't we agree to keep it closed at all times?"

Spouse: "Oh, I was carrying in all my work stuff plus Johnny's hockey gear, and my hands were too full to hit the wall button. Then I forgot to go back outside. I'm really sorry."

You: "Well the cat got in again—I think he waits by the driveway—and the garbage is all over the floor. I'm really getting tired of cleaning the garage every day when I get home."

Spouse: "You're right. I know we have to keep it closed and I just forgot. I'll clean it up right now. And I'll really try to remember the next time."

You: "Thanks."

Your partner gets up and goes outside to clean up the mess, and you sit down with Johnny to look over his homework.

This is a simple example of a small disagreement that would be okay for your child to witness, because it demonstrates so many things that resolve conflict in a relatively calm way. He sees the two of you speaking in controlled voices and not using harsh words, sarcasm, or name-calling. He hears you each listen to what the other has to say. He sees one spouse take ownership of something and another spouse be quick to let it go and move past it. He sees a resolution that is valid and involves no drama, no emotional outbursts, and then notes how quickly normal life resumes. If your child can witness an occasional healthy disagreement like this, you will have significantly increased his odds of success in future relationships of all kinds. Well done!

Life is filled with disagreements, and arguing in a healthy way is a useful skill that will help your children in their own arguments now and when they grow up.

That being said, many people's arguments can quickly degenerate into angry, hostile accusations that have no resolution, especially if a couple is in trouble. If you've already got a list of "sins" in your head that your spouse has committed, you'll be quick to jump on him for leaving the garage door open and be ready, even eager, to let him have it for his forgetfulness.

This sets the stage for a noisy, nasty fight that your wide-eyed child will have to hear. Is that fair to him? Should he be witness to these displays of venom and loss of self-control? No way.

So if you can't disagree in productive way, at least keep these toxic fights away from your children. Until you and your partner can better control yourselves, adopt the rule of never arguing in front of your children. This is a difficult habit to break if you've gotten used to erupting when something goes wrong, but it may be the single best thing you can do for your kids at this time.

The key here is to have a signal or a key word that you both have previously agreed upon that simply pauses the upset person and promises that you will give them an opportunity to be heard at a more appropriate time and place. The place should have already been agreed upon by the two of you and should be someplace where the children can't hear the rage and unkind words. I recommend a car, as it is a confined space and is small, so there is no need to shout and no room to pace around and steam. You are both required to sit there, inches from one another, and discuss what is wrong and how to resolve it. And it's best to do it sooner rather than later. In a healthy relationship, when someone feels hurt or slighted, it's usually okay to wait awhile before talking, because your basic compatibility often reasserts itself and there doesn't have to be a fight after all. But when you've got a lot of other resentments stored up, it's much better to air your grievances as soon as you can so they don't get added to the pile of issues you're already carrying around and make you even angrier.

Why do you need to make your disagreements invisible? Because when children see and hear your fights, they have a fear response. They begin to automatically fear the worst: divorce. If you've already gone through a divorce, then you know firsthand just how that affected your children—for them, it can feel like their universe has been torn apart at its seams. Further, what your children witness will stay with them as they grow. Their brains don't have a "delete key" to conveniently rid their memories of unpleasantness. It's more than likely they will absorb what they've experienced and adopt your poor fighting techniques when they leave home, go out in the world, and found their own families. Do you really want them to copy you and your partner's bad behavior and carry it into their own lives? Of course not; you want better than that for your children.

You and your partner can decide now to take your fights out of the family spotlight. It is never too late, no matter what the age of your children. They will quickly absorb the new example you set.

So, how to do this when you've spent years in circular, visible arguments? You make the mutual decision to table the disagreement until you are alone with each other. You do this out of respect for your children. You do it because you love them. As I mentioned, you agree on a password or phrase that you both promise to honor when tempers rise. I call it a Peace Pause; you could call it a time-out, you could call it broccoli. It doesn't matter what you name it; just make sure you both know it means *stop*.

Stop means no more talking *right now*. It means an immediate cessation of hostilities, a cease-fire. It means you set up a time to resume the argument that you both agree to. You say, "Peace Pause until 10 clock?" And then, with dignity and with your children watching, you both nod in agreement and completely drop it for the moment. To make the cease-fire work properly, you cannot pout, you can't make a sarcastic follow-up. You have to stop talking *completely*. For example, if your spouse requests a Peace Pause, your response should not be, "Oh sure. Use that as a way to avoid dealing with this!" Simply honor the request as something you both have already agreed to in the past as a way to spare your family unnecessary suffering. Have enough respect for the sanctity of your home and your children to accept the Peace Pause.

This will *not* be easy. Let me repeat—this will *not* be easy. It will be a true test of your love for your children. If you can muster the self-control to stop your anger mid-boil, you are showing them that you care more about them than you do about winning a fight. You are showing them that even if you feel you are absolutely right, and even if you hate your partner so much that all you want to do is unleash your rage, you stop. Your children will register this even if they're not sure what's going on. It will be a powerful teaching moment for them. But you know what? It will be a teaching moment for you, too, to realize you can pull yourself back from the brink of destructive behavior.

Unfortunately, if you refuse to let go of your fury, it is also a teaching moment, but a much sadder one. You will then be telling your children that nothing, not even seeing their eyes filled with worry and fear, is enough for you to let go of the satisfaction of venting. If your partner refuses to join you in pausing in your fight, you can just walk away yourself. Simply leave the room. It is very difficult to argue with an empty room. Or, if you need to resolve things right then and there, invite your spouse to come sit in the car with you, as we discussed above. Your refusal to engage in the presence of your children will eventually take some of the air out of the argument.

In a family that is torn apart, this one decision to take you and your partner's fights offstage and stick to the plan can make a bigger difference than you think possible. Firstly, your home will be more peaceful for your children, and secondly, you might begin to fight less. When you talk after a Peace Pause, you're both likely to be calmer, able to discuss things more rationally, and more likely to come to a resolution. And even if you don't resolve the matter, you've given your children a huge gift. That gift is the stability of knowing that regardless of whether mom and dad are having a good day or a bad day, this family is still safe and it will always get worked out. Your child needs to be able to go to sleep every night knowing, "It will be okay." That's a gift fewer and fewer children seem to possess. Can your children be some of the fortunate ones?

2. Respect your children's parent.

One of greatest gifts you and your partner can give your children is to openly love each other. When a child sees parents who clearly care for one another, their sense of security is almost immeasurable. They feel safe because they know they can depend on their parents to stick together, even in the rough times. They know their parents are *there for them* no matter what. It allows them to feel free—free to express themselves, free to have fun, free to be a kid.

Additionally, by loving, honoring, and respecting your spouse, you are showing your children how to properly build healthy relationships when they are older. Like it or not, they will likely model your behavior when they start their own families. They will treat the women and men in their lives the way they see you treat your partner.

Think about this. How many of the people we see on the news being arrested for abuse were abused themselves as children? How many divorced people come from divorced households? How many of the little bullies at your child's school may have been bullied in their own homes? On the other end of the scale, how many kind, polite children come from wonderfully kind, polite parents? What you do as a parent has a tremendous effect in shaping your child's personality and future way of dealing with people.

This, of course, doesn't do you much good if you and your partner are fighting like cats and dogs and are in a terrible place in your relationship. But, guess what? Even if you're angry, fed up, and frustrated with your partner, you can still treat him or her with respect. Far too many children are being raised by parents who openly discuss their hatred for one another. Don't let that be you. Bad-mouthing your partner to your children is a form of abuse to your children. You're telling them their other parent is no good, which may be true in your eyes but is very hurtful for their own relationship with their father or mother. You are setting them up to feel disdain rather than love in their own future relationships. And you are forcing them to take sides between the two people who are most important to them, which borders on cruelty.

Instead, treat your partner with respect in front of your children, no matter how much it privately pains you at times. Even if you think he's a terrible father, they deserve to make up their own minds on such an important figure in their lives. If you attempt to poison their minds about their other parent, they will resent you for it when they are older. Instead, allow them to form their own opinions of the other parent.

If you are a single parent, I suggest a similar path. Treat your children's other parent with courtesy. Don't use your kids as a weapon against your ex by trying to turn the kids against him or her. This may be oft-heard advice, but it needs to be repeated here because it's so important.

Even if they have already formed a poor opinion of their other parent on their own, I still urge you to speak of him or her with dignity and respect in front of your kids. If you try to poison your kids against your ex, I promise you that one day they will grow up and realize exactly what you did. And then you risk losing their trust or even your relationship with them. Don't play with this fire; you stand to lose too much. By taking the high road now, your kids will respect you so much more when they're grown.

In my work on *The Locator* and in my own career of locating family members, thousands of children of divorce have come to me as young adults asking for help in finding their fathers. When they provide me with details of their separation, they usually start by blaming their mother, who had spoken poorly of him.

If you are already guilty of this, at any level, admit it, sit down with your children, own it, and then work to fix it. Change your tune immediately. No excuses here for this kind of trash-talking. Even if you know for a fact that your ex is saying terrible things about you, you need to stop reciprocating if you value your relationship with your children. Right now.

3. Don't be a hypocrite.

"Do as I say, not as I do." You've heard this old saying before; heck, you might have said it to your kids today! I'm sorry, but this hypocrisy gets an "epic fail" status in my book. How can you expect your words to hold any meaning at all if your actions directly contradict them? Your child would be a fool to believe or obey you, and you and I both know your kid is no fool.

Hypocrisy is never good for children who need principled guidance on how to live their lives, but it's particularly unfair to kids in troubled homes. They are already being asked to cope in so many difficult ways because their home life is unsettled. And then you hold them to false standards that you don't even act on yourself? Don't smoke even though I smoke? Don't spend so much time at the computer even though I'm glued to the television set from the minute I get home from work? Hypocrisy just adds turmoil to confusion and disorder.

When life is difficult at home, show your children you love them by being honest with them. Don't act one way in front of them and then another way when they aren't around. The idea is to live, and I mean *really* live, each day the way you hope your children will live. Live an honest life. They will trust you and know they can rely on you regardless of your relationship with your partner. They will model your behavior. By way of example, you are teaching them how to be successful adults.

Actions Speak Louder Than Words

Children are far more likely to mirror their parents' behavior than their attitudes, according to a 2005 University of Washington study that tracked smoking habits of parents and their children. Adolescents of parents who smoked were twice as likely to pick up the same unhealthy habit between the ages of 13 and 21 than were kids whose parents didn't smoke. What was intriguing to Karl Hill, the director of the University of Washington's Seattle Social Development Project, was that it was the smoking *behavior* by the parents, rather than their *attitudes* about smoking, that was the determining factor in whether the children smoked.

4. Give your kids a compass.

When I was growing up, my mother always made Jell-O for us as an after-school snack. She had several molds—a starfish, an octopus, a happy face, even a brain—and would pour the liquid Jell-O into a mold, stick it in the refrigerator, and let it slowly thicken into a solid, ready for us to devour when we got home.

Imagine for a second trying to make Jell-O without a mold of some kind to pour it into. You'd end up with a big, red, sticky mess all over the refrigerator. The same is true with your kids. Without a solid structure supporting them as they grow, they can't thrive, and they, too, could end up with messy, unhappy lives.

Even if you and your partner are struggling with your own relationship, you both owe your children a clearly defined set of principles, or morals, that you both agree is the best way to raise them. From this foundation, a set of clear household rules needs to be built that will govern all of your day-to-day lives. Every child needs loving, consistent, structured parenting, but especially those children who are living in troubled homes where there is a lot of volatility and unease.

Of course, your children are free to alter these principles and establish their own household rules when they go out into the world. But because you are the founder of your family, it is your responsibility to give them a good moral compass to guide them. That compass will be the bedrock upon which they learn what's expected of them in your family and your lives outside it, and it will help them move forward with security and the confidence to make their own decisions and lead successful lives once they leave your household to start their own families.

If they're getting different messages from you and your partner, or no guidance at all, your kids will be confused, torn between you and your partner, and likely seek another structure outside the family, through peers or other adults. This could be dangerous territory, because there are predators who seek out children from homes like yours. These predators come in all sorts of packages—drug dealers, pedophiles, online sexual predators, and even other damaged children who find comfort in the misery of others. Do you really want your children to come under the sway of such people and be shaped by forces completely outside your control? Do you really want to risk their happiness and perhaps their futures by your inconsistent parenting?

You *can* change the way you set the rules in your household. Firstly, sit down with your partner and identify the areas in which you've been sending mixed, or no, signals—bedtimes, homework, chores, sleepovers with friends, time on the computer, etc. This could be difficult if you and your partner are arguing a lot, but I have to assume that despite how you feel about each other, you both want the best for your children. So please agree to let go of your hostility and pride for their sakes. Then, hammer out one set of rules—writing them down helps a lot if you've never done this before—and agree to abide by them. In fact, write them here:

_____

_____

_____

_____

_____

_____

_____

If yours is a blended family, it's *very* important that *all* the adults— ex-spouses, stepparents, grandparents, and any other relatives—who have involvement in the children's lives agree to these rules and to the consequences for violating them (more on that below). This will probably be a lot harder than sitting down with the children, as you adults are most likely all carrying around various degrees of resentments and hostilities toward each other. You, likely, will have to be the one to take a deep breath and be the first brave soul to initiate this concept among the various parents and stepparents.

Work hard to put aside all feelings of bitterness and hurt that you might have toward a former spouse and agree that when it comes to your shared children, there will be a united front. Keep the focus on the fact that you're doing this for your children and that all of you will benefit when the kids know the rules and learn to abide by them. It should also be very clear to everyone that the primary mother and father are the authors of the new code and that, when it comes to your children, the others need to abide by it.

Below are some of the areas where consistent rules are important. Setting rules for these areas and following them will assure your children a wonderful stability. They will also recognize—probably not right away, but down the road—that your consistent enforcement of the rules is a sign of your love for them. Feel free to change or expand the suggestions below to suit your own family's needs.

- Bedtime
- Chores
- Sleepovers
- Internet

- Texting
- Cell Phone
- Curfews
- R-rated movies
- Dating
- Smoking/Drinking
- Earning Money
- Discipline
- Church
- Guns
- Pets
- Lying
- Violence
- Manners
- Cleanliness
- Racial Issues
- Service

Okay. You've outlined some new, better ways for your family to function. Your work isn't done! Now you have to bring your kids on board, which requires a family meeting.

Jen and I have had weekly family meetings since our first child was born and still do today. Our meetings are a time to discuss upcoming calendar events for the week, recognize the various accomplishments of some of the family members, and then allow everyone to voice their opinions and feelings. Some meetings go better than others, but they have been a real blessing in our life. It is a time when the entire house stops moving for a moment. Instead of televisions blaring, phones ringing, kids texting, we all agree to just talk together in a quiet, reliable environment that facilitates healthy discussions.

Handled with sensitivity to all involved, a family meeting is a very good way to keep a family on track.

If you've never had a family meeting, your children's reactions to the idea will range from skepticism, fear, discomfort to curiosity, even enthusiasm. So be very specific and nonthreatening when you announce that you'd like to get everyone together on a regular basis to talk about important matters. Explain that the meetings won't take long but that you'll need everyone's attention and cooperation.

At your inaugural meeting, start in a positive way, telling your children that you're very glad they agreed to this and that your hope for the meeting is to make things better at home. Then you can introduce your ideas for setting some new rules for the household. Take full responsibility for why the rules and procedures hadn't been clear and organized to this point, without laying blame on anyone. If you would like a script to guide you, here is one to use of you want to:

> Well kids, Dad and I have called this family meeting because we want to talk with you about a few things. As you have probably noticed, things have been kind of tense around here. There seems to be a lot of bickering between each of you and between us and you as well. We, as your parents, have made a couple of mistakes in the way we have been running our family.
>
> For example, we have not been very consistent. Some days we tell you not to do something and other days we don't seem to care. Some days I will tell you one thing and Dad will tell you something different. We've decided it isn't fair to you kids to have rules that change all the time, so we sat down and talked a lot about how we can make life in our family calmer and happier. One of the ways we are going to do that is to share with you the rules of the family so you never have to wonder about them and we can all stop arguing about them so often.
>
> So, here is a list of our family rules, which we will go over right now, and then I'll tape a copy inside the kitchen cabinet in case you ever want to look at them.

Then you simply take out the list you devised above and start reviewing it. Allow room for discussion or questions so your children can clarify what they think you mean. Make this a safe place for them to question, but remain a firm and united front in responding to any pushback.

Tell them you're setting up these clear boundaries because you love them and want what's best for them. After you go over the rules, despite all of the groaning and eye rolling which will likely follow, you again tell them you're doing this because you love them and want the best for the whole family.

A vital part of this exercise is to explain the consequences for violating the new rules. In fact, write the specific consequence for violating each family rule right next to each category on your list. That way there will be no misunderstandings or misinterpretations about consequences weeks, months, or years down the road. It's right there in black and white.

When your kids test the rules, which they are bound to do, both you and your partner must stand by what you have established here. Soon enough, they will realize you mean business, that these boundaries are solid, and they will adapt. As they do, remember to give them recognition and praise for good behavior. This is a long-term commitment, and results come slowly. The payoff won't come in days or weeks but rather in months and years. So, continue to be diligent and it *will* pay off.

5. Discipline isn't a dirty word.

When a couple is in trouble, disciplining children can be a nightmare of extremes. A mother who is barely speaking to her partner feels so guilty about the antagonism her children have to live with that she lets them get away with murder. Temper tantrums, not doing chores, talking back to her are excused because "they're having such a rough time."

Equally disastrous is when the upsetting fights and ugly incidents between partners make them so short-tempered and irritable that they take out their frustration on their child, whose only mistake is being in the wrong place at the wrong time. This, too, can result in kids who act out in inappropriate ways.

If you have a child whose behavior is erratic—some days well behaved and other days out of control—the chances are high that you are not disciplining him or her properly.

Discipline is just as important to the growth and well-being of a child as good nutrition. And like good nutrition, it should be provided consistently and with love. When you prepare a meal for your children and it includes vegetables that they hate, are you giving them those vegetables because you are mad at them and want to see them choke and sputter? No, of course not! You want them to be healthy. This concept must be applied to discipline as well. You are correcting behavior, balancing their actions just as you balance their diet, because you want them to learn proper boundaries.

If one reason you don't discipline your children properly is because you don't want to "punish" them, think again. Discipline is a *consequence*, not a punishment. In the world, there are consequences for almost every action, good and bad, and your children need to learn this just as much as they need to learn to look both ways before crossing the street. If you don't, you are letting your children down big time. They will be ill-prepared and unarmed for life. When the cop stops your daughter for reckless driving, he's not going to say, "Oh, dear, you're going too fast." He will simply hand out the consequence: a big, fat ticket.

There are some important dos and don'ts for disciplining a child effectively. Taking these suggestions to heart will go a long way toward stabilizing your child's behavior.

To avoid turning your discipline into a punishment, don't discipline when you're angry. We've all been there. You overreact, say or do something you regret, feel guilty afterward, and, to say the least, do not use the incident as a teaching moment. Remember, look at discipline as a consequence, not a punishment, for crossing an established line.

Another important one: don't call names. Telling your child he is being a "bad boy" is name-calling; telling your son he has done a bad thing is different. This goes back to making certain you are disciplining as a teaching moment, not punishing out of anger. Children should be treated as you would expect to be treated when you have erred. Allow them their dignity and self-worth. Teach them what they have done wrong and remind them of what the right thing is.

I consider the word "discipline" to be another word for "teach." It takes time and sometimes lots of energy to discipline/teach your son or daughter. There are too many parents who skip this important part of parenting. You've probably seen them at restaurants, their child running laps around the dining room, or on a plane, when they're sitting behind you and letting their child kick your seat from takeoff to landing. Choosing not to discipline simply means you are choosing not to teach your child. Yet, this lack of effort only results in your child learning poor behavior.

An important "do" is to breathe! When you hear the ominous crack of the stair banister and run to the front hall to find your son has knocked out a row of balusters because he was using the banister like a piece of gym equipment, take a breath. Count to 10 slowly and evenly. Give yourself some time to tamp down your initial anger. Knowing how much it's going to cost to fix the banister, you may want to scream at him, "What were you *thinking* in doing such a stupid stunt?" But don't say aloud what's on the tip of your tongue; instead, tell him through gritted teeth that you'll discuss this later. And then you'll have time to figure out what he can do to make things right.

Discipline is only to be administered out of love, not anger. Your goal is not to use your child's misbehavior as an excuse for losing control and venting your own frustration, but to get your kids to understand why what they did was wrong, and to learn that there are consequences to their bad or thoughtless behavior. (By the way, spanking or hitting shouldn't be one of those consequences. There are far more effective and productive ways to let your kids know the difference between right and wrong than physical punishment.)

In my years of work with families, I've identified some of the most common excuses parents use for not properly disciplining their children. The biggest one—"I'm too tired"—is *never* a good reason to blow off disciplining a child for misbehavior. If you're simply too exhausted to deal with a situation, tell your child you will talk later, but don't let her poor behavior go unchecked.

Another biggie is wanting to avoid conflict, yet uniform discipline actually *minimizes* conflict because your child begins to self-discipline to avoid the consequences of poor behavior and bad choices. Real conflict occurs when a child is undisciplined and grows to be difficult to handle at home, in school, and in social settings. You're doing your child a disservice by not teaching him rules to live by to ease his place in the world. Remember, kids need that Jell-O mold!

Finally, there's the lame, "I don't want the child to not like me." And that leads us right into . . .

6. Don't let go of the reins.

A temptation, when you're fighting your way through a bad relationship, is to lighten up on your parenting. In the same way you might be loath to discipline your child because life at home is so shaky, you might back off from your full role as a parent. It's not that you don't love your child and want the best for her, but you're so consumed by worries in your relationship that you step away from your parenting responsibilities. This can wreak havoc with your kids.

There are two common ways parents do this.

The checked-out parent is the one (usually a father, but not always) who just isn't there, either physically or mentally. A checked-out parent is not involved in his child's life in any real way. He doesn't know what position his son plays on the baseball team, what his grades are like, the names of his teachers, or who his friends are. He rarely steps into his daughter's bedroom, has no idea what she wants to be when she grows up, rarely engages in conversation other than those involving chores or day-to-day logistics. On the rare times he attends a school function like a play, no other parents know who he is.

If any of this sounds familiar, you are likely a checked-out parent. There can be many reasons for your absence—work demands, a partner who discourages your involvement, social discomfort in general, geographic distance if you live away from your children—but this is a terrible situation for your child. You must make an effort to go to your child, engage in conversation, be a part of his or her life. You need to sacrifice time from other activities to attend your son's game or your daughter's recital. You need to be there.

The second common way to drop the parenting reins is to try to be the "cool" parent. This mother or father is really hard on a kid. The cool parent is making parenting decisions based on how her child will think of her, or how the child may describe the parent to friends, rather than on what is in the long-term best interests of the child. Sometimes parents assume this manner to ingratiate themselves with their children when times are bad at home. Others seem to be trying to relive their youth by striving for popularity with their own children. Still other well-meaning parents, reeling from their own parents' indifference or neglect of them, honestly think they can be better parents to their own children by being *friends*—they've never learned the proper boundaries of good parenting.

No matter the reasons, these sorts of "popular" parents generally raise incomplete children. They let go of boundaries and structure in an effort to make their children always happy. The result is that the children never learn what I discussed above—the values of responsibility, discipline, and consistency. These children eventually grow up to quietly, or not so quietly, resent their upbringing once they come across peers who are far more prepared for life and, ultimately, are far more successful.

To be a truly good parent, popularity will be fleeting at best. There is nothing easier than doing the easy thing. It's easy to put off repairing the leaking sink for another day, it's easy to overeat your favorite dessert, and it's easy to say yes to whatever your child asks of you. But that's not parenting. The hard thing is very often the right thing. Remember that and you will be a better parent.

7. Own your parenting imperfections.

Much of childhood is a lesson in how *not* to do things. Everything your child does in childhood is being done for the very first time, so failure and temporary setbacks are a part of his daily life. Heck, it's a part of our lives, too. Your kids are not perfect, and neither are you.

But some parents, in an effort to look like they know what they're doing, feel uncomfortable admitting to their children that they make mistakes, too. Do you let your children see your occasional imperfections, and do you willingly admit when you are wrong? Have they ever heard you apologize for doing or saying something you regret? Could your children tell me one of your fears, or one of the areas of life in which you want to improve? Or do you work overtime trying to always appear "perfect" in their eyes?

It's really *okay* to let on that you're not perfect. It's actually important *not* to act like you're always right. Children want *human* parents, not flawless, robot parents. Having a "perfect parent" can be discouraging; it sets an unrealistic standard. A child of parents who try constantly to appear perfect can struggle with depression and anxiety as they start off every day with the realization they will likely disappoint their parents. Would *you* like to feel inadequate every day of your life? The ideal role model isn't a perfect person, but rather a person always striving to improve and grow. That is someone your child can aspire to and relate to.

So be authentic when owning your mistakes, especially when those mistakes involve your children. When you flip out after tripping over a pair of shoes left in the den, screaming at your daughter for being so careless, apologize for losing your cool. When you and your son disagree about when he's supposed to be at school for a play rehearsal and he's right, acknowledge that you blew it. Let your kids hear the words "I was wrong" or "I'm sorry" from you once in a while. They know you aren't perfect; it would just be nice if they knew *you* know that, too.

One note: You don't have to take truth serum here and completely lay bare your mistakes. You still need to be in *charge* of your children. If your young son confesses he tried marijuana for the first time and is feeling bad about it, don't comfort him by saying, "Don't worry. Marijuana is nothing! I was addicted to meth for two years!"

Disclosing your colorful drug past may likely lead him to decide, "Hey, meth didn't kill my dad, so it might be worth a try for myself." He might decide to increase the amount of marijuana he smokes tomorrow because, after all, at least it's not meth!

Far better to help him work through his feelings, acknowledge we all feel badly when we make a decision that goes against our personal moral code, and then encourage him to start fresh today and move on making better choices tomorrow.

8. Initiate kid dates.

We're all familiar with date nights with your partner as a way to bring healing in a relationship. But when your family is in turmoil, and the kids are sometimes unwitting pawns in the hostility and antagonism that is coursing through your home, what about a *kid* date?

Doesn't your child deserve the same time-out from your family's troubles to take a breath and relax? I think so. Asking your child on a kid date tells him you think he's important, you love him, and you want to spend time with him outside of your normal day-to-day activities. What you actually do on your kid date often isn't as important as making the date itself.

Whatever you do together should be something you both enjoy. It could be a movie, or something as simple as going to the park to play catch. Use the time to talk to your son or daughter, but mostly to listen and learn. Spending time with a child outside of the daily round of school and home allows you to come to know him in a different, fresh way. He has a life and personality apart from being your son, and discovering that is a

wonderful experience. You might see this already during the drive home after you pick him up from school or after sports practice, but making the extra effort to set aside special time with him will pay off. You are showing him you value him by putting in place a structure for a stronger connection with him as he grows up. It is wonderful bonding time and can lead to some very important discussions. He will appreciate your interest in him and be grounded by it. Your partner, too, can have dates with your children. The more the merrier!

9. Catch them being great.

I want to end with this advice, because if you're going through a hard time with your partner and also reading in this chapter about how you might be making some parenting mistakes, this is your reward. You should enjoy and take pride in telling your kids how great they are!

Sometimes you may find yourself so busy doling out discipline you forget to really catch and appreciate the moments when your children are behaving well. What sort of recognition do they get for being good kids? Do you verbally thank them for using their manners, or do you only chastise them when they burp in public? Do you give them credit when you see they cleaned their room or are doing their homework without being told?

Share the good news! The more you do it, the more they will continue the behavior that earns them compliments. They notice. When you see your children playing nicely together, stop and tell them how happy it makes you to see them getting along and being so kind to one another. Did your son take the garbage to the curb without his usual argument? Immediately respond by telling him how much you appreciated his lack of grumbling.

In our large family, when I see that we have had a pretty good day overall, with chores and homework done, no fights, and generally good behavior, I will sometimes shout, "Midnight ice cream!" The kids come pouring down the stairs from their rooms, some in their pajamas, and we hop in the van and go to the 24-hour McDonald's for dip cones. The fact that it's midnight and it seems so illogical is half the fun. On the way to the restaurant, I thank them for all of the great things I noticed that day. It's not a speech, just a thank-you. But I can see the pride on their faces. If you haven't experienced the fun of catching your children being good, I highly recommend it.

Parenting can seem perilous when you're in a rocky relationship, but with perseverance and proper discipline, you can raise healthy, successful children even in the most trying circumstances. By acting with responsibility, steadiness, love—and a healthy dose of humor—you will teach your children well. And down the road, they will recognize and honor what you have done for them, regardless of your relationship with your spouse. Your investment in their future will greatly enrich your own.

Life-Changing Action Plan: Step 4
Embracing the Good

Healing, letting love back in, recreating intimacy—these are some of the seemingly magical feelings I have seen among families who have pledged themselves to fixing what's wrong in their relationships. During my time on *The Locator*, guiding families to reunions where they could rediscover each other's affections and deep love was a reward beyond measure. I was humbled by the courage, will, and generosity these mothers, fathers, sons, and daughters showed for each other as they worked to reunite their frayed bonds.

I don't use the word "magical" lightly. It *is* truly magical to me to see people facing seemingly impossible odds—long separations, bad behavior, long-held grudges—and choosing to do the hard work to open themselves up to the idea of change and new beginnings. The same healing takes place among the couples I talk to who yearn to improve their marriages and then take the necessary steps to make it happen. And believe me, it can happen to you and your partner and family as well.

Rebuilding a good marriage is, in my mind, simply doing what comes naturally. By naturally, I mean behaving in ways you know are good and honorable, ways that you probably *did* behave before the pressures and stresses that come with long relationships (and life!) strained you and your partner's feelings toward each other.

The next six chapters talk about six changes you can make to dramatically enrich your marriage. They are things you already know, really, and have probably just got out of the habit of doing, so this is a chance to reacquaint yourself with the good news that comes with a strong, intimate relationship. They all require you to think in new ways about your relationship, and to commit yourself to the discipline it will take to shift your behavior. But each chapter is structured in a very practical, step-by-step way to guide you through setting and reaching the goals yourself.

By learning (probably *relearning*) these basic behaviors, and practicing them regularly (including sex!), you will find you and your spouse in a far better place—more grounded, happier, and having a lot more fun together!

Good #1: Take Ownership of Your Uglies

15

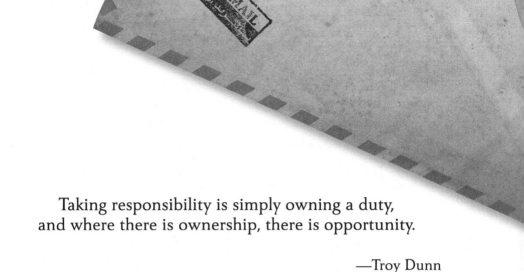

Taking responsibility is simply owning a duty,
and where there is ownership, there is opportunity.

—Troy Dunn

I'll never forget that Oklahoma day in the fall of 1983 when I arrived at high school in my first car, which was a used but incredibly cool Chevy Malibu, painted black with eye-popping seat covers, chrome wheels, and a great-sounding stereo system. It wasn't new, not even close—heck it was older than I was! But as I drove slowly through the parking lot seeking the perfect spot to park her, my head faced forward but my dark sunglasses hid the fact that my eyes were darting back and forth to see who was noticing it was me driving this cool car! I was very proud of it.

Opening my locker later, I overheard a couple of my buddies asking each other whose black Malibu was parked out front. I spun around eagerly and said, feeling like a million bucks, "That's mine!"

A cool car is one thing, but it's a lot more difficult to spin around and say "It's mine" when what you're taking ownership of doesn't make you proud but instead ashamed, sometimes *very* ashamed. However, it is in those moments, the ones in which we "own the ugly," where we change our own life and the lives of those around us.

As I've told you earlier, my father was an alcoholic. I didn't know that term as a child growing up, and it certainly doesn't define in my mind who he was or what he represented. He was a loving man who adored his family and made huge sacrifices for us. But he did battle "the drink" for many years.

Some of my saddest memories of my parents fighting were during his drinking years. I was very young then and don't remember much about his slow descent into that dark hole of alcoholism, nor all of the suffering it triggered, but I remember enough. And I certainly remember what I call the grand finale.

Dad came home drunk one time too many and Mom simply said, "That's it." She had threatened to "take the kids and leave" many times when Dad's drinking got out of hand and would pile us in the car. But always, after tearing out of the driveway and driving around for a couple of hours until we fell asleep in the car, she would wake us and we would be parked back in our driveway. My Dad would come out and carry my sleepy brother and sister up the steps and into the house. It would be over . . . until the next time.

But this night was different. Mom didn't shout at Dad or talk to us with gritted teeth about him. She just said to me (I was the oldest at 13), "Troy, honey, it's time to go." And go we did. That night, she gathered the three of us kids and loaded us and the luggage into a waiting taxi. We boarded a plane out of Alaska and flew into Portland, Oregon, where we settled into a little rental house—just mom, my brother, sister, and me. There was no bluff this time. There was no circling the block. She had actually done it. She'd taken us and moved hundreds of miles away from Dad.

I kept thinking he would follow us in a day or two, or that we'd all pile back onto the plane and go home. But with every item Mom unpacked into that rental house, it became clearer and clearer this was now home. It was strange to be there without Dad in the house. It was a very conflicted time for me because I both missed him and was so proud of my mother for finally taking a stand and rescuing herself (and us) from a bad situation. My father was an amazing man with a heart of gold, but alcohol had become more important to him than us, his wife and family. That my mother was having none of it anymore made me proud and so sad all in the same moment.

Weeks went by, and it was as if Dad didn't exist. Other than a family photo on a shelf, there was no evidence in the house we even had a father. There was a gaping hole in our home, and all of us kids felt it.

Then one day, about two months later, I came home from school to see Dad's truck in the driveway, and he was sitting out on the front step, waiting. I was elated! I ran with tears in my eyes right into his arms. As I hugged him, I saw Mom in the front window looking out at us, and she was smiling. I knew then that something good was happening. Dad asked me if I'd like to go for a ride and get some ice cream, and I said, "Sure."

So we climbed into his truck and as we drove, Dad did something I'd never seen him do before. Heck, I didn't even know what it was, really. He began to take ownership, to take responsibility for every single negative event that had occurred in the recent memory of our family. He started with, "Do you remember the night I didn't come home and you and Mom went out looking for me, thinking I had been in an accident?" Of course I remembered. Mom had cried her eyes out thinking Dad was dead, and we'd gone looking for him and found his truck parked in front of a bar and him inside.

He said, "That was my fault, and I'm sorry for that. Your mother did nothing wrong, and neither did you kids." He then went to the next negative memory, and then the next and many more after that. I sat in stunned silence just looking at him, listening and nodding my head. I had never seen my father like this. He was so calm, tender, and humble. As he talked, tears were streaming down his cheeks. Each of his stories ended with the same words: "That was my fault, and I'm so sorry."

He must have said that 30 times in that two-hour ride around town.

I don't know why, but as he spoke I felt myself wanting to cry, too. I fought back my tears for as long as possible until I eventually interrupted him and burst into sobs, saying, "I love you, Dad." He stopped the truck immediately and turned and hugged me for a long time. I will never forget that embrace or the way I felt that day in Dad's truck, when everything changed for our family.

I would later learn that Dad had gone to Alcoholics Anonymous and dedicated himself to sobriety after Mom left with us. He didn't race after us, because he knew he was the cause of our leaving and he wanted to make things right before resurfacing in our lives.

The result was nothing short of a miracle. I had resigned myself to the idea that our family was broken beyond repair. I was already thinking ahead to how hard Christmas would be without my father, and the fact that I was going to have to be "the man of the house" was just starting to settle on me like a truckload of boulders. And suddenly, it was like I'd woken up from a bad dream.

You know the huge feeling of relief that washes over you when you open your eyes in the morning and realize that the nightmare you were living isn't real? That's exactly how I felt! I couldn't believe things could go from so bad to so good in an instant. My whole worldview changed. It sounds silly, but truly, everything looked and felt differently as I realized my family was back together. Colors seemed brighter, birds seemed to whistle louder, jokes were funnier, and I felt happier than I think I had ever felt. I never saw my father drunk again. And as far as I know, he never had another drink in his life.

That day in Dad's truck was my first experience watching someone truly taking full and complete ownership of his mistakes, without any excuses and without assigning any blame. He could have mentioned some of the hateful things my mother said to him when he was drunk, or he could have insinuated that it was somehow her fault, that she drove him to drinking, but he didn't. He "owned the ugly." He just stood up, put his big boy pants on, and took ownership of the worst thing to ever invade our home—alcoholism.

His decision brought more change to our family than I ever thought possible. Gone were the fears of unpredictable rage or listening to Mom on the phone calling around looking for him. Suddenly, laughter echoed throughout our home. There was plenty of weekend time together as a family, more trips to putt-putt golf and the movies. We were a family without alcohol as an unwelcome member. If you, or someone you love, has lived with this demon and went on to defeat it, you know what I'm saying. It was fantastic.

Sole Proprietorship: It's on You!

My father's turnaround is a dramatic example of what happens when someone is willing to look in the mirror and assume responsibility for his own ugly. (I hope you know that by "ugly," I'm not referring to your looks but to behaviors that you would rather not talk about.) Personal accountability takes a lot of humility and a lot of courage. And that's why so many people don't do it!

It's human nature to look for the easy way out. Let's say you're trying on pants in the dressing room of your favorite clothing store (something which I *loathe* myself) and they are way too tight where they shouldn't be. You shake your head that the designer is so off the mark in his sizing and try on the next pair. But *this* manufacturer has also screwed up—the pants are cut way too tightly! What's going on with these people? Finally, after you've tried on half a dozen pairs of pants, all of which are sized "wrong," it begins to sink in that maybe it's not the designers that are cutting their pants too skimpily; maybe it's that your own "sizing" is wrong—you need bigger pants! Guess what? You need to accept responsibility for the fact that unless someone is force-feeding you potato chips and ice cream while you sleep, what you see in the mirror is a result of nobody's choices but your own. You have to own your own uglies.

It is no different in your relationship. If you want to fix what's wrong in your marriage, you have to look in the mirror with the same honesty and take responsibility for your own role in the resentment, acrimony, and distrust between you and your spouse. If you don't, your relationship will fall victim to the uglies that you try to push off on others.

If you start a business, the Internal Revenue Service (IRS) asks you to name the type of business you're forming. They need know who will be responsible for the taxes. The first choice is a sole proprietorship, which means that you alone are responsible for taxes. The buck stops with you.

This is a helpful way to view your role in your relationship. While you can be a partner in your relationship and share responsibility for what you and your partner do together, when it comes to your own bad behavior and its consequences, it is your name on the tax bill, and you're the one who has to write the check.

Unfortunately, when you're in the heat of an argument, when taking responsibility for what you've done wrong would be most productive, it's a lot more tempting to hand off the ugly side of your behavior to your partner, close your eyes, shut down your conscience, and hope that he or she will pay for it.

But what if you take a different route, a route that allows you to embrace the power of owning your uglies?

What About *Your* Uglies?

What would it feel like if you could find the courage to take responsibility for the mistakes you have made in your marriage, take a deep breath, and say "I'm sorry"? I can tell you. It will feel wonderful. When you and your spouse disagree, and you assume your share of the blame for whatever happened and don't try to push everything off on him, amazing things happen. You will feel a deep shift as you let your guard down and relax into the truth of what just happened. The first few times you try this will feel very strange, as if you're in a new, unknown place. And your partner, stunned by this new honesty, might jump in and take advantage of the situation, agreeing vehemently that yes, you really screwed up and that yes, you're totally, completely wrong.

But being consistently honest and taking responsibility for your mistakes will have a slow, steady healing effect on your spouse as time goes on. Almost always, he or she will begin to respond in a healthier way.

Let's say your mother-in-law is a major buttinsky, subtly criticizing your mothering skills. One evening she's over for your husband's birthday dinner and makes a crack about how long your daughter's hair is—"Maybe I could take you for a haircut, dear, since your mom's obviously too busy."

You suddenly have had it. You completely lose your temper at the table, tell your mother-in-law that you're sick and tired of her interference, catalog all the ways she's undermined you over the years, and in a final flourish, remind her that it's not like she did such a great job mothering judging by her deadbeat, two-time-divorced daughter.

When you finish your flare-up, there is an astounding silence at the table. Then your daughter starts to cry and runs upstairs. Your mother-in-law gets up and follows her, and you, your husband, father-in-law, and your two other children sit like statues looking down at their plates.

You get up and start to clear the table, and your husband follows you into the kitchen and says you have no right to speak to his mother that way. He's furious.

You've got a choice. The fact is, you're right: your mother-in-law has been out of line for a long time in criticizing your parenting. Also, it's your opinion that your husband hasn't stood up to her on your behalf. So you could feel well within your rights in finally letting her have it.

However, by losing your temper at the table, you upset a lot of people besides your mother-in-law, including your children who adore her. And while it felt great to let out all your stored-up feelings, it's not as if yelling at her in front of everyone is going to induce her to change her behavior.

So, do you defend yourself to your husband? Do you tell him he has no right to be angry at *you*, pointing out that his mother is a first-class b****, and it's *his* fault that you lost your temper because he never stands up to her for you? After all, *someone* has to stop her.

Or do you say, "Look, let's talk later when everyone's gone home."

And when that time comes, do you say, "Listen, she drives me crazy, and I do think her crack about Maggie's hair was way out of line, but I should have never lost my temper that way. It wasn't fair to you and the kids. I'm really sorry I acted the way I did and wrecked your birthday dinner."

If you choose the latter, you open a window into healing. Firstly, you're acknowledging that it's not your husband's fault that you lost your temper.

Your loss of control is on *you*. Secondly, you're apologizing for the unfair consequences of your outburst, wrecking your husband's special day with his family. And thirdly, you're giving your husband room to step in and acknowledge his part in what happened. When you have the courage to be honest, it's more likely that he will, too. He may agree that his mother has been too hard on you and that she should back off. You might actually have a conversation about how to make that happen.

The two of you, instead of each nursing your hurts—your belief that your husband favors his mother over you; his belief that you're unfairly blaming him for your terrible temper—surprisingly feel *closer*. Together, you can begin to solve the problem of your mother-in-law.

This is the great gift that comes from owning your uglies.

Sorting Out the Uglies

I worked with a couple who we'll refer to as Ralph and Suzanne. Within minutes of meeting them, I knew what the problem was: his temper. He was belligerent about how much he didn't want to be here, didn't think he *had* to be here, didn't believe in counseling, it was a waste of time, and every other excuse imaginable.

"So why did you agree to come?" I asked.

"Because *she* made me," he growled, glaring at his wife, who seemed completely intimidated and looked at me, her eyes as big as saucers, as if I was her last hope.

She told me about an incident the previous week when they'd argued over a vacation she wanted to take to her mother and stepfather's house in Florida, and how he had slammed the bedroom door so hard he'd split the door frame.

"I hate how he yells," she said in a meek voice.

"You know I can't stand your mother's husband," he said in a loud voice. "The last time we were there, he kept making fun of me and laughing in my face. Why did you even bring it up? I think you just like to upset me."

He looked at me for confirmation, but if you'll remember from earlier in the book, I am a firm believer that there are three sides to every story— his, hers, and the in between, which is usually the truth. So I don't take a side until I have heard all three versions.

"And you had to break the door down, too?" she interjected in a soft voice.

"It's your g**d*** fault, Suzanne! You drive me crazy." Now he was almost bellowing.

If this guy was so out of control in front of me, I could only imagine what he was like at home. Their relationship was completely run by his temper, and she tiptoed around him like a scared rabbit. I wondered if he had ever been physically abusive to her.

When I asked him, he was taken aback by my question.

"No," he said, his voice suddenly toned down. "I would never do that s***."

A quick glance at his wife confirmed that he was telling the truth.

So that information, combined with the fact that he did show up, offered hope that somewhere in his bullying heart there might be a glimmer of self-awareness.

In truth, both Ralph and Suzanne were perfect examples of the problems that come up when you don't take responsibility for your behavior.

I had zero sympathy for Ralph, bashing his way through his relationship, refusing to acknowledge that his bullying was way out of line. But Suzanne, by not standing up for herself, wasn't helping things either.

It took a few visits to dial down Ralph's noise level and as many tissues as I had for Suzanne to wipe the constant flow of tears that rolled down her cheeks, but they finally began listening to each other in a neutral atmosphere.

Then I talked them through owning their uglies.

To his credit, Ralph listened carefully when I told him the damage his temper was doing to his relationship and to himself, which made me believe that deep down he knew his behavior was wrong and he wasn't happy with the way he acted. But even though Suzanne was the one who had pushed for counseling, she was less pleased with what I had to say.

She hated the terrible fights she and Ralph had, but when he began to control his temper, she realized that she had to learn to stand up for herself better. This represented a challenge for her, because her husband's outbursts had saved her from having to face her own contribution to their dysfunction. She had always believed (and perhaps rightfully so) that she was unable to defend herself or even get a word or opinion in because his raging outbursts left no room for discussion. But when he stopped taking all the air out of the room, she realized she could no longer justify her silence. The microphone was now hers.

That they were both able to admit that they'd thrown their relationship out of whack by not taking responsibility for their behavior—he for his bullying temper and her for not standing up for herself—was a credit to them. Next, under my guidance they began the harder work of putting what they'd learned into action. When they disagreed and Ralph's voice rose, Suzanne learned to overcome her fear and tell him that if he wanted to speak to her, he had to control himself. And then he had to take a breath, calm down, and rephrase what he was saying in a way she could hear. They began to communicate more rationally, hear each other more clearly, which gradually meant they had fewer blowups. These changes didn't happen overnight, but over several months, as they both stepped into these new, healthier roles, they started to see the benefits—less acrimony, more pleasure in each other's company, a calmer home life. That's the benefit of these kinds of changes—slow but steady improvement that lasts.

About six months after we'd worked together, they video-chatted me one afternoon to update me and to say thanks. It was a surreal experience watching these two acting like newlyweds, and *she* did most of the talking. I loved it! To see a long-married couple become closer as a result of owning their uglies was a good day for me.

Owning the Ugly with Your Kids, Too

You are stretched out on your recliner in your den, exhausted after a terrible day at work, and the traffic on the way home didn't exactly improve your mood. Suddenly your young son races through the den making a loud engine sound for the imaginary car he's driving. There was a time when your reaction would have been to hop up out of your chair and chase after him with your own "vroom-vroom" sounds as the two of you raced around the living room. But today as your little boy zooms past you, your reaction is to grab him by the arm and bark, "Why do you always make so much noise? Stop running around screaming all the time! Go to your room!"

Shocked and horrified, your son retreats to his bedroom in tears. He throws himself onto his bed and wails into his pillow, having no idea why you did what you did. As you lean back in your recliner contemplating what just went down, you know you overreacted. You also know you should apologize, but it's really the last thing you want to do. Instead, you think to yourself, "He *was* making lots of noise, and I deserve to come home at the end of a hard day to a peaceful home!"

See what's happening here? Feeling guilty, you shift some of the blame for what just happened onto your son, who was doing nothing out of the ordinary. Now you have essentially stolen some of his childhood by impressing upon him the idea that normal childlike play is actually wrong, and he's going to alter the way he plays in the future. Gone will be the sweet sounds of a pretend race car and the playful giggles of a boy enjoying a simple childhood moment. Instead, he will tread lightly in your presence, afraid of enraging his seemingly unpredictable, grouchy parent.

Is that the result you wanted when you yelled at your little boy? Of course not! So you shift back, own the consequences of what you did, get out of your chair, march right into your son's bedroom, scoop him into your arms, and take responsibility for your actions, your ugly. You say something like, "Son, I am so sorry for yelling at you. You did nothing wrong. I love the pretend race car you drive around here. I had a rough day at work and I'm tired, but that's not your fault and I shouldn't have yelled at you. Please forgive me? Now let's go race! Vrooooom, vrooooom!" You've righted a wrong, and your son's respect and love for you grew a little more.

Taking Ownership

Shifting responsibility in your relationship to let yourself off the hook can be very subtle. If you've been doing it for a long time, you might not even be aware of how you've slipped into the bad habit of not owning up for something you've done. Below is an exercise that can help you change the way you handle disagreements with your partner or family members so that you can take more responsibility for something you do.

Think about your own habits, your own issues. It might help to start small—for instance, admitting that you're the one who finished off the milk, because the person who polishes off the milk is supposed to buy more and you forgot.

Then move on to deeper things. How often do you not acknowledge responsibility for your insecurity, disloyalty, unwillingness to forgive, or sense of martyrdom when it causes trouble in your relationship? Select one thing you know you do as you complete the following sentence:

I need to take full responsibility and ownership of _____ .

Now think of who would be touched and healed if you took owner-ship of what you did. This could be your partner, your child, someone else in your family, or a friend. Enter the name of the appropriate person (or names, if there's more than one) as you complete the following sentence:

_____ *should hear me take full*

ownership of this.

Now let's take a giant leap in personal growth and commit to doing it—apologizing to whomever you wronged and admitting what you did. This should happen sooner than later. Write down the date and the location you will do this in the blanks below.

I will tell these people on _____ *at* _____ *that I own it without any undertones of blame to other people or circumstances.*

Now go do it! Be the humble hero in the lives of others. Bring about instant change in your life and the lives of those you love. Remember that taking ownership is the first step. The second step is to explain how you are changing your behavior so this issue goes away. And the final step is to actually change that behavior. I am inspired to do this because of my father, and if you have a mentor who inspires you, let the thought of that person help you.

If no one comes to mind, I urge you to seek someone whose input you value and whose life you want to emulate in some capacity. Ask for truthful feedback, opinions, and insight as you move forward until you have established a pattern of doing things in alignment with your mentor's own actions and thoughts.

I want to conclude this chapter by stating that when it comes to taking responsibility for our actions, I'm talking to myself as well as you. I don't profess to have perfected each of these tools and skills in my own role as a husband and parent. I, too, try to stay on top of my uglies, checking to be sure that I am indeed walking the walk and keeping it real in my own life. Not all of the things we talk about here come automatically. But they are all doable, and you really can build a better, happier life for yourself and the people you love when you consistently work to own your uglies. We all have them. Let's not let them get the upper hand.

Good #2: Let in Forgiveness

16

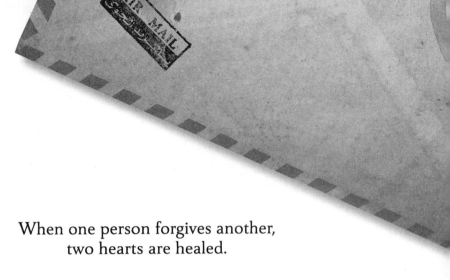

When one person forgives another,
two hearts are healed.

—Troy Dunn

Choosing forgiveness—both asking for it and receiving it—stabilizes and enriches a marriage like nothing else. If there is one thing you can do to cut through the silences and distrust in your relationship and heal wounds, create intimacy, and rekindle love between you, it is to practice the art of forgiveness. Like owning your uglies, practicing forgiveness opens the doors to trust and builds and strengthens your connection to your partner.

When you can forgive the insults and wounds that you've inflicted on each other (that *all couples* in long-term relationships inflict on each other), amazing things happen. First, there is an instant sense of relief when you and your partner have resolved a problem. It's not as if you've forgotten what made you both so angry and hurt, but you've agreed not to let it keep you apart. You can put your hands back on the steering wheel of your own life, and that life includes a new feeling of warmth toward your spouse and family. You see that you've made a brave new investment in your relationship.

The second thing that happens is not as instantly dramatic but just as definite. A healing begins. Notice I said "begins." When my son Trevin falls and scrapes his shin, I wash it and place a little ointment on it along with a bandage. He immediately wipes his last tear and runs off to continue playing. Now, I didn't erase the scrape; I just treated it and set it on the course to recovery. Left untreated, it could have become infected and gotten worse. But now it won't. When you engage in the action of forgiveness, you, too, are triggering the healing process that, over time, makes things better. Forgiveness is the ointment that heals emotional wounds and allows for couples, entire families even, to return to the joys of life with no long-term suffering.

Not only is the damage repaired after you forgive your partner, but your relationship gets even stronger than it was before. By choosing true, honest-to-goodness forgiveness, you will find you treat each other with renewed trust. Your feelings for each other grow deeper and more intimate. I always get very excited when I can watch two people rediscover each other in this way because I know what the future holds for them. It makes me feel like I have the best job in the world. (Well, second only to Santa Claus, of course. He's got the best job.)

Does this all sound foreign and impossible to you? Can you not even imagine being in this place with your partner? Then it's likely that you need to learn about the power of forgiveness more than anyone!

Is it hard to forgive? Of course! It is the opposite of many behaviors that may be deeply entrenched—pride, blame, keeping score. If you're like many people in troubled relationships, you may have gotten used to protecting yourself from your spouse, maybe even nursing the hurts and wounds she's inflicted on you. You might in fact be proud of the way you have taken her insults and buried them, not letting them "get" to you.

But where has this gotten you? When you wake up in the morning, do you feel a sense of ease and well-being, or are you already mentally slipping on your bulletproof vest to take whatever your partner throws your way? If it's the latter, wouldn't you like to be able to relax, knowing that you and your partner are allies and will look out for each other?

This is what can happen if you can learn to practice forgiveness, humility, and saying, "I'm sorry." You will not regret it.

Forgiving is not the same as forgetting. "Forgive and forget" is such common advice that it might surprise you to know that it doesn't work. It isn't possible. In fact, note that I put the word "forget" in quotes, because I don't believe that once you forgive you ever actually forget. The human brain is very powerful, like a supercomputer, but unlike a computer, the brain has no "delete" key.

You will likely not forget harsh words spoken in anger, the betrayals and insults that you and your partner have exchanged—they are locked in your memory forever. They're always lurking, tempting you to pick at them like a scab, so that all the anger, pain, and ugliness will come flooding back into your mind, causing you to go backward in your healing.

But you *can* choose to banish them. You can consciously replace the painful memories of past wounds with thoughts of the happier present, of the kind and loving things your partner has done recently. You can learn not to bring up old hurts in your conversations with your partner or anyone else. You can resist pulling them out to use as a weapon in a new argument, or as another brick in your wall of martyrdom. Changing your behavior in these ways is doable. Forgetting isn't really an option, but choosing to put your problem behind you is a realistic goal.

And by moving your relationship toward forgiveness, it opens up untold opportunities for new beginnings.

And besides, what's the alternative? What happens if you hold on to all your resentments and anger and never try to introduce forgiveness into your marriage or relationship? What if you're doing this right now?

Let me tell you about what happened to my old car. (In fact, the same one I mentioned in the last chapter, the Chevy Malibu.)

One Saturday morning in the summer between my junior and senior year of high school, I was sitting at a red light, clicking through radio stations on my presets (yes, the buttons on our radios used to click—don't judge!), when all of a sudden I heard a sound that gave me chills: the screeching of tires very near me and then, in an instant, a loud crunch as my car shoved forward several feet. I had just been rear-ended! I climbed out of my car to discover the back of my car was bashed in so much that I couldn't open the trunk. Since the accident wasn't my fault, I got a check from the insurance company to cover the repair costs. But being a broke teenager, I kept the money instead of repairing the car and learned to live without my trunk.

At first I was uncomfortable driving around in my wrecked car. It was embarrassing. I felt like everyone was staring at the obvious damage and wondering why I would drive around in such a piece of junk. I went out of my way to drive alternative routes that helped me avoid friends' houses or the mall, and when I parked, it was always out of sight from other people. But after a while, I really didn't notice the damage anymore. I no longer gave it much thought and just kind of accepted it. It became my new normal.

Now, think about all the dings, scratches, and even smashed-up trunks in your relationship. Is there any unrepaired damage from the past, any emotional wounds left open because no forgiveness has occurred to speed the healing? Maybe at first you experienced feelings of awkwardness or discomfort, but over time, you've come to accept the damage as the "norm." The relationship works okay, but not as well, or as completely, as it did before. Does this ring true for you?

Well, my decision not to repair my car eventually came back to bite me. About a year later, I was driving in a rainstorm and suddenly I felt water filling my shoes! At first, I couldn't figure out what was going on because my windows were rolled up and there were no holes in the floor. Where was all the water coming from? I pulled over under a bridge to take a look at the car. And then I spotted it.

Back in the corner of my car where it had been hit, the bent body panel had rusted through and was now a gaping open hole. The splashing water from the puddles I was driving through was getting into my trunk and flowing along the floorboards to the driver's compartment, soaking my feet. Sure, I could live without the use of my trunk, but with this leak, my car was now vulnerable to further damage and unsafe to drive. I couldn't ignore the problem anymore.

Just like my car, damage in your relationship doesn't repair itself; in fact, it can spread and lead to new damage. Rust sets in and before you know it, you're taking on water. I had to take my car to a body shop and pay an enormous amount, way more than I'd received in insurance money, to fix my car. Don't let this happen to your relationship.

When the End Becomes the New Beginning

A remarkable example of allowing forgiveness in when a relationship is up against the wall came to me through an e-mail. I get hundreds, in some weeks thousands of e-mails asking for assistance in bringing two people back together. But this one was just the opposite. Mary and Tony wrote me as follows:

> We are not sure if you ever get letters asking for the best way to separate as opposed to reunite, but that's what we are asking you for help with. We have seen the number of people you have brought together, so we can only hope your experiences have also given you insight into the best way to dissolve a relationship. We have decided to get a divorce, but don't want to go to war in the process. We have three children who deserve to still have intact parents when this is over. Will you offer some suggestions for a peaceful closure of a different type?

This was a first for me—asking me to break up a relationship instead of fix it—but it certainly got my attention. Two people who were concerned enough about their life and children to want to end their relationship thoughtfully may just have enough fight left in them to actually save their relationship. I read on and learned of the events that brought them to this point. Mary was going to Alcoholics Anonymous meetings and had been sober for two years after nearly a decade of alcoholism. Her husband, Tony, had recently ended an affair he was having when the husband of his lover caught them in bed at her house one afternoon. After that horrible confrontation, made even worse because Tony knew her husband, the two broke off their affair. Between the two of them, Mary and Tony had created more trouble for themselves than two couples put together. They were furious with each other, and both just wanted to call it quits. They said it would be easier just to split up and share custody of their kids than to try and fix what was broken.

I agreed that on one level, divorce *would* be easier. They wouldn't have to wade through all the issues that had brought them to this impasse, and they wouldn't have to resolve anything between them if they lived apart. They could just go their separate ways.

On the other hand, all those problems they were choosing to ignore would surely resurface somehow, either in their co-parenting or in new relationships they would begin. So, I suggested while they were preparing for an amicable divorce, they should attempt to sort through some of this for the sake of their children, who were 8, 11, and 14.

Mary agreed and Tony was more reluctant, but since his own parents had divorced when he was young, he was persuaded to continue our talks for the sake of his three sons. They both came from troubled families, had married at a young age to escape those families, and they had very poor communication skills, with a lot of blaming, angry fights, insults, and long, hostile silences.

First, I helped them clean up the way they spoke to each other (by sharing with them the same tools you and I are working through in this book), which significantly reduced the tension between them. They began to listen to each other more carefully, and then, surprisingly enough, they began to say kinder things about each other. Mary, who had obviously learned a lot in her AA meetings, thanked her husband for putting up with her alcoholism for so many years. "I was a terrible drunk, and you took care of the kids," she told him. Tony, instead of agreeing with her about how awful she'd been, just said, "Thank you. You're welcome." He then took ownership of his selfish act of infidelity and asked for forgiveness, and Mary, very aware of her own flaws, gave it.

They asked to continue talking to me periodically over the next several weeks, during which time they used their new communication skills to sort through a lot of things they'd never discussed except during loud arguments. They began to experience some empathy for each other as each shared their insecurities, fears, even their dreams.

One afternoon I suggested it was time to discuss the best approach for telling their children they were divorcing. And then it happened, the moment I had secretly hoped and planned for. They looked at each other, then at me, and shook their heads.

"We were thinking we might give it another try," Tony said in a gruff voice. "For the kids, you know."

"And for us," Mary said to him.

The emotions in the room were so intense I felt like electricity was in the air around us. This couple was actually breaking through the dysfunction of their relationship and beginning to repair their marriage. Tears came to my eyes.

"That's great news," I said. "Your kids are lucky to have parents like you."

These two did a very brave thing—they forgave each other. They didn't take the easy way out, and now their lives are richer than they have ever been before. I told them that I had rarely seen a couple in so much trouble work so hard to stay together and that I admired them a great deal.

In truth, their family histories didn't exactly set them up for marital success. Just the opposite, in fact, as many of their problems were a reflection of what they had experienced within their given families. These deeply embedded behaviors are very hard to address and unlock. But for the sake of their children and, importantly, themselves, they chose to chart a new path.

Because their turnaround was so dramatic, I've made a point of keeping in touch with Tony and Mary, partly to just say hi and partly because I want to know how things are going. They regularly use many of the strategies I've written about in this book. It's not as if the past doesn't intrude—there's always the temptation, when they disagree or are tired or stressed, to dredge up old insults or wounds—but the more they practice forgiveness (and enjoy the results of their newfound companionship), the less often old hurts come up. And they especially work very hard to make sure they communicate regularly and resolve conflicts before they become serious. Their oldest son is about to go off to college, which makes them very proud, and their other two boys, who once had behavioral problems in school, are also doing well.

In fact, Mary told me they have even been approached by some of their friends asking them about their secret to a happy marriage! They both get a real laugh out when *that* happens, as it is a reminder as to how far they have come. And getting to that amazing point took a lot of courage, and a lot of forgiveness.

Asking for Forgiveness

Is your relationship in need of forgiveness? Do you have issues in your marriage that you've swept under the rug hoping they will disappear? Are you resentful, angry, and hurt, but feel too overwhelmed to talk about it? Do you feel bitterness toward your partner? Would you like to try to repair the hurts that have built up over time and corroded your relationship but don't know how? Practicing forgiveness could release a lot of the anger and frustration that are keeping you from a full, rich relationship. It's worth a try!

I've developed a four-step Forgiveness Recipe to help people find their way toward forgiveness. Asking for forgiveness is not easy, especially at first. You have to let go of your own pride in order to reach out to another person in humility, which can be difficult when you've never done it. Not only are you admitting that you screwed up, but you're opening yourself up to your partner, hoping she will love and trust you enough to forgive you so you can move on together. If your usual interaction with your partner is like two boxers circling each other in the ring, this takes a lot of courage.

And the same applies when your spouse asks *you* for forgiveness. You have to think about how difficult it is for her to ask you at all, and then make the brave decision to let go of how much you were hurt. Not easy.

The results, however, are awe-inspiring. In my work on *The Locator*, teaching people the art of forgiveness was the "secret sauce" in my recipe for successful reunions. It still is.

I developed the Forgiveness Recipe over the many years of my career to help people with very serious problems, a prime one being the number-one home wrecker—infidelity (see box on pg. 255). But no matter what resentments and anger you're holding on to, from forgetting an anniversary to selfish behavior to lying or deceit, these steps can lead you to forgiveness and resolution. The Forgiveness Recipe can mean the difference between a healthy, growing relationship and one that slowly corrodes and grinds to a halt.

The Forgiveness Recipe

This is a time-tested technique for seeking and giving forgiveness. Depending on the situation, you have either hurt the one you love the most, or he or she has hurt you. The recipe can be used either way, and I explain how as we go along.

Okay, you have done something wrong. You know it, your spouse definitely knows it, and it's hanging in the air between you like a dark rain cloud or, worse, a huge boulder. You've called your wife a fat cow in front of her skinny sister because she kept nagging at you to turn down the television. You've thrown away your husband's prized collection of car magazines that were piled in the den because you were so mad that he never helps you around the house. Or more seriously, you haven't kept to the budget you and your partner agreed on and now you've got some serious money problems. Or you told your mother about your husband's drinking problem after you promised not to because he's getting help. Now he's found out and he's hurt and feels betrayed.

Ingredient #1: Empathy

When you ask for forgiveness, you have to mean it. This is when you let go of your pride, your habit of rationalizing ("If you hadn't been so sarcastic, insulting, impatient," etc.), and begin to empathize with your partner. Look at the situation from his point of view. Did your husband total the car on purpose? And how did your calling him names for doing so make him feel? Or imagine how your wife felt when you called her a fat cow, and especially in front of her skinny sister. Humiliated, helpless, as if he or she was a complete loser. Is that how you want her to feel?

Put yourself in your partner's shoes and feel how sad and hurt he or she is. Whatever you did or said needs to wash over you with the same power it did to your partner. Let its destructive impact settle in on you. When you've done that, you're ready to apologize.

Tell her how sorry you are for what you've done. And be specific, as in, "I should not have called you such a cruel name, and especially not in front of your sister. It was mean and thoughtless, and I know I need to learn how to control my temper. I'm really, really sorry I hurt you."

If you're sincere—and she will know that right away by your tone and manner—she will listen carefully to what you say. Then it's your turn to listen to her.

Ingredient #2: Regret

When you've apologized, your partner needs time to let your words sink in. She's got to be able to replace her anger toward you with her feelings about your apology.

While she's doing that, this is a productive time for you, too, to think about your own behavior. Do you regret letting your temper flare, or calling names, or fighting in front of the children, or waiting so long to seek resolution? Taking time to inventory what you regret now can arm you for the next time you're about to do it again. Then you can respond differently. When you do this, you're not only helping the healing process; you're starting to modify your behavior.

If you are the partner who's being asked for forgiveness, and your spouse has apologized to you and you believe that he understands and is remorseful for hurting you, give yourself enough time to work through your feelings. Weigh your own anger against the sincerity of his words. It may not take long—you might be able to shrug off a minor slight—or it may take long indeed to accept his apology for something that really wounded you. Whatever your reaction, take the right amount of time to cleanse yourself of the toxic effect of what your partner did.

Ingredient #3: Asking for Forgiveness

When you feel your partner has had time to think about what you've said, or she tells you so, it's time for the next step.

Simply ask, "I'm so very sorry for what I've done. Will you forgive me?" You know she *can* forgive you; the question is, *will* she?

If she says, "Yes, I do," great! You will both feel a powerful emotion, which is the beginning of healing. Savor the moment when both of you have come together to repair the rift between you.

If she says, "Not yet," you have to accept that, say it's okay, and step back. Then continue to behave in a kind, patient manner until you feel you can try again.

If she says, "No, I don't," then you have to accept that, too. But if you feel you've apologized fully and are truly remorseful, ask why she doesn't forgive you and what you could do to have her reconsider. See what she says. If you've done something really hurtful, the process of asking for forgiveness and receiving it could take time. But stay with it and you will most likely receive your partner's forgiveness. If she truly will not forgive you, you will be calmed by the knowledge that you tried your very best to atone for what you did.

If you are the person being asked for forgiveness, you have a responsibility on the other side. Saying "yes," "not yet," or "no" should all reflect your serious consideration. If you feel you're not ready to forgive your spouse or if you won't forgive him, you should try to be clear with him and with yourself about why you're withholding forgiveness.

It's one thing if you're still reeling from whatever he did and need more time to adjust. Or if you don't think he's sincere in his apology, which you should tell him. But don't withhold forgiveness as a weapon or as a way to get back at him, as in, "I'll let you know when I'm ready to forgive you, but don't hold your breath." If he's trying to improve the way the two of you resolve conflict, you owe it to both of you to play fair yourself.

Ingredient #4: Moving Forward

Once you, the victim of the offense, have listened to your partner share his regret and ask for your forgiveness and you say yes, you've got to hold up your end of the bargain. Let's say your partner did something that you'd call a 4 on a scale of 1 to 10. It's not divorce material, but it was pretty lousy, like the example of calling you a fat cow. He's told you that he was way out of line, apologized for his bad temper, his rude remark, and especially for saying it in front of your sister. Even though your feelings were badly hurt, he's apologized sincerely and you know he wishes he could take back what he said. You thought about what he said, have gotten over your fury, so you agreed to forgive him.

But the next time your sister comes over, the memory of what happened starts swirling around again, and you can feel yourself getting angry. This is when you've got to take a deep breath and put those unconstructive feelings away. If it helps, remind yourself that he loves and respects you enough that he did the soul-searching necessary to apologize, that he wants to move forward with you. It's really hard to do this when you're used to carrying around your resentments like rocks in a sack on your back, but that is what accepting forgiveness means.

It does get easier with practice. If you continue to practice forgiveness, you will find you don't want to hold on to those hurts anymore. It's much better to move forward. You apologize to each other, patch things up, and are good to go. Being "good to go" means letting it go. For real. (Besides, the next time around it might be you who messes up, and you'll need forgiveness yourself!)

If you're the person asking for forgiveness and your spouse said she forgives you, you need to learn from your mistakes. Work on controlling your temper, slowing down your reaction time when something goes wrong or you get annoyed by something your partner has said. Promise yourself not to repeat your behavior.

The Other Big One: Infidelity

Infidelity is one of the most dangerous threats to a relationship, if not *the* most dangerous, so I applaud any couple who doesn't throw in the towel and works to climb out of the pain and chaos caused by an affair. In this, more serious Forgiveness Recipe, the first ingredient is called "Broken Heart" and is aimed at the person who had the affair. The broken heart I refer to is not the person who's been victimized by the affair but rather the offender.

If you've been unfaithful, you must get to a place where you are keenly aware of how much hurt and suffering you have brought to your partner. You need to own this ugly. You are not allowed to rationalize your behavior or blame it on your partner by saying you didn't have enough sex or that your relationship was terrible. The bottom line is that there is no justification for an affair and for hurting your partner so deeply.

When you truly allow the full scope of what you have done to your mate settle in to your heart, when you really look at the hurt in your partner's eyes, hear the devastation in her voice, your own heart will break into pieces. Let it. Let the full destructive impact of what you have done settle in on you. Then, feeling the weight of the damage you have inflicted, be open with your partner. Tell her how you feel; express the depth of your regret and your deep desire to repair what you have done. Make certain as you are owning this that you use the words "I" and "me," not "we" and "us." Do not make any attempt to share the blame with the one you have victimized with your personal choices. Do not ask for her forgiveness yet. Letting her know that you really understand the seriousness of what you have done will open a slight crack and hopefully begin the healing process.

The second ingredient in this Forgiveness Recipe is called "Grieving." When somebody close to you dies, grieving is one of the vital steps toward healing. It's natural and expected that you embrace your sorrow and feel the sadness of your loss. Yet there seems to be this mythical belief that the healing from a marital tragedy (that's what an affair is—a tragedy) is an event rather than a process. It is unreasonable to expect that an affair is something that can be fixed and healed in a single moment, a single statement of apology. Like any serious wound to the body that requires days, weeks, and sometimes months to heal, so does a tragic attack on a marriage require a healing process that can take significant time.

If you are the victim in an affair, allow yourself a reasonable grieving period. You know how much time you need to absorb the wounds you have suffered. For many I have spoken with, the feelings of loss are the same as the wrenching agony felt at the death of a loved one. The pain cuts deep and wide. You have to find the balance here between honoring your feelings and sensing when it's time to take a deep breath and move forward.

If you are the offender, you need to accept that this will take time to get through. Your unfaithfulness has critically undermined your partner's trust in you. If forgiveness is going to evolve so the marriage can climb up out of the grave you dug for it, time and an extended period of humility is required of you.

You can't rush this. If you're getting impatient, tempted to say things like, "Get over it. Let it go. It's been long enough. Move on," do not. You lost control of this situation when you cheated on your spouse. It is now your partner's decision *if* and when to move this relationship forward. Demanding to be forgiven is just a form of emotional abuse and could mean the end of your marriage and family.

The third ingredient, like before, is "Asking for Forgiveness." When your partner has had time to think about what you've said and believes that you really understand how much you hurt her, betrayed her trust, and are truly remorseful, it's time to ask for forgiveness. Keep it simple and sincere.

The final ingredient is, again, "Moving Forward." Once you, the victim of the offense, have listened to your partner share his regret and sincerely request forgiveness, and after you have had sufficient time to process it, you have a decision to make. If, despite what has occurred, you still believe in your spouse, love him, and want your family to live through this dark chapter, then you must arrive at a formal decision. The decision process starts with confirming in your own heart and mind that you are definitely willing to work through this damage and are prepared to stay in the marriage. The next step is to confirm it with your partner.

Your partner needs to understand that trust has been broken and must be re-earned. If he agrees to your terms and is as willing to work on moving forward as you are, then you let him know you are willing to forgive him and start the rebuilding process. From this moment on, the two of you make every effort to return your behavior and conversations to a normal place. It is a delicate time, and it can be difficult to maintain equilibrium when both of you are trying to move forward, but it can be done. I have seen it happen when two people are willing to reach deep into themselves and commit to trying again.

Use the Forgiveness Recipe

The more you use the Forgiveness Recipe in your relationship, the better your relationship will be. These four steps can nip quarrels and misunderstandings in the bud and lead you to a much healthier marriage.

I'm not suggesting that you and your spouse wander around asking for and receiving forgiveness as if you're at a Sunday prayer service all the time. Hardly. But a relationship grows much stronger and is much happier when each member of a couple recognizes and owns up to the mistakes they make, apologizes to each other, and asks for forgiveness. And the sooner you apologize and ask for forgiveness after you've done something wrong, the less your mistake will affect your relationship. Ideally, you and your partner will get used to timely apologies and forgiving each other. And you will find your relationship getting stronger and more loving with each passing day, resulting in fewer reasons to have to ask for forgiveness in the first place.

Asking for forgiveness is the icing on the cake, solid proof that you understand and regret how you have hurt your partner. And everyone knows that the icing is the best part of the cake.

Good #3: Sex:
The Great
Healer

17

Make love. It doesn't make itself!

—Troy Dunn

Wait a minute, Troy! Didn't you already talk about sex as a *roadblock* in relationships, how sexual problems mess up marriages and create misunderstandings and resentments? And now you're talking about it as a *good* thing, suggesting that by jumping into bed I can heal the rifts between me and my partner? What's up here?

Well, I understand your confusion over why I'm writing *two* chapters about sex, but there's a reason for my emphasis here. Yes, sex is a volatile area in many relationships, and in chapter 13 I outlined some of the most common bedroom troubles couples experience in their marriages.

But I also believe very strongly in the healing power of sex and it's power to do good. And I believe further that the act of making love can be a tool toward repairing a relationship and not just the pot of gold at the end of the rainbow, the final reward when you think you're back on track at last.

So, in this chapter I want to tell you about the good news that comes when you *do* have sex, even if you and your partner are having a hard time in other areas of your marriage. I want to persuade you that just as you've been learning how to change your behavior in other areas of this book, communicating in more positive ways with your spouse, reaching out to him or her in new ways to show your love, you can also learn to reintroduce sex into your relationship in a way that's loving and natural.

Like taking responsibility for your actions and learning to practice forgiveness, reintroducing sex into your relationship is a way to open up to your partner, to increase intimacy and encourage loving attitudes. If this is a completely foreign idea to you, if you think good sex can't happen if you and your spouse are in a tough place in your marriage, please take a moment to hear me out.

Sex in every manner, shape, and form is ever-present in our minds and culture. We can all agree on that. But what I rarely see or hear on television, in books, or on the Internet is what I know to be true—that sex delivers intimacy and pleasure and strengthens relationships in a way that almost nothing else can. When two people make love, they give each other tremendous pleasure. Trust and affection builds between them. Their warm feelings toward each other strengthen the bonds that connect them. The disagreements and obstacles in their marriage don't seem so significant anymore. Healing happens.

And if you can use it to rebuild your relationship, why wait?

You *can* reignite sexual feelings for your partner and choose to guide yourselves toward a new harmony at the same time that you're working on other problems in your relationship. Sex, in fact, can become a vital building block in repairing your marriage. Awkward at first? Of course. Rewarding? Enormously.

Start Up the Fire

It may seem odd to introduce sex by way of a winter camping trip, but that's where I learned a basic principle that has shaped my life, and one that I hope will help you and your spouse enjoy renewed sexual intimacy. It is the basic law of action and reaction.

As a young boy living in Alaska, I was a member of a Boy Scout troop. One January, we were on an annual campout properly named "The Freeze-a-ree." Yes, we were camping in Alaska in January. It seems nuts but was actually a lot of fun . . . for those who were well prepared.

I, however, was ill prepared. We had just moved to Alaska from Phoenix, Arizona (talk about culture shock!), and my parents had no clue how to equip me for the frigid cold. Other campers donned heavy down parkas; I was layered in cotton sweatshirts and thermal underwear. Bedtime arrived and the other kids climbed into their heavy-duty "tundra-tested" sleeping bags that would keep them warm to 50 below zero, while I wrapped myself like a mummy in the roll of bedding my mom had stripped off my bed as we were leaving the house.

Late at night, shivering and too bone-chilled to stay in the tent, I ventured to the campfire to thaw out, but when I got there, I gasped when I saw that the fire was no longer burning. One of the adults still sitting by the dying embers heard my gasp and asked what was wrong.

"I'm freezing and wanted to come out by the fire to warm up, but the fire is out," I replied. The scoutmaster said, "We're headed to bed, but if you want to restart the fire, go gather some wood and toss it in these smoldering coals. It'll start right back up."

"But I'm too cold!" I protested. He laughed and said, "Well, you have to build the fire before you can warm up, silly!"

I did, and I warmed up enough to survive that long, cold night. I also learned a lesson: life is a series of actions, followed by the results of those actions. If you fail to take certain actions, you will not get the results you want. But if you do take action, you *will* be rewarded.

Think of this in terms of your sex life. It is difficult to feel love if you don't make it, figuratively and literally. It's called "making love" because when sex is part of a committed relationship, the act of sex can conjure up feelings of love.

If your relationship is lacking intimacy, you can create it yourself. Truly. Just like I took steps to get the fire going at my campsite. Positive actions trigger positive results. Negative actions trigger negative results. It really is that simple.

So if the primary reason you and your partner are not making love is because you don't "feel like it," then gather up some firewood, light it up, and let the warmth envelop you! Don't be discouraged, and don't let pride, stubbornness, or awkwardness keep you from doing what needs to be done to repair your relationship.

Gender Jumble

A word here about the differences between men and women. It's never a good idea to generalize, but if we're going to talk about making love as a means to strengthening your relationship, let's at least address some commonly held beliefs about each gender's attitudes toward sex.

You may have heard the comedian Billy Crystal's line about men and women and sex: "Women need a reason; men just need a place."

So let's just say that even when there are problems in a relationship, men will usually be more likely to agree to sex than women. I say "usually" because there are exceptions to every rule—there are men who are reluctant to have sex when there is little emotional commitment. On the other side, while most women enjoy sex more when there is an emotional connection, there are a good number who like to have sex regardless of their feelings.

So when you are thinking of reintroducing sex into your lives, it helps to be mindful of these potential differences when talking to your partner.

If you are a woman and the idea of making love with your partner as a way to ease tensions between you makes sense, but you are more than a little reluctant at the thought of initiating sex with your spouse because of unresolved issues between the two of you, you will have to take a deep breath and commit yourself to trying to change. It will help to remember the good sex you've had in the past, no matter how long ago, the warm feelings that came from the intimacy, how pleasurable sex can be, and how nice it would be to feel that comfort again.

If you are a man, you need to be sensitive to your partner's feelings, be aware that you might need to build up to the invitation to sex by small kindnesses and thoughtful gestures—smiles, a touch on her shoulder or butt as you pass her, even a surprise bouquet of flowers—so that she feels more warmly toward you.

Talk Your Way Back into the Bedroom

Okay. You're open to the idea of trying to make love despite the challenges you're facing in your relationship. It's daunting, feels awkward, and you're more than a little afraid of rejection. What do you do? How do you bring up the topic?

Below are the steps that can lead to an invitation, a "yes" answer, and to lovemaking. Having said that, it's *very* important that you tailor these steps to your own situation. No one knows your partner better than you, and you need to proceed with tenderness and care to increase your chances for success.

Here are the steps you can take to activate your sex life. Let's call it "Operation ST"—Sex Tonight!

Step One: Get the Word Out

You want to let your partner know what you're thinking in one or all of the following ways. Talk about this new idea, the idea of making love as a way to improve things between you. Ask if your partner would be willing to try this out even though things haven't been great between you.

Or, depending upon how you relate to your partner, you may skip the explanation and just send a clear message, be it in person or by a call, a text, or a note on the steering wheel. If you're reaching out to your husband, you could say something like, "Sweetie [or honeybun or stud muffin or whatever tender pet name you might call your spouse], we haven't made love in quite a while and I miss you. I want you. Let's get the kids in bed quickly tonight and I'll meet you in our bed by 9:45. Come ready for an awesome massage!" Yes this is cheesy, yes it is not the way you normally speak to your spouse (or you might be having more sex!), and yes it is going to be awkward.

If you're a man inviting your wife to the bed, the aforementioned signs of affection will really help before you actually ask her if she'll make a bedroom date. Either way, know that if you haven't discussed the idea beforehand, your spouse may not be as receptive to your sudden proposal as you'd hoped. He or she might logically wonder what has gotten into you, what has changed, and be skeptical. If so, you can explain that you've got this new idea, that you think it's worth a try, so why not? Most likely, your partner will be curious and say yes. He or she has most likely been missing sex as much as you. You have planted the seed to bring it back into your life.

Step Two: Show Up!

Follow through with your suggested plan. Get the kids to bed fast, get yourself emotionally psyched up, and get to your bed! (Or wherever you have chosen Operation ST to take place.) Be enthusiastic, but understand this—it is going to be awkward. Set things up to be comfortable, relaxing, and a little spicy. You know best what you and your partner like. Thank your spouse for showing up. You'll both be a little nervous, but excited, too.

Step Three: It's Time!

Think back to what pleased you both when you were first discovering each other and try those things again. The fact that you're both willing to try will go a long way toward easing the path to intimacy. You both will likely feel awkward, but it will be a fun awkward in many aspects. You will be rediscovering one another and will have to learn to dance together again, but the pleasure will come.

Step Four: Linger

Afterward, be quiet and be close. Don't be quick to shift to opposite sides of the bed and get to sleep. Don't let the conversation suddenly turn to what things need to get done tomorrow, something that happened with one of the kids that day, or anything else. Just let the moment linger as long as possible. That silence and the close physical proximity will be the sound and feel of healing. Let it happen. The ice has been broken, the dry spell is over, and a new winning streak has begun!

Step Five: Rinse and Repeat!

Don't let more than a day or three pass by before you meet again in the bedroom. Sex needs to become a habit—a part of your life. You have to get used to it again. There isn't any *right* number here that defines how much sex to have. Just go for it—you will find out what works best for you, depending on your feelings of affection, your need for connection, and, of course, your son's baseball practice schedule. (Only half-kidding here!)

Look, the reality is that your intimacy might feel a bit forced at first. You have to work at rebuilding your connection. So do your best to make your time together special. Banish talk about your daughter's problems in school or the fact that the tree in the backyard needs to be taken down. Talk about yourselves. Remember together the time you made love in your mother's den and the dog started growling, or your amazing vacation in Puerto Rico before you had children. Retrieve your good memories.

Understand that you both might be a little gun-shy from perceived rejection, that you might be worried about opening yourselves up to each other. That's okay. The fact that you're trying to get through this together will carry you along as you rekindle the feelings you once had for each other. Hang in there, and you will get the results you want.

Making love isn't a cure-all for a marriage that's been in trouble, but it does an amazing job of blurring the edges of your unhappiness with each other, softening your feelings, reducing tension, and helping you put things back into perspective.

And after making love, you have a wonderful opportunity to begin to repair or grow your relationship. If this sex is coming in the form of "make-up sex," this is a grand time to apologize. But if this sex is simply an effort to bring your relationship back to the top of your priority list, or an effort to remind yourselves how much you love one another, then just acknowledge within yourself that sex is an important part of a healthy relationship, and that sometimes, *not* being in the mood is a good reason to have sex—to bring back that mood to your relationship, your life.

It's almost magical how words that previously fell on deaf ears suddenly ring with power and impact after a healthy lovemaking session. If you're not sure what to say in these moments, try something like, "I love *us* and want to work together to save this marriage," or, "I know the past few days/weeks/months haven't been what they could have been, but I know we can make it. I love you and I choose us." These are just suggestions; adapt them in your own words so whatever you say will have the most impact and the best chance to kindle affection between you. If you can say positive, kind words right after a successful lovemaking session, and mean them, you will open the path toward humble communication and gradual healing.

By the way, "successful" lovemaking means different things to different people. For some, the sheer fact there was sex at all is enough, especially after a long drought. That's success! For others, it may mean sex that was fulfilling, didn't feel demeaning or abusive in some way. Or that sex triggered positive thoughts about yourself and your spouse. The best way to define success is that you and your spouse are happy enough after your lovemaking that you want to do it again!

Sex can be a magic ingredient in your relationship. It is fulfilling, gives pleasure, and creates intimacy. Satisfying sex is one of the key markers for successful, long-term relationships. Unlike in the movies, great sex doesn't just happen. It takes imagination, kindness, tenderness—a sense of humor helps, too! If you find yourself long on enthusiasm but short on imagination, this would be a great time to get ideas and support by confiding in a close friend or sibling who you believe has a successful relationship. If the sheer thought of doing that completely creeps you out, then I'd suggest you go to your favorite Internet search engine and type in these exact words: "creative ideas for spicing up marriage." The results will astound you, and I am confident you will find some suggestions in those results that will make you laugh, maybe make you blush, but will definitely give you hope that you too can build—or rebuild—a beautiful and satisfying relationship by reigniting your sex life.

Good #4:
Creating Tools
to Succeed—
Putting Down
Your Weapons

18

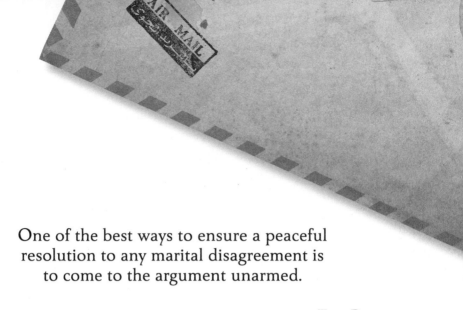

One of the best ways to ensure a peaceful resolution to any marital disagreement is to come to the argument unarmed.

—Troy Dunn

Even the most compatible couples have fights. Let's face it, you're never going to agree on everything. Nor should you—think how boring that would be if every time you had an opinion or made a choice to do something new and different, your partner echoed exactly what you said, felt, or did. Heck, it would be like being married to yourself, and who needs that!

But when you *do* get angry at your husband or wife, you don't have to resort to guerrilla warfare and the prospect of endless conflict. You can learn to resolve your disagreements peaceably by one simple switch.

Replace weapons with tools.

Weapons are retaliatory, like sarcasm, anger, blame, silence, or withdrawal. Their aim is to inflict harm, to punish your partner as much as he is hurting you. Success can feel jubilant but it's short-lived, mainly because your partner is responding to your weapons with his own. He inflicts just as much pain on you as you did on him, and each time, there is more hostility and the problems either stay the same or worsen. It's an endless cycle.

Tools are a different story. Tools comfort you and help you get answers so that the problem resolves itself. Communication, compassion, forgiveness, kindness, psychological help, and religious faith are examples of tools.

We all know what it's like when a fight brews. You and your husband can't agree on what kind of a car to buy, or you're upset that he won't stop smoking. He thinks you're too hard on your daughter's boyfriend, or keeps nagging you to stop buying so many holiday decorations each year—he says the basement looks like the Christmas tree shop.

When an argument looms or is underway, it's tempting to grab anything you can to fight back. In a troubled relationship, you go to your emotional closet, check your arsenal, and pull out the weapon you think will inflict the most distress on your partner—accusing your husband of being a spendthrift for wanting to buy such an expensive car, or telling your wife she's jealous of her daughter. The original disagreement gets lost as your fury and hurt feelings spiral into a real hate fest. Not only is the issue left unresolved, you're both even angrier than when the problem first came up.

But *tools* solve problems and strengthen relationships. The same differing points of view are there, but they are respected and discussed. Instead of attacking each other, you listen to each other and use your conversation to find a solution that you can both live with. You recognize that your husband has done his homework on the cars and that a bigger car does suit your family's needs, and he listens to your concerns about getting locked into a higher monthly car payment than you think you can afford. You together decide on a car that meets both your criteria. And not only do you get a new car; your relationship is stronger. You've worked through a problem and come out the other side, and there is more trust and respect between you than there was before. A win-win situation!

Here are some steps you can take to help you replace your weapons with tools.

1. Write a list of the weapons you use when fighting with your partner or other members of your family. These could include sarcasm, questioning motives, accusing, shouting, slamming doors, tossing pots and pans, or just walking away and refusing to talk.

2. Now write down tools—listening, trying to understand the other point of view, having a desire to come to a solution, kindness, forgiveness, taking responsibility for words spoken in anger.

3. Next, think of a recent argument you had with your partner and write a short synopsis of what the fight was about. Write down how each of you responded and then what happened.

An example . . .

The setting: in the kitchen cleaning up after a holiday dinner. Helen is standing over the sink, up to her elbows in dishwater, scrubbing the roasting pan, and her husband, Paul, comes into the kitchen to grab a beer.

"Another one?" she says sarcastically.

"No, Helen," he replies, equally sarcastically. "It's for your father."

"Nice that *someone* can enjoy the party," she says.

"I told you I'd help you later," Paul says, his voice angry. "You know I'm not wild about having your family here in the first place."

Slamming of pan as Helen lifts it to rinse it off. "Really? I never would have guessed. You were *so* kind when you teased my sister about taking a second piece of pie."

"C'mon, Helen. You're always going on about her weight yourself. You're such a hypocrite."

"*I'm* a hypocrite? You make fun of people's weight when your beer belly's so big I can't remember the last time I saw your belt."

"F*** you, Helen," he says in low, icy voice and walks out of the kitchen. Helen smiles.

So we have sarcasm, anger, cruelty, and withdrawal. Helen feels put upon, alone in the kitchen with her greasy pan, resentful that no one's helping her, wishing her husband was nicer to her family. Paul is in an equally dark space because a quick trip to the kitchen turned into a grudge match.

Now imagine the same encounter using tools instead. Helen would verbalize that it's depressing being alone in the kitchen; Paul could suggest she join them and he will help her clean up later. She says she wishes he hadn't teased her sister, and he apologizes—"You're right, teasing your sister isn't my job, it's yours," said with a smile. They leave the kitchen together and go back to the den to join the rest of the family.

Replacing weapons with tools is a simple way to effectively change the atmosphere in your family life. Every time you can behave this way, you are promoting harmony and respect and strengthening your relationship. Soon it will become a habit. Try it.

Good #5: Build Up Walls!

19

An example . . .

The setting: in the kitchen cleaning up after a holiday dinner. Helen is standing over the sink, up to her elbows in dishwater, scrubbing the roasting pan, and her husband, Paul, comes into the kitchen to grab a beer.

"Another one?" she says sarcastically.

"No, Helen," he replies, equally sarcastically. "It's for your father."

"Nice that *someone* can enjoy the party," she says.

"I told you I'd help you later," Paul says, his voice angry. "You know I'm not wild about having your family here in the first place."

Slamming of pan as Helen lifts it to rinse it off. "Really? I never would have guessed. You were *so* kind when you teased my sister about taking a second piece of pie."

"C'mon, Helen. You're always going on about her weight yourself. You're such a hypocrite."

"*I'm* a hypocrite? You make fun of people's weight when your beer belly's so big I can't remember the last time I saw your belt."

"F*** you, Helen," he says in low, icy voice and walks out of the kitchen. Helen smiles.

So we have sarcasm, anger, cruelty, and withdrawal. Helen feels put upon, alone in the kitchen with her greasy pan, resentful that no one's helping her, wishing her husband was nicer to her family. Paul is in an equally dark space because a quick trip to the kitchen turned into a grudge match.

Now imagine the same encounter using tools instead. Helen would verbalize that it's depressing being alone in the kitchen; Paul could suggest she join them and he will help her clean up later. She says she wishes he hadn't teased her sister, and he apologizes—"You're right, teasing your sister isn't my job, it's yours," said with a smile. They leave the kitchen together and go back to the den to join the rest of the family.

Replacing weapons with tools is a simple way to effectively change the atmosphere in your family life. Every time you can behave this way, you are promoting harmony and respect and strengthening your relationship. Soon it will become a habit. Try it.

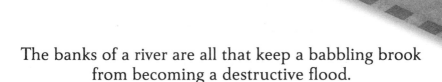

> The banks of a river are all that keep a babbling brook
> from becoming a destructive flood.
>
> —Troy Dunn

I spend most of my life and career helping people take down the walls in their lives so they can share intimacy and love with their partners and families. Healthy communication is essential to a vibrant and happy relationship.

But . . .

Building *up* walls is an important ingredient in strong relationships, too. It means that you know when to share and when to zip your lips. Too **much** talking can lead to unnecessary problems in your marriage, and building up walls will help you define limits.

Let's look at the *Titanic*. Despite all of the extraordinary engineering and forethought that went into the design and construction of the *Titanic* over a two-year period, once crisis struck, it took only two hours and forty minutes for it to sink.

The cause? Poor compartmentalizing. The hull of the ship was divided into "watertight compartments," as they were called by the engineers. But that was simply untrue. While the horizontal sections of each compartment could be thought of as watertight, the vertical walls did not go all the way to the top. When one compartment filled with water, it flowed over the top of the wall and into the next compartment. This spillover effect repeated itself until so many compartments were flooded and weighed down by incoming rushing water that they dragged the front end of the ship down until it snapped in half and sank to the bottom of the ocean.

In the same way, if you too easily let the negative emotions and effects of the different areas of your life spill over into each other, you're making trouble where there shouldn't be trouble, and perhaps even creating unnecessary risks to your marriage.

Give Your Partner the Gift of Compartmentalizing

Your own life has different compartments, including your personal feelings, your marriage, your role as a parent, your career, your physical health, and your finances. In each, there are ups and downs, rewards and disappointments, victories and defeats.

You wake up one morning after a horrible dream, feeling grumpy. Your daughter was caught stealing something out of a locker at school, you've got a sore throat, a report is due at work, there's a weird clicking noise in your car. These can all cause you various degrees of stress, especially if they all happen on the same day!

But when you keep the bad news in each of these areas separate from each other, you are giving those you love the gift of sparing them unnecessary problems. When something negative happens in one "compartment," and you don't let it spill into the other compartments of your life, you are keeping the bad news contained, where you can take care of it.

I'm not saying you shouldn't mention to your husband that you had a bad dream, or your worry about your daughter, your report, or your sore throat. Part of a partner's job is to comfort you when no one else can. But what I am suggesting is that you give thought before you automatically spill all your bad news into all the parts of your life. After all, what can your partner do about your work project except feel bad for you? And then he feels bad himself because he can't help you. If you keep your bad news to yourself, he and your children can go off to their days without the cloud of your troubles on top of their own. Your home life has just dodged a bullet.

Another good reason to practice compartmentalizing is to help you better understand your own behavior. When something bothers you and you don't blurt it out to your loved ones right away but instead try to figure out why you're so troubled, you can come upon clues to your reactions. A flip remark from a friend really bothers you, but instead of complaining about your friend to your husband, you spend a little time thinking about why you reacted so strongly and eventually realize her sarcasm is exactly the way your sister behaves toward you. That insight takes most of the heat from the encounter, calms you down, and no one has been bothered by it except you. End of story.

Holding back the bad news and keeping it where it belongs requires forethought and discipline, but there are a lot of payoffs. Firstly, you spare yourself and your loved ones unnecessary trouble. And secondly, when you keep bad news where it belongs and take care of it yourself when it's right to do so, you will find your loved ones more supportive when you *do* have troubles they can help you with. It's kind of like not crying wolf—they'll know it's serious and will be eager to ease your worry.

The best way to begin to build *up* the walls is to write down the different compartments of your life as described above and add any others that might be relevant: relationships with your partner, children, parents, friends; your home and work lives; hobbies and interests. Just writing them down so they are distinct from each other in your mind will help you identify how you spend your days. You can add additional compartments as things change in your life, but for now, just keep this list someplace where you can refer to it when you need to remind yourself to compartmentalize.

Walls or at least dividers should separate your numerous compartments. It may be an action or a thought. If your job is stressful and you walk in your home with that stress attached to you, then you need a divider between the office and home. Stop at the gym, take a walk, anything that will create a calm transition between compartments.

Another way to create a divider between compartments is to stay in the moment more often. If you are home, be home. As your child tells you about his exciting day, don't allow your mind to wander back to something that happened at work. Center yourself. Remind yourself this moment is important. Your children need you and deserve your respect. Listen to them and engage with them, right now.

Great tools for maintaining your life's compartments are simply a clock and a calendar. There is a time to discuss work, and there is a time to discuss family plans, just like there is a time to eat and a time to sleep. You wouldn't sleep at the dinner table, and you wouldn't wake the family for dinner at 3:00 a.m.

When our daughter, Josalin, was seven years old, we discovered she had cancer. It was devastating to hear a doctor tell us that news. Our heads were spinning, our hearts were crumbling, nothing else outside of the doctor's office even existed. We were just sitting in a dark hole called cancer. But when we had a follow-up appointment with the oncologist treating Josalin, he snapped us back into reality with these words: "Mr. and Mrs. Dunn, I have been treating children with cancer for many years and have been quite successful at it. But I have been unsuccessful at saving the marriages surrounding these ill children. Half of the parents with terminally ill children end up divorcing as a result of the stress and strain of life with cancer in it. They blame, they withdraw, they are too depressed to make love, they ignore each other while they care for their child. The other tragedy I have witnessed is the forgotten siblings. The healthy children are left at home while their sick sibling gets all of the attention and gifts. I cannot count the number of times I have greeted a sibling of one of my patients by saying, 'How are you,' and hear them reply, 'I wish I had cancer.'"

With those wise words, Jen and I embraced each other and began developing various rules for the compartments of our family so we could still manage our marriage and raise our other children while supporting Josalin in her battle against this horrific disease. Happily, she is now 16 and doing well, thank God.

When you realize you are not in a good place emotionally, and someone attempts to engage you in something that may not go well based on your current state of mind, acknowledge that and in the most humble and nonthreatening way possible, tell that to the person who is engaging you. It is far wiser to reschedule certain conversations than to engage in them at the wrong time.

Everything in your life does not have to be reactive and spontaneous. Regain some control of your life and increase the odds of better outcomes and results in all areas by placing some dividers in your life to keep compartments from flooding one another. Your relationship will be much stronger, and you will increase the odds of pleasure in your home. What's not to like?

Good #6: Walk a Straight Line

20

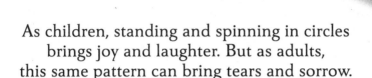

As children, standing and spinning in circles
brings joy and laughter. But as adults,
this same pattern can bring tears and sorrow.

—Troy Dunn

I've worked with a lot of couples eager to repair their marriages, but the ones who have the most staying power in creating new, more intimate relationships have learned how to shed their old patterns of behaving with each other and replace those patterns with a new, positive path for themselves.

It's the difference between walking in circles and walking a straight line.

It Feels Like a Straight Line . . .

I recently read about a series of fascinating experiments that sought to prove or disprove the theory that lost people walk in circles. Beginning in 2007, psychologist Jan Souman from the Max Planck Institute for Biological Cybernetics in Tübingen, Germany, placed study participants in various outdoor settings and asked them to walk in a straight line. In some of the experiments the subjects were blindfolded while in others they were not, and they walked in deserts, forests, or open fields, on cloudy, overcast days as well as sunny days and bright nights. Strapped onto all of them was a tracking device, similar to a GPS, allowing Souman and his colleagues to follow their paths. And almost everyone walked in circles.

The only ones who successfully were able to walk a straight line, in fact, were those who could see visual guides outside of their own senses, such as the sun, the mountains, a far-off radio tower, the moon, or other markers that they could use for orientation. The rest walked in circles!

One of the most interesting findings of the experiments to me was how surprised the participants were to find out they'd been walking in circles. They'd trusted their instincts to guide them in a straight line and couldn't believe how wrong they'd been.

This same instinct can trap couples into returning to old behaviors and getting restuck in patterns that got them into trouble in the first place. Old habits and emotional triggers lurk behind every change they try to make and pull them back into unproductive interactions. But when two people can keep their eyes on the goal of treating each other in more forgiving, caring ways, they can start walking on a straight line toward a much healthier relationship.

You might recognize that straight walking is somewhat similar to the steps to change that I discussed in chapter 4, including committing to change and making a "Ramp." But I bring it up here because straight walking is a very practical way to embed this behavior in the day-to-day workings of your marriage. Turning your relationship away from circle walking and becoming a straight walker is very rewarding for couples who are eager to repair their relationships but clueless about how they're sabotaging themselves.

Circle Walking Makes You Dizzy

Many times (most of the time!) people don't even know they're walking in circles but are very grateful when they learn to walk straight. An example was a couple I met on a business trip to the Midwest. Our meeting was very odd, arranged (or commandeered) by the executive who had hired me to make a keynote speech at his annual convention. In fact, I was not thrilled when, after I finished my speech and was heading for the airport, he asked me to meet his daughter. I hesitated, but as I was there on his dime and had a few hours before my plane left, I somewhat reluctantly agreed to visit his daughter's home.

When I got to her house, "Tina" and her husband, "Jeff," greeted me like an out-of-town relative they hadn't seen in years. A tight hug from her and a firm, rapid handshake from him coupled with a big smile made me more than uneasy, and I wondered why in the world I'd agreed to this meeting.

"We wanted you here to help us reunite with each other," Tina said. "We have seen how you fix those people on TV, and we want to know what you think we need to do because we are stuck. Broken."

Jeff chimed in, "I can't do this anymore."

I started to tell them that I wasn't a therapist or a priest, but Jeff interrupted me to say, "We don't need a therapist—got one. We don't need a priest—got one of them, too. We need the Locator."

By now I really wished I hadn't come. I was completely uncomfortable sitting in the living room with these two very intense people. But as I sat, looking across at them both staring hard at me, my discomfort was slowly replaced by the realization that these two people were deadly serious and borderline desperate about their marriage.

So I said, "Well, let me just ask you a few questions."

I proceeded to ask them the questions listed below. As they answered about their arguments, their goals, their role models, their choices, their long-term plans, one thing became crystal clear to me: they were circle walkers, endlessly repeating behavioral patterns that locked them into treating each other with a lack of respect and hurtful behaviors. Not only that, but nothing was resolved by their endless bickering and repetitions. They couldn't even agree on what color to paint their kitchen—they both hated the green color it was but went back and forth between yellow, her choice, and blue, the color he wanted.

I began to explain circle walking to them, pointing out how they repeated their fights. I explained that if they could commit to the larger goal of deciding what they both wanted in their marriage—to stay together, to fight less in front of their children, to have fun together like they did when they were first married—they had to set a new path for themselves and be alert to the circles that popped up in their relationship. As we talked, they started nodding and softly repeating "yes, yes, yes" to the things I was describing to them. By the end of our long conversation, they both had tears in their eyes, and I saw they had connected the dots. They now better understood why they felt stuck and how they could change. The breakthrough that I see when people are motivated to change had occurred for them. I asked them to let me know how things progressed as they converted from circle walkers to straight walkers. Then I dashed out of the house to catch my plane.

Family: The Good F-Word

285

I didn't give much thought to Tina and Jeff until, almost a year later, a card arrived at my office. When I opened it, there was nothing written inside other than a straight line drawn down the middle of the card and signed at the bottom, "Thank you. Tina and Jeff."

I would like to encourage you, in the same way I was able to help Tina and Jeff, to embrace the world of straight walkers. Below is a short questionnaire to set you on your way.

Circle the Answers

1. When you argue with your spouse, is it usually about the same two or three topics over and over (finances, sex, laziness, insecurities, bad habits, etc.)?
   Yes   No

2. When you two make love, is it usually the same general way, positions, places, time of day, frequency, etc.?
   Yes   No

3. When you discipline your children, is the type of discipline you use the same one or two punishments repeated over and over (time-outs, grounding, extra chores, etc.)?
   Yes   No

4. When you set goals for yourself (if you do), are they usually the same ones over and over because you failed at them in the past (weight loss, deciding to stop smoking, being more patient or more productive, etc.)?
   Yes   No

5. In your job or career, do you find yourself doing the same type of work for the same type of income without ever moving up the ladder in title, opportunity, or income?
   Yes   No

Getting Straight Answers

These five questions are a quick but accurate way to determine if you are walking in circles in any part of your life, or many parts of your life.

Answering "yes" to any of them is a good indication that you may be a circle walker, which is why you might feel that you're in a rut. You are in a rut!

Why does it matter if you walk in circles? Well, first of all you never get anywhere! The scenery of your marriage, job, and life never changes, and the same bad things keep happening. You lose hope. Secondly, you're shutting yourself off from being happier with yourself, your partner, your family. Walking out of your troubles and into a far more satisfying and pleasurable relationship is possible when you look up from the deep trough you've dug for yourself.

No one chooses to be a circle walker. The trait usually creeps up on people when they're not paying attention or when no one has given them guidance on how to move forward and resolve problems.

But when you become a straight walker, you can, like the successful participants in the study in Germany, get where you want to go if you create landmarks and goals for yourself. You can aim for change.

Look back at the five questions you just took in the circle walker test and revisit the ones where you circled "yes." These will be the areas you need to concentrate on.

Let's say you circled "yes" for the first question. This means you and your spouse may be walking in circles when it comes to your way of communicating and disagreeing. The most efficient way to learn how to stop going in circles in this area is to seek a role model in a couple who communicates well, who resolves their disagreements and moves on, a couple who walks straight. When you hang around with them, you will pick up important information on how to talk to your own partner. Try to think of a couple you know who seem to get along well, who treat each other with respect and kindness. Compare your own interactions with theirs. Are they supportive of each other in a way you and your partner are not? Do they seem to enjoy each other's company? Show physical signs of affection? Don't be shy—copy them! It might seem awkward at first, but taking new actions has a way of becoming habit.

If, however, among your friends and family you come up empty here, then you can create your own roadmap for change. Think of your last argument with your spouse and make a list of all the unproductive things you did. (Not what your partner did; what you did.) Choosing the wrong time to argue (too tired, after a glass or two of wine), name-calling, interrupting, not listening, shouting, and bringing up past arguments are all common. Then beside each of those things, write down its opposite. These include choosing the *right* time for a talk, which is when there is calm and the kids aren't around; refraining from name-calling or interrupting; *carefully* listening to what your spouse has to say so you can try to understand where he's coming from; keeping the conversation focused on the incident at hand; using phrases like, "I appreciate you listening to me," and, if you can say it truthfully, "Regardless of this issue, I love you very much."

Questions two through five deal respectively with sex, parenting, yourself, and your job. Answering "yes" to any means you're likely walking in circles and aren't able to break out into moving forward. For each question, again I ask you write down an example of what you have been doing the same way for a long time and next to it an example of what you would like to do instead. This becomes your straight-walking list of goals to aim for. The list makes it easy to identify a behavior you want to change and choose the one you want to replace it with.

Pick one and try it. Changing even one of your old ways of doing things or saying things will free you to step outside the circle.

What's exciting about this tool is that you can feel the dynamic changing as you speak. It's subtle, but in the pauses and thoughtfulness that come when you're approaching a tired pattern with new insight, you can sense the possibilities for change.

If you have been walking in circles for a long time, you have probably dug a deep rut that is unhappily all you know. You will feel resistance as you start, so don't be discouraged when it requires more than one attempt. Most importantly, remember that if you keep your eyes on your destination, every step forward is a step closer to a more fulfilling relationship and farther away from the old circle. Many before you have taken this path, so keep walking, keep walking, keep walking. You *will* get there if you do.

Conclusion

We've come to the end of the journey of guiding you to a stronger and happier family with the LCA Plan. The plan, based on so many years of my experiences with so many different people, is both practical and, I hope, inspirational. It gives you the tools and, just as importantly, the belief that you can improve your life and the lives of those closest to you by following a slow, steady path to change.

Change is never easy. It takes commitment, discipline, motivation, faith, and maybe even a little luck. But the rewards of identifying a better life for yourself and taking the necessary steps to get there are rich and long lasting. I've seen so many families take these steps together and be, in a way, reborn by their new commitment and love for each other. It is from their deep well of strength and courage that I drew my passion to write this book in the hope that others could do what they have done.

I hope you have found these pages useful and that you are encouraged and willing to continue making changes in your life. It is never too late to embrace new tools and new thinking to strengthen your relationship, improve your parenting, and fulfill goals for yourself. This book can be a perpetual resource for you, and so can the notes you've taken to help you on your journey.

My belief in the power of families continues to grow and informs everything I do. If you have caught my enthusiasm and are newly grateful for the family you founded and now nurture, then I'm doing my job.

If you would like to continue your work with your family, you can go to a website I've created for the readers of this book. TroyDunnBooks.com will be a place for those of you who want additional tools or would like to interact with other readers, swap ideas, and share with me your successes or failures. I'll be there often, as will my wife, Jennifer, so come hang out with us if you've got a minute. You can also find me at facebook.com/troythelocator.

After successfully reuniting a family on *The Locator*, I walked away as soon as I could because I wanted to give each newly repaired family their privacy. My work was done, and it was time for my former clients to begin their own journey together. So it is with this book. I have shared with you what I've learned from my many years of work fixing families. I have introduced you to the LCA Plan, which I designed to encourage people to make the changes they yearn for. Now it is your turn to go forward.

Thank you for your belief that you can make a difference. I wish you all the joy and love that a strong and healthy family can bring, and I leave you with my last three action items.

Be faithful to the one you're with.
Be patient with the one you're raising.
Be forgiving of the one in the mirror.

God bless.

Sources

Chapter 1:

"Family Structure and Children Living Arrangements," ChildStats.gov, accessed October 29, 2013, http://www.childstats.gov/americaschildren/famsoc1.asp.

"Are We Happy Yet? Marriage Trumps Parenting as a Predictor of Happiness," Pew Research Social and Demographic Trends, accessed October 29, 2013, http://www.pewsocialtrends.org/2006/02/13/are-we-happy-yet/21-3/.

"Marriage May Make People Happier," *Michigan State University Today,* accessed October 29, 2013, http://msutoday.msu.edu/news/2012/marriage-may-make-people-happier.

Chapter 11:

"Myth," www.merriam-webster.com, accessed October 2, 2013, http://www.merriam-webster.com/dictionary/myth.

Chapter 12:

Stephanie Jacques, "Researcher finds correlation between financial arguments, decreased relationship satisfaction," Kansas State University News and Editorial Services, accessed October 31, 2013, http://www.k-state.edu/media/newsreleases/jul13/predictingdivorce71113.html.

Chapter 13:

Kathleen Doheny, "10 Surprising Health Benefits of Sex," WebMD, accessed October 17, 2013, http://www.webmd.com/sex-relationships/guide/sex-and-health.

Pew Internet and American Life Project, Pew Research Center, July 25–28, 2013, accessed October 17, 2013.

Chapter 13 (*continued*):

TopTenREVIEWS, *Tech Media Network*, 2013, accessed October 17, 2013.

Chapter 14:

"Children whose parents smoked are twice as likely to begin smoking between 13 and 21," *MNT*, accessed November 18, 2013, http://www.medicalnewstoday.com/releases/31304.php.

Chapter 20:

Susanne Diederich, "Walking in Circles," Max-Planck-Campus, August 20, 2009, accessed July 14, 2013, http://www.tuebingen.mpg.de/en/news-press/press-releases/detail/walking-in-circles.html.